SAFE AT HOME:
A Season in the Valley

By Austin Gisriel

To Moira,
Hope you enjoy!
Austin Gisriel

Layout and Cover Design by:

Augusta Free Press
PO Box 1193
Waynesboro, Va. 22980

*To the citizens of New Market,
Virginia, who each year welcome a
new group of young baseball players
into their homes and into their hearts.*

CONTENTS

FOREWORD

For a little over two months in the summer of 2009, I regularly left my home in Williamsport, Maryland, and drove 90 miles to my home in New Market, Virginia, in order to gather material about the New Market Rebels. To clarify, I do not own a house in New Market — not yet, anyway — but since the inception of this project, it is a place where I have always felt at home. During the fall and winter of 2008 and the spring of 2009, I attended league meetings and interviewed folks associated with the team and the town, and at every point, I was not only told to "make myself at home," I was *made* to feel at home. I was welcomed into Bruce and Lynne Alger's home and into Larry and Sharon Smith's home and into Mo and Dorothy Weber's home. Once the season started, I was welcomed into the coaches' office by Lucas Jones and his staff and onto the team bus by driver Vic Moyers. I was welcomed into the webcast booth by Charlie Dodge and Jay Hafner. I was welcomed into the bullpen by the relief pitchers, and even into the dugout by all the players. I was welcomed onto the field to shag fly balls during batting practice and welcomed to the postgame meals. I could not have felt more at home anywhere I went in New Market than if I had been related to every person I encountered. Indeed, by the end of those two months, I felt as if I had been taken in by and had become part of the New Market Rebel family. For such hospitality, I am eternally grateful.

Naturally, there are several people whom I wish to thank specifically for their help and encouragement:

Head Coach Lucas Jones, his coaching staff, and all of the players from the 2009 Rebels made themselves available to me at all times and welcomed me — a civilian, so to speak — into their midst. I was honored to be there.

Publishers Chris and Crystal Graham of Augusta Free Press believed in this project immediately and have offered their support and constructive criticism.

The Dodge family not only hosted two different players, they also hosted me for several nights. Charlie graciously welcomed me into the webcast booth, and Melissa not only served as my eyes and ears for events that I could not attend, she also provided her perspective as a host mom. Melissa's photographs are an invaluable contribution to the present work.

Larry and Sharon Smith, owners of the Cross Roads Inn—a wonderful bed and breakfast in New Market, one block from the ballpark—not only put me up on occasion, they bade me sit on their beautiful, breezy front porch whenever I was in town. Their parlor became a second office for me.

Dorothy and Mo Weber also put me up on many nights throughout the season. I am indebted to Mo for how much he taught me about the game I love.

Bruce Alger, his wife Lynne, and their sons Trey and C. B. welcomed me into their home and into their lives. This book would not have been possible were it not for the time that Bruce was willing to give me.

Thanks to Vic Moyers for getting us up and down the Valley safely on the Rebels bus. Thanks for all the peanuts. Thanks most of all for the fellowship and friendship.

Thanks to the Kipps family for feeding me during the postgame meals with the team. Knowing the dedication with which those meals were served made them even tastier!

Thanks to Kay Helsley and Dick and Nan Powell for sharing their perspectives in writing and to all the members of the Rebel family for sharing stories and tidbits about the players and the season.

Thanks to Al Smith, my friend and teammate since high school, who still pitches great batting practice and whose support for this project has been most appreciated.

Thanks as well to Kurt Britner, who has never attended a baseball game in his life, but whose encouragement has been most meaningful to me.

Finally, thanks to my daughters for their support and to my wife Martha whose love and understanding allowed me to write this book ... and who edits a mean manuscript.

A Note About Language
Baseball players are wonderfully talented at stringing together curse words that would make a sailor's hair stand on end, although the vocabulary of the 2009 Rebels was not as colorful as many teams around which I have been. I have included such language only where it is relevant, and in all other cases, I have simply used the old-fashioned cartoon method of indicating what words or kinds of words were spoken.

PROLOGUE

With two outs in the top of the 9th inning of the last regular-season game of the 2008 Valley Baseball League in Virginia's Shenandoah Valley, New Market Rebels' manager Nolan Neiman motions for centerfielder Kevin Dietrich to come off the field. It is a traditional gesture of respect in the game of baseball. Kevin has played three straight summers for New Market, and such longevity is rare in the college summer circuits. The 200 or so Rebel fans, seated in the bleachers between home plate and the home team dugout, clap wildly and call his name. His teammates are out on the warning track and greet him with handshakes and hugs. Kevin doffs his cap to the fans and smiles.

New Market needs only one more out to clinch a victory over the Front Royal Cardinals. On the mound for New Market is another third-year Rebel, Dale Brannon. Dale has been a very versatile player for New Market, and to recognize this, Neiman has played Brannon at all nine positions this evening. His final spot is on the pitcher's mound, and he is trying to preserve what would now be a 7-5 victory. Brannon has allowed a run in this inning, and the tying runs are on second and third, but he has struck out two.

Brannon and Dietrich were honored for their tenure with the Rebels in a pregame ceremony. Dale Brannon has not only played for New Market for all three summers; he has also lived with Bruce and Lynne Alger and their two sons for each of the past three seasons. Bruce — the Rebels' president, general manager, and public address announcer — notes for the crowd that although Kevin has not lived with them, he has consumed his fair share from the Alger refrigerator. Lynne and Trey, the Algers' older son, present the two with gift bags, each containing an official Rebels coach's jacket, a framed copy of "The Man in the Mirror," an inspirational poem that hangs in the Rebels' locker room, and, lastly, a key to the Alger home. By the time Lynne pulls this last item from one of the bags to show the crowd, she is having a hard time holding back her tears, as is Trey. Kevin and Dale hug them both.[1]

"God bless you, my sons," says Bruce over the loudspeakers from his perch in the press box. "It has been a joy for me to announce your names for three years." Bruce does a magnificent job maintaining his own emotions; his smooth, rich voice revealing his feelings ever so slightly. Everyone in the stands, as well as players from both teams, is standing and applauding as Bruce concludes with "The last four words from the movie *Hoosiers*, 'I love you guys.'"

Bruce quickly announces the New Market starting lineup, and each boy runs to his position as his name is called. The game begins.

The Rebels build a 5-4 lead through six innings and have added two runs in the bottom of the 7th on Murray Watt's line-drive two-run home run, and now it has come down to the 9th inning with Dale Brannon needing one more out.

He doesn't get it. Brannon yields a double to right field tying the score, but the Cardinals batter is out at third trying to stretch the drive into a triple.

The Rebels fail to score in the bottom of the 9th, and Dale returns to the mound. After recording one out, Brannon gives up a towering home run to Front Royal's cleanup hitter, Bennet Davis. Two singles put Cardinal runners on first and second, but Brannon wriggles out of trouble, striking out the final batter of the inning on a called third strike.

The Rebel faithful have not given up, however. Bruce plays the theme from *Rocky* before the 10th inning gets under way, while the first two Rebel hitters loosen up in the on-deck circle, unconsciously swinging their bats over their heads in sync with each other and in time with the music. A leadoff double has the crowd clapping and stomping on the metal bleachers, but an intentional walk brings Steve Owens to the plate. Owens

---

[1]Dale is the third Brannon to play for New Market. Oldest brother Evan played in 2003 and served as head coach in 2007 when middle brother Nolan played for the Rebels.

is normally a pitcher, and between the fact that it is the last game of the season and the shuffling of players into the lineup to accommodate moving Brannon around the diamond, Owens has been inserted in right field. During Front Royal's 9th-inning rally, a ball fell in front of Owens that a regular outfielder most likely would have caught. The Cardinals expect a bunt, but after working the count to 2-2, Owens spanks a hit through the left side, loading the bases. The crowd is in a lather now, but a collective groan goes up when the next batter hits a pop-up behind second base. It sails high in the air, but since the batter is right-handed, it is spinning away from the second baseman. He is in trouble, and it tips off his glove, tying the score and keeping the bases loaded. Front Royal protests that the infield fly rule should have been called, but the field umpire has determined that catching the pop fly required more than the "reasonable effort" that the rulebook states.

Rebel fans are ecstatic. As it is, a festive mood has gripped the ballpark since before the opening ceremonies.

"It's a bittersweet night," says Melissa Dodge, upon spying me in the pavilion near the Rebels' bullpen eating dinner and jotting down notes before the game. Melissa's husband, Charlie, broadcasts games on the Web, and they are, as are the Algers, a host family. For Melissa, any night of Rebel baseball is sweet, and the ceremonies for Dale and Kevin will make the evening even more so; but the end of the game will bring goodbyes and a 10-month hiatus for baseball in New Market.

Melissa has been snapping photographs throughout the game, as she usually does. When the "Chicken Dance" is played, she joins another host mom, Kay Helsley, who *always* and fervently rises and does the Chicken Dance.

Fred Miller, a longtime Rebel fan, is in his usual seat in the front-row bleachers by the Rebels' on-deck circle. He keeps up a constant chatter with Dale Brannon whenever Dale appears on deck. He also gives it to the umpire in a good-natured way and rings his cowbell. This is most appropriate, since Fred showed his prize black Angus cattle at the Shenandoah County Fair for 55 straight years.

On a close call that goes against the Rebels, Fred yells, "You watch 'em, ump, and I'll call 'em!" Later, after another comment from Fred, the home-plate umpire responds with a little wave as he squats behind the catcher, the gesture seeming to say, "That was a good one, Fred!" A silver-haired lady with eagle eyes in the last row of the bleachers spies the gesture and hollers, "At least he can hear!"

Booing every close call that goes against them and cheering almost every move a Rebel makes, the crowd is determined to eat up as much of this baseball game as possible, knowing that it will be 10 more months before they will be able to feast again.

With the game now tied and Fred ringing his cowbell, shortstop Michael Mooney steps to the plate. He has lived with Melissa and Charlie this summer. At 5'8" and 155 pounds, he is the smallest player on the team, but he leads the league in walks. Sure enough, Mooney adds to his total, drawing ball four and forcing home the winning run to the delight of the Rebel faithful. Final score: New Market 9, Front Royal 8.

After the game, fans mill about collecting autographs and greeting the players. Nan Powell, who along with her husband, Dick, has hosted at least one player every season for 15 summers, thanks each player for coming to New Market to play as he exits the field and ambles across the gravel parking lot to the locker room.

The players eventually make their way to the pavilion where the postgame meal awaits them. Becky Kipps has volunteered to coordinate these meals. She and her husband Bruce are celebrating their 29th wedding anniversary on this day. Tonight she is serving chicken nuggets and homegrown tomatoes, among other items spread across two picnic tables. Her daughter, Anna, a rabid Rebels fan, is helping to serve. Earlier this summer, Anna received a message from Brad Ziegler, a Rebel in 2000, who texted to tell her that he had just been called up to the Oakland Athletics.

Folks are proud of what Ziegler has accomplished. The night before, the stands were buzzing about Ziegler, a submarining relief pitcher, called up to the A's in June, and who just set the major league record for the most shutout innings to begin a career, breaking a mark that was over 100 years old.[2] It seems that Rebel fans speak of Ziegler as if he was a native son, but upon listening closely, it becomes clear that they speak of him as if he was their own son.

Bruce Alger finds Steve Owens in the buffet line, slaps him on the back, and smiles.

---

[2]Ziegler made his major league debut with Oakland on May 31, 2008, which happened to be Opening Day for New Market. On July 27, 2008, he threw his 26th and 27th scoreless innings against the hard-hitting Texas Rangers to break the record for consecutive scoreless innings to begin a career. The record of 25 had been set by Phillies' right-hander George McQuillan in 1907. Drafted in the 20th round, Ziegler spent parts or all of six seasons in the minors before getting called up by Oakland. Ziegler's consecutive scoreless inning streak eventually reached 39 before he allowed a run to Tampa Bay on August 14, 2008, in his second inning of work that day.

"Why didn't you tell me you could hit like that?!" exclaims Alger, referring to the pitcher's clutch single in the 10th that kept the inning going.

"I've been trying to tell the coaches, but they just wouldn't listen!" smiles Owens.

Upon finishing his plate, the 6'9" Owens walks over to the table at which hitting coach Mo Weber is seated. Weber is 85 and stands all of 5'5", and though Owens towers over him, it is obvious that the pitcher from the University of Richmond regards Mo as a man of great stature. Owens thanks Weber for all he has done for him and for the team this season, and Weber promptly tells him to call pitching coach Rick Smith if he needs any "reminders."

One by one, other players make their way to Weber's table, and he can't help but repeat the instructions that he has given them since May.

"Remember, boom-boom!" he tells Brannon, as he gestures how the bat should go back and then forward in an instant as the pitch approaches.

"Boom-boom, Mo," smiles Brannon, who gathers up his team picture and walks out of the pavilion and into the night. Mo talks baseball to me while he finishes his ice cream.

The game itself meant nothing. New Market at 16-28 has tied for the second worst record in the league; only Front Royal's record is worse, and both teams have already been eliminated from the playoffs. Furthermore, this was a makeup game from a rainout earlier in the week. No game could have been more meaningless, yet no game could have been more celebrated by the fans, many of whom linger still to say good-bye to players for whom they have developed a genuine affection. The host families, the Rebel staff, the concession workers, the ticket takers — volunteers all — have given countless hours to ensure another successful Rebel season. In spite of the team's record, it is agreed that the season is indeed a success, the only regret being that it has ended too soon.

This is baseball in New Market, Virginia, or, more specifically, this is Rebel Baseball. It is a giant family reunion, held annually, beginning the first of June or thereabouts and not ending until sometime in late July or early August. It is replete with laughter and storytelling, hamburgers and hot dogs, and 22 home games played by the adopted sons of the towns-folk who feed and shelter them, cheer for them, and hold them up as an example to their own flesh-and-blood children. If baseball is no longer America's pastime, it is certainly still New Market's pastime.

At the risk of sounding like Yogi Berra, every baseball season is unique — that's what makes it so typical. Indeed, the mathematical combinations of possible outcomes in a baseball game are as infinite as the combinations of human genes; thus, no two people and no two baseball games are ever the same. The very first pitch of any game may result in a strike; a ball; a foul ball; a single; a double; a triple; a home run; a hit by pitch; catcher's interference; six assisted infield outs (if you count the pitcher and catcher); three assisted outfield outs resulting from a batter trying to stretch a hit, but being thrown out; and nine unassisted putouts. This list does not include such esoteric outcomes as a strong-armed rightfielder throwing out a batter/runner at first base; or the batter, incensed with some action of the umpire, being thrown out of the game before or immediately after the first pitch. Neither does this list include the quality of the hit or of the out, for as any baseball fan knows, a bloop double is not a sign that the pitcher has nothing that day, but a scorching lineout that just about rips the glove off a fielder's hand might be a sign of an early shower. Nor does this list consider the location of that first pitch, for again, as every baseball fan knows, there is a big difference between a languid curveball that flops lazily into the dirt in front of home plate resulting in "ball one," and a 95-mile-per-hour blazer that nearly scorches the stubble on a batter's chin.

Yet, in spite of these unique combinations of events in any *given* game, there are certain universal rhythms that may be observed in *every* game.

Every baseball game begins with the starting pitcher throwing 10 warm-up pitches, the last one of which the catcher pegs to second base, where one of the middle infielders catches it, applies a tag to an imaginary runner, flips it to the other middle infielder, who throws it to the third baseman, who takes a few steps toward the pitcher, and tosses the ball — and often a comment such as "Go get 'em, big boy"— to the man on the mound. The pitcher then toes the rubber, looks in to the catcher for the sign, and delivers that first pitch, and a baseball game, with its unique combination of genes is born.

As that first pitch hurtles toward the batter, reaching him in approximately 4/10ths of a second, the fans don't know yet if they'll see a no-hitter or a blowout; a nail-biter or a slugfest. That uncertainty is part of the game's rhythm, which is dictated by the game itself and not by the inevitable tick of a clock. And, of course, there is a sensuous rhythm to the game that is almost as old as the game itself, from the sound of metal cleats crunching along a stone-chip warning track to the smell of hot dogs drifting through the stands. The hum of the crowd, the cry of the vendor, the flapping of myriad flags along the upper most concourse; the crack of the bat, the crack of the catcher's mitt, the distinct swish of dirt swept away by a sliding runner. Merely hearing these sounds can transform old men into time travelers who could open their inner eyes and see the last ballpark they were ever in, or perhaps the first. They would open their eyes and see Eden-green grass and the effortless grace of young men in their prime. Or perhaps they would open their eyes and find that they are not in the stands, but are themselves gliding across that lush green grass, looking up into the sky, tracking a lazy fly ball, drifting under it ever so gracefully.

It's the unique aspect of baseball that makes it such an intriguing game, but it is these eternal rhythms of the game that take us home again.

We often forget how easily that can be accomplished. We spend the first 10 years of our lives adding the phrase "and a half" when stating our ages. We yearn for those seemingly unreachable milestones: 10 and double digits; 13 and teenhood; 16 and a driver's license; 18 and legal; 21 and an adult. By our third decade, some of us have started lying about our ages — and always on the younger side of the ledger. By 50, a year is nothing, and we begin to measure our lives not by "and a half," but by full decades. We want to slow life down, but we continue to live in a hurry. We forget the way home because we forget the magic of the moment.

This is also one of the allures of baseball, for it is a game of moments, each influencing the next and each containing a multitude of possibilities before a particular actuality comes to pass and is recorded on the scorecard. Becoming aware of baseball's sensuous rhythms is a simple matter of taking a moment and *seeing* what it is you're looking at, *listening* to what you hear, inhaling deeply.

The rhythm of the game in New Market runs deeper and beats more strongly than the rhythm that one may observe at other ballgames in other places. Seeing another crop of Little Leaguers run onto the field for the National Anthem, taking their places alongside their much taller and older collegiate counterparts is part of that rhythm. The chance to guide a young man or a whole house full of them toward his baseball dream — or, more importantly, toward being a successful adult — is also part of that rhythm. So is the chance to share a summer's evening with a friend.

My first Rebels moment came in June 2002. My wife Martha and I and our two daughters, Becky and Sarah, were spending the weekend in New Market, enjoying the impending end of school and the sights of a place other than home. While walking around town after dinner, we saw a large, hand-lettered sandwich sign proclaiming "Baseball: Rebel Park 7:30 Tonight." If it was a baseball game, I wanted to go, but something about an old-fashioned sign comprising the team's advertising campaign was as intriguing as the game itself. Becky, our oldest, was (and still is) a daddy's girl, and she was eager to join in the adventure.

We walked to the ballpark — Rebel Park — and approached the man at the folding table, which functions as the ticket booth. We paid our admission and looked over the photocopied program listing the rosters of the Rebels and their opponents that night. Being early, we milled around, taking in the park with its green wooden fence that ran from both dugouts to the outfield wall, which in turn was covered with advertising from local businesses. We spied an older gentleman pulling a uniform top out of the trunk of his car and asked him about the team and the league and the game that we were about to see. With the zeal of a prophet, he regaled us for 10 minutes about all three, and he was obviously pleased that I was there, and even more pleased that I had brought my daughter. We didn't know it at the time, but we had just been baptized into Rebel baseball by Mo Weber, hitting coach extraordinaire, who would turn 80 a couple weeks after that game.

It was a great game in a beautiful setting, and Becky and I were hooked. Though we lived (and still do) in Maryland, we thought nothing of the

180-mile round trip to take in a game over the next few summers. We began to introduce other people to Rebel baseball and to accumulate precious moments watching the games and being together. One such moment came at a 2004 playoff game in Luray that lasted a month — or at least that's the joke we passed around in the stands — as the game, begun at 7:34 p.m. (according to our score sheet) on July 31 meandered well past midnight and into August 1st. With two out in the bottom of the 17th inning, Rebel hurler Sandy Jacobs threw a low-and-away strike to Luray Wrangler Brandon Pope, who drove the pitch to right. At first, everyone still remaining in the stands thought right-fielder Marion Knowles would catch it and, at worst, that he would have to play the carom off the wall. He turned, but the ball sailed just over the fence for a Luray victory. I see that moment still: Marion waiting for the carom that never came, the split second of silence before the Luray players erupted in celebration, the stunned look on Becky's face.

The tears started to well in her eyes. "That's not fair," she said. The tear that trickled down her cheek was like the water that flows from a fountain of youth. I was 7 again, and Becky's tears were my tears.

We have all been 7 years of age, full of faith and innocence, and that 7-year-old lives inside us still. We are all 7 and 17 and all the ages that we have ever been, and if we take life moment by moment, rather than year by year or decade by decade, we will find our way home. Too many people have no time for that internal 7-year-old, or they think it somehow inappropriate to let him come out and play, what with a world that seems headed to chaos and ruin.

In baseball, however, it's possible, even with two outs in the 9th and no matter how far behind my team has fallen, *it's really actually possible* that my team will pull together the most improbable of rallies and win the game. I wouldn't let the 7-year-old in me miss that for all the money in the world. The unbridled glee that my inner 7-year-old enjoys during such a triumphant moment will make a better day for the 52-year-old man who he has become. It will make him, that is to say, it will make *me* a better man. Indeed, the Luray side of the field that night was nothing but little children jumping up and down, both on the field and in the stands.

One of the benefits of maturity (a euphemism for getting old) is appreciation for the joy that my opponent has in his victory, even as I must accept defeat. As we get older, we learn that faith is not always or even often rewarded, but the mere exercise of faith, like the exercise of one's muscles, becomes increasingly important if we wish to maintain our health. For the night that the Rebels lost in Luray, I was not only 7, I was also 47, and I knew that Becky and I had witnessed an epic and had done it together and had shared it with strangers who for a night were family.

You don't have to attend many games at Rebel Park, however, to discover that soon, there are no strangers there, only family. Membership in the Rebels family is not an opportunity to go home again; it is an *invitation* to go home. Consider this book an extension of that invitation — at least for the 2009 season — which, of course, begins the day after Kevin Dietrich and Dale Brannon have led the Rebels to their season-ending victory over Front Royal.

Chapter 1
Life is So Simple

Baseball has been played for at least 140 years in New Market, the southernmost town in Shenandoah County, which is about in the middle of Virginia's Shenandoah Valley. The fans have always been passionate about their team. Newspaper accounts from 1922, the first year of the "Shenandoah Valley League," constantly refer to the huge turnouts for New Market games. The 1922 opener against Strasburg "was witnessed by one of the largest crowds ever attending a ball game in New Market."[1] In June 1923, approximately 2,000 fans saw New Market lose to Harrisonburg 4-3 in 13 innings: an amazing crowd for the time.[2] (This would be a good attendance figure even today. Four teams in the low Class A South Atlantic League averaged fewer than 2,000 per game in 2008.[3])

Sometimes the crowds were passionate to the extreme, as evidenced by the July 4th riot of 1923 when New Market faced Harrisonburg. That day, some 500 cars overflowed the streets around the field and encircled the diamond itself. According to the *Shenandoah Valley*, many fans had come from Harrisonburg; and they were "peeved" by a 7-3 loss that their team had suffered to New Market that morning at home. New Market was leading the afternoon contest and had the bases loaded with none out in the 8th inning when a Harrisonburg fan "flashed with a hand mirror the

---

[1]*Shenandoah Valley*, June 22, 1922.
[2]*Shenandoah Valley*, June 7, 1923.
[3]Retrieved September 22, 2008, from http://web.minorleaguebaseball.com/milb/stats/stats.jsp?t=latt&lid=l16&sid=l116

sun's blazing light into the face of a man at the bat at the time and caused him to strike out. Besides two other batters similarly treated before the offender was caught in his nasty acts and removed from the field." This apparently touched off a "melee" in which New Market Police Sergeant — and Bruce Alger's great-great uncle — George A. Tidler was hit with a bottle, and several others were injured. New Market's mayor, Thomas A. Andrick, fined two offenders (one the grand sum of $25) and issued warrants for the arrest of several others.[4]

The current form of the Valley Baseball League (VBL) was begun in 1946, and New Market joined the league in 1949. Until 1961, the league essentially consisted of old fashioned "town teams" that used local talent. That year, however, the league was sanctioned by the NCAA, and the rules were changed to allow two players on each club "to come from a distance greater than 100 miles." [5] This was the beginning of the Valley League as a summer collegiate league. In 1993, the VBL mandated that traditional wooden bats be used, instead of aluminum bats, primarily so that professional scouts could make a more accurate judgment of a player's hitting ability since it is much easier to drive a baseball with an aluminum bat than with a piece of ash or maple.

Various towns throughout the Valley have had teams in the league, which consisted of 11 franchises in 2008 and included the Fauquier Gators, Haymarket Senators, Winchester Royals, Front Royal Cardinals, Luray Wranglers, Woodstock River Bandits, Harrisonburg Turks, Waynesboro Generals, Staunton Braves, and Covington Lumberjacks, in addition to New Market. The Rockbridge Rapids, based in Lexington, were added to the league beginning with the 2009 schedule.

Of all these teams, the "New Market Base Ball Club, Incorporated" is unique in that the team has no owner. Fauquier is owned by a nonprofit corporation, and the other 10 teams have individual owners. Many assume that the town of New Market owns the team, but this is not so. The team owns itself and is run by a board of directors.

Although it is the smallest town in the Valley League, New Market enjoyed the largest fan following during the 2008 season. (See Appendix A for VBL member populations.) While ranking fifth in total attendance in 2008 by averaging 403 fans, New Market "attracted" 1,873.3 fans

---

[4]*Shenandoah Valley*, July 5, 1923.
[5]*Shenandoah Valley*, May 4, 1961, p. 1.

per home game, when webcast listeners are included.[6] This represents approximately 100% of the town's population.

As impressive as the Rebels' attendance figures may be, the real measure of New Market's regard for its team is in the number and dedication of its volunteers, who make improvements to the field, feed and house the players, run the concession and souvenir stands, man the ticket booth, serve as official scorers, and even call the games on the Internet. New Market's volunteers don't resemble an organization so much as a family, and their patriarch is Bruce Alger.

At 6'0" with an athletic build and limitless energy, his appearance belies his 55 years. Quick to smile and quick to laugh, he seems to know everyone's name, to which he almost always adds the phrase "my friend." To be addressed by Bruce as such is to be complimented, for he does not use the word "friend" lightly. His Virginia drawl and his resonant voice call to mind the image of a true Southern gentleman.

Bruce is president as well as general manager of the Rebels, positions he has held since the middle of the 2001 season. The president at the time, Tom Linski, had held the office on and off for 20 years and was ready to relinquish the responsibility. More or less by the acclaim of all concerned, the position fell to Bruce, whose involvement with the Rebels dates back to 1965.

It was a great uncle, Lem Tidler, who introduced Bruce to working for the ballclub, albeit in a rather inauspicious way. "Uncle Lem was involved for years, and he got me involved. He needed someone to hang the numbers on the scoreboard: the big old tin numbers. He couldn't find anyone else to do it, and he saw me walking down the street and he said, 'Hey, Bruce, let's do your great uncle a favor and come on down to the ballpark and help me out down there a little bit.'

"I said [to myself], 'Sure! I get to play ball!' Right! — That never happened. So he sent me with hammer and nails out to the scoreboard to make sure I had all the nails in place before the season started. He said, 'Now every half inning, you run in, and I'll give you the summary, and you run back out and hang the numbers.' He said, 'You can add, can't you?' And I said, 'I think I can,' and that's how it got started."

---

[6]Figures are from Doug Barret of Futuremedia, the league's 2008 webcast host.

Bruce Alger (center) shares a story with Charlie Dodge (left) and author Austin Gisriel (right).

Baseball has been a lifelong passion for Bruce, who recalls stealing a ball from a local grocery store in order to have something with which to play. "There were two ladies who ran this store, and I remember stealing a red rubber ball, because we couldn't find anything else to play with. It cost a nickel," he laughs, "but I actually remember stealing that ball to go play. Of course, I went back and apologized and gave 'em a quarter or whatever it cost," he laughs again, "because I felt so bad afterward. We would be at Rebel games and get foul balls, and back then, you got a hot dog for turning them in and, of course, we'd keep a couple to play with, and we'd sneak in the ballpark and play."

Bruce laughs at himself as he tells this story, but there is no doubt that in some way, he still feels the sting of having disappointed Miss Eula and Miss Bernice, the sisters who owned the store.

New Market offered no organized baseball for boys past the age of 16 during the time Bruce was growing up except for the Junior Deputy League, which featured "about a four game schedule," according to Bruce. Not even the local high school, Stonewall Jackson High, offered varsity baseball then, so Bruce and his friends played pickup games. And he followed the Rebels. To this day, he carries an encyclopedic knowledge of who played for New Market and what college the player attended. He also carries with him an abiding love of history.

"To be right here where Stonewall Jackson was and to walk the streets where he walked ...that does something to me; to be in a place where history was made. That still gives me goose bumps!" marvels Alger. "The idea that Stonewall Jackson was in this town, and he looked at this very same building that I'm looking at ... that's amazing to me! History just grabs me like that and pulls me into it."

Then again, to live in New Market is to live with history, and a walk through town evokes a sense that a variety of historical eras are alive and flourishing. Founded in 1796, New Market was designated a Historic District by the Virginia Historic Landmarks Commission in 1972. This official acknowledgment of its historical significance is itself fading into history.

On any given evening at Rebel Park, fans in the third-base bleachers can see the headlights of cars winding their way through New Market Gap and down Massanutten Mountain. This is State Road 211, "the Old Cross Roads" that runs from the town of Luray and its famous caverns. It is the same road over which Stonewall Jackson marched his troops during his Valley Campaign of 1862. Where the Cross Roads now intersects with Route 11 in town sits a white brick building that was a store in 1862, and a plaque on its front wall, dedicated in 1952, reads:

> *General Jackson, seated upon his horse "Little Sorrel," reviewed his troops as they passed this corner.*

This is the same corner at which sits the large, hand-lettered sandwich sign proclaiming "Baseball: Rebel Park 7:30 Tonight."

Houses that existed during the War Between the States are marked as such; and though Jackson and his foot cavalry passed this way often, New Market is most famous for a battle that took place in 1864, a little over a year after Jackson's death. The May 15 Battle of New Market would mark the last Confederate victory in the Shenandoah Valley, but it is most noted for the fact that the students from the Virginia Military Institute were called out to serve in the little army of Confederate General John C. Breckenridge.

The General, a former Vice President of the United States under James Buchanan, was very reluctant to send in the 258-member Corps of Cadets, but when a gap in his lines opened, he had no choice. "Put the boys in," he said, "and may God forgive me for the order." The cadets of VMI charged across the Bushong Farm just north of town through a driving thunderstorm until they struck the Union lines and captured a battery of artillery, securing victory for Breckenridge and the South. The Corps suffered a casualty rate of almost 25%, including 10 killed.

5

Outside the Reformation Lutheran Church, Bruce Alger's church, on North Congress Street stands a single gatepost with a 3-inch artillery shell lodged halfway from the top. As the battle began to unfold, General Breckenridge surveyed the Union position astride his horse in the middle of the street by the church. Union artillery shells soon rained down on the general and his staff, and one — the 3-inch shell — struck the gatepost but failed to explode. A small plaque at the foot of the gatepost tells the story. A miniature cannon rests atop the post. Rebel Park sits a long home run to the northeast of this spot.

Thus, the single biggest event in New Market occurs every year on or about May 15 when the battle re-enactment takes place on the Bushong Farm. Within about two weeks of the re-enactment every year, another group of young Rebels comes to town, this time armed with bats and gloves.

"New Market begins each season 1-0, because the Rebels beat the Yankees at this time every year," laughs Bruce.

New Market saw its fair share of armies and war for the same reason that most towns do: its location along an important road. Route 11, the "Old Valley Pike," as it's known throughout the Valley, was the main thoroughfare from Harrisburg, Pennsylvania, all the way to the Tennessee border until Interstate 81 was constructed. Route 11 was built on the wagon road that brought the first settlers, mostly Germans and Scotch Irish, to the Valley. The wagon road itself was built on a well worn Indian trail. Half the Valley Baseball League lies along Route 11, including the teams in Winchester, Woodstock, New Market, Harrisonburg, Staunton, and Rockbridge (in Lexington).

New Market is only three streets wide at its widest, and it runs for about a mile along Route 11, or Congress Street as it's known through town. Rebel Park, on the north end of New Market, evokes a scene from the 1930s, with its ad-filled plywood fence and intimate seating. It is located immediately behind what was once New Market's school. Built in 1931, the building is now the community center that houses, among other things, the Rebels coaches' office. A little side street, Dixie Lane, runs from Route 11, past the New Market Rescue Squad building on the right, across John Sevier Road, and into Rebel Park.

On the southern end of town sits, appropriately enough, the Southern Kitchen Restaurant. Opened by Lloyd and Ruby Newland in 1956, son Randy and his wife Rebecca run the Southern Kitchen today. They offer a free steak dinner to any Rebel who hits a home run at Rebel Park and a 10% discount to players in general. The décor hasn't changed much since its opening. Gold and green ovals suggesting rockets — a popular design during the time of Sputnik — adorn the classic Formica tops of the booth tables, and even though the jukeboxes are now digital, the sounds of "Rockin' Robin" or "Goodnight, Sweetheart, Goodnight" may suggest a scene from *American Graffiti*. Indeed, manager Lucas Jones remarked during his interview that dining at the Southern Kitchen is like being "in a movie."

Next to the Southern Kitchen lies the Shenvalee Golf Resort. Bobby Jones opened the then 9-hole course in 1927, the same year that the Valley Pike became U.S. Route 11. In 1944, the Shenvalee housed "Italian prisoners of diplomatic rank."[7] Built on ground that saw the opening of the Battle of New Market, the original hotel still stands and is still used.

Three miles south of the Southern Kitchen lies Endless Caverns. Discovered in 1879, the caverns have been a longtime tourist destination. About 20 miles south of the caverns, in Rockingham County, lies the city of Harrisonburg, home to 17,000 students at James Madison University.

New Market has preserved something of much greater historical significance, however, than its buildings and battlefield. New Market has preserved a certain way of life; in truth, a certain innocence that has disappeared in many areas of the United States. This is a community with a new town hall, a new library, new businesses, and an old-fashioned sense of what it means to be a good neighbor and a good person.

"People will call up and say, 'I'm going into Harrisonburg, do you need anything?' which is really nice," says Sharon Smith, wife of Mayor Larry Smith. "Friends always check with friends to see if they need anything if they're going into town. That's just something people do."

When the new library was ready, 100 volunteers showed up with wheelbarrows, hand trucks, and little red wagons to move the 5,000 or so books from the old library. In 30 minutes, the move was complete. The land on which the new library sits (as well as a great deal of construction money) was donated by Anna Hildreth, and the library is staffed entirely by volunteers, including Becky Kipps, the Rebels meal coordinator.

For the players, this old-fashioned neighborliness can sometimes result in a very positive culture shock. Lynne Alger recalls their first host son who was from Philadelphia and attended Xavier College in Cincinnati.

---

[7] Retrieved September 22, 2008, from http://www.shenvalee.com/about_us.html.

On the player's first trip into New Market, "Bruce jumped out of the car and left it running, and our player's going 'What're you doing?! What're you doing?! You leave the car running with the keys in the car?! What're you doing?"

She laughs at the memory and then recounts how often she leaves her mailbox keys at the post office, only to have Gary Comer, a town councilman who also cleans the post office pull into the Algers' driveway to return them.

"It's so simple. Life is so simple," says Bruce in such a way that he clearly intends his statement to apply to more than the way of life in his hometown. Born and raised in New Market, Bruce Alger has never taken home for granted and, indeed, it is home in the deepest sense of the word. "I drank my first beer here. I smoked my first cigarette here. I found Jesus here. I bump into people who steered me in the right direction when they saw me doing something wrong, you know, *'If your grandmother knew you were here ...you get yourself home!'* — 'Yes ma'am!' That all made me what I am. And for those people, *all* those people, some of whose names I don't even know. I thank them ... I could never repay this town for what they've done for me and my family. I'm trying to. I don't feel like I've given enough, because you know what? They're still doing it," says Alger, who is probably the only one of New Market's 1,845 citizens who thinks that he hasn't "given enough."

"Dad has a real passion for the Rebels," says Greg Alger, Bruce's son from a previous marriage. Greg, age 30, adds that his father "has done a great job building up" the organization.

Mayor Larry Smith notes that Bruce is "very modest" about his contributions to the Rebels. Sharon adds, "There are many who contribute, but Bruce is the one who keeps heading them in the proper direction."

Describing her father's work as "amazing," Amanda Alger, 32, Bruce's daughter and Greg's sister, marvels at the growth that Bruce has brought to the Rebels' organization.

"It wasn't always like that when I was growing up," she said. "There were no signs, no press box, no scoreboard ...to see the way it is now," she pauses, and simply adds, "I'm very proud of him."

In fact, while baseball is Bruce's passion, an intense desire to thank his neighbors for making him the man that he is drives Alger's involvement in the Rebels. Because of the Rebels' unique relationship with the town of New Market, the amenities that Bruce and other volunteers purchase and install at Rebel Park become the property of the town and, therefore, are enjoyed by the New Market Shockers, the local adult league base-ball team; and Stonewall Jackson High School, Rebel Park's other residents. All three teams now enjoy excellent field lights and an electronic scoreboard among many other amenities. In years past, as Amanda Alger noted, the bullpens, the concession stand, and the press box were built by Bruce and the other Rebel volunteers.

"That's why we do it; to give back to the community," Alger says of the time and energy he devotes to the Rebels.

It is never "I" with Alger, who instinctively credits his many helpers. In fact, Bruce describes his job as general manager as "easy, because I can't recall anyone *ever* telling me 'No'; that they wouldn't or couldn't do something that was asked with regard to the Rebels."

Bruce Alger marvels at the fact that no one turns him down when he asks for their help, but that's what families do.

"He sets the tone," says Becky Kipps, "to make it be that way; to make it be the Rebel family."

Chapter 2
Baseball Withdrawal

B ruce Alger has been at Rebel Park every day for a month since the season ended, taking down banners, packing away equipment, straightening the press box, and cleaning the offices. At least it doesn't take him long to get to the park—his backyard ends a few feet short of the visiting dugout.

"We didn't want to leave the offices there today," he says at the end of August, "because it's Rebels. It's gotten to the point where there's nothing else we can do there, so we're gonna have to go home and do Alger stuff."

Doing "Alger stuff" keeps Bruce as busy as doing "Rebel stuff." Alger and his wife of 17 years, Lynne, have two sons: Trey will be heading into 8th grade, while brother C. B. will be a 7th grader at North Fork Middle School come fall. Lynne is an accountant in nearby Harrisonburg. Naturally, therefore, Lynne holds the position of secretary/treasurer for the Rebels. She also oversees the operation of the General Lee concession stand and the Rebel Yell souvenir stand.

"Lynne has embraced my commitments to community service and to the Rebels as her own, and I can't thank her enough," says Bruce who goes on to extol the virtues of his "beautiful bride," a phrase he often uses to describe Lynne. He sounds more like a husband of 17 days rather than 17 years, and ultimately summarizes his love most eloquently when he says, "She is my best friend and together, we make a perfect team, both on and off the field."

Trey and C. B. play baseball, of course, including fall baseball for the first time in the autumn of 2008. It is the first time because heretofore, New Market did not have a team in the local fall ball league until the Alger boys expressed an interest, and Bruce and Lynne stepped in and organized it.

"I don't know when the man sleeps," comments Rebels hitting coach Mo Weber, an observation echoed by Greg Alger.

Labor Day finds Bruce and a few friends reseeding the area between the backstop and the home-plate circle. On the following rainy Saturday, he uses the time indoors to make three dozen calls regarding reserved-seat sales. Already 73 out of the 86 reserved seats — regular fold-down stadium seats that sit directly behind home plate — have been sold.

As general manager, Bruce makes all the off-field decisions in consultation with other members of the Rebel Board of Directors. The first "Board meeting" following the 2008 season takes place the evening after the season ends, when several members gather to erect a second picnic pavilion beyond the Rebel dugout. It is an unofficial meeting, but an important topic of conversation is first-year manager Nolan Neiman. Rookie managers make rookie mistakes, but there is a strong desire to bring him back.

"The Board of Directors 100% wants Nolan to return," says Alger. "Don't want to waste one year's worth of training; that's very valuable, very valuable in this league."

Bruce Alger is not the only person who must "wean" himself from the baseball season. It is equally hard for Lynne Alger to accept the end of another year. The Algers not only comprise three-fourths of the Rebels' administration, they are also a host family. They housed five players during the 2008 season, and Lynne always finds it difficult to say goodbye, even in a year such as this, when the Rebels had a losing record and she has lost three recliners to tackling practice. Riley Cooper, an outfielder for the 2008 Rebels, and a wide receiver for Florida (his roommate was 2007 Heisman Trophy winner and Gator quarterback Tim Tebow) broke the recliners demonstrating tackling techniques.

"He was something," marvels Lynne. "Those recliners have been declining, anyway," laughs Bruce. Lynne, accountant that she is, has obviously entered her three lost chairs into the books under the "Boys will be boys" column.

Indeed, Lynne and Bruce are not the only host parents who find it tough to part with their summer sons. Melissa Dodge, 43, a 1st-grade teacher at

W. W. Robinson Elementary in Woodstock, likens the experience to sending one's own child off to college. "However, at least you will most likely be seeing your child again, come the first break from school. We never know if we'll ever see our players again. For me, I guess that's what makes saying goodbye so difficult," she says.

Melissa's husband, Charlie, 47, teaches at Skyline High School in Front Royal, while her daughter, Hannah, attends Lord Fairfax Community College; and her son, Noah, attends Stonewall Jackson High School. They live in Mount Jackson, the next town north of New Market, about 7 miles up Route 11.

"For us," continues Melissa, "hosting a ballplayer isn't just about providing a place to stay and food to eat. We endeavor to make this young man a part of our family and to make him as comfortable as possible. I try to look at it from the player's perspective. They are coming to live with complete strangers in a place that is most likely foreign to them — I mean, really; where in the world is New Market or Mount Jackson, Virginia, anyway? Though the Valley is awash with many cultural experiences, I'm betting none of them are on the players' Top-10 List of things to do. It's not exactly a cosmopolitan hotbed of excitement. So, I do what I can to provide the comforts of home to make their stay as enjoyable as possible. It's not a major sacrifice to keep the pantry stocked with his favorite cereal or snacks.

"Now that the season's over, it's strange to not have a game to go to every night, and our mealtime clock is taking awhile to adjust back to normal. It's nice to not be so scheduled, but I sure do miss it, too."

Kay Helsley, 54, a dietitian from Edinburg, a town 15 miles north of New Market, often leaves notes, which may include a game critique for her players. In 2008, she attended 43 of the 44 games that the Rebels played, to root for her boys.

"I can't even not go to games because I'm always afraid that I'm going to miss something," relates Kay. "A local newspaper wrote a headline about the team's fortunes: 'Rebels 2008 Is One To Forget,'" she continued. I resented that, as I never want to forget any Rebel team.

"The day the players leave — it is always hard to go down to their room and see it empty. No matter how much you disliked their clutter, it was still a symbol of the season being in progress. I am never really ready for the end; even though I know I couldn't take much more than 2 months of baseball, mentally or physically, whether the team is playing well or poorly. I am so pumped up during the season that I can't ever make up for the lost sleep until it's all over."

Dick and Nan Powell are a retired couple living in Basye, a ski and golf resort located 19 miles northwest of New Market. They have been hosting players for 15 years.

"Winning seasons and favorite young men are the hardest to give up. When Brian, our first 'favorite young man' left, I cried and was miserable for a few days. Then I got a hold of myself and realized they were 'on loan' for two months, and that is the way I look at it to this day," says Nan.

"It just ends so fast," says Bruce, referring to the season, "and when it's over, it's over. When the last game of the season comes, there's no going back home and sitting on the front porch to talk about the game. Those players become part of your family and part of your life, and they're *yours*. I mean they are *yours*," adds Bruce with intensity. "If you're sitting in the bleachers and if somebody hollers something about #28 — 'He stinks' or something — it's like it's your own kid! Among New Market people, even. [They'll yell back] 'It's not his fault!' They will defend those guys to the end!"

In early September, Nolan Neiman informs Bruce Alger that his schedule will not allow him to return as head coach of the Rebels, and so Alger and two additional members of the Board of Directors begin a search for a new skipper. Since the head coach is solely responsible for recruiting, this has put them behind several other clubs in the league. Woodstock, for example, already has 23 players under contract.

Lucas Jones, 26, is one of the candidates to replace Neiman and is brought to New Market for an interview. He played in the Valley League for the Winchester Royals in 2005, and served as an assistant coach in 2007. Jones is an assistant baseball coach at Randolph Macon College (RMC), and he comes highly recommended by RMC's head coach Ray Hedrick, an esteemed member of the New Market Rebels family. Hedrick coached the Rebels to their last Valley League championship in 2002.

A self-described introvert, Jones is polite, addressing everyone as "sir." As the interview progresses, he is not afraid to acknowledge that he will make mistakes and that he will need to rely on the experience of someone such as his mentor, Ray Hedrick. "If you let me learn, then I'll do a good job," he tells the board members. Bruce Alger informs Jones that New Market will not send a player home if he turns out to be less talented than was thought, as do some other teams in the league. All three board members emphasize that committing to a player is also a commitment to the player's family, as well as to his host family.

"We're not going to sell out for the sake of winning," states board member Dave Beaver, age 66 and a maintenance worker for the town, who also doubles as Rebel Park's official scorekeeper.

Jones listens intently as the board emphasizes the importance of recruiting players with good character. "Do twice as many character checks as talent checks," states Bruce. Dave tells Lucas that players may go unnoticed walking down the streets of a large town such as Winchester, but they are practically celebrities in a little place such as New Market. He even reminds Lucas that the players will have to watch their cursing on the field.

Executive Vice-President Jim Weissenborn, also 66 and a lawyer in town, laughs, adding, "Mo Weber told our players one time, 'Boys, if cussing will raise your batting averages, we'll bring in a professional to teach you how to do it well.'"

The three men assure Jones that they will not interfere with the way he runs the club. "It's your team and your season," Alger tells him. Weissenborn adds that the fans will let him know how he's doing. Everyone chuckles, including Jones, who quips that he was afraid "Front-Row Fred" was going be present at the interview, throwing zingers his way.

After answering and asking questions for almost 90 minutes, Jones exhibits a quiet sense of confidence. Having heard what the job is all about, he knows he can do it. Beaver and Weissenborn depart, but before Jones leaves, Alger reviews for him a checklist of impressions regarding the interview. The would-be head coach has scored well, and there is no doubt everyone in the room is impressed by his baseball knowledge and his personal character.

Some two weeks later, Lucas Jones is offered the Rebels' managing job, which he joyfully accepts. On Columbus Day, he signs his contract and is officially welcomed into the New Market Rebels

Lucas Jones

baseball family at a gathering at Rebel Park where the message board flashes his name in greeting as he arrives. Within three weeks, he has some 20 players lined up to play with the Rebels, although he is still looking for more left-handed pitching, as is everyone from the New Market/ Mount Jackson Little League to the Tampa Bay Rays.

No sooner has Lucas been hired, however, than another problem arises; this concerning the 2009 schedule. In September, the league had approved a two-division format in which each team would play six games against its division rivals, but only two games against non division opponents. New Market was placed in the Southern Division, while their two biggest rivals — and two biggest gate attractions — Luray and Woodstock were placed in the Northern Division. Alger informs the attendees at the league's October meeting politely, but in no uncertain terms, that the schedule is "detrimental" to the league's "smallest organization." He goes on to explain that he is in danger of losing two large sponsors if the schedule is not changed. Other teams also raise objections to the schedule. Several, including New Market, would like to see three 4-team divisions, a format that was shot down back in September.

The discussion is orderly, even friendly, but motions to change the schedule are improperly made, and no one is quite sure what question, if any, is being called. When someone states that the original schedule was already approved and, therefore, is "written in stone," a wag from the back of the room deadpans, "Must have been sandstone."

Finally, after an hour's discussion and a 10-minute break for pizza, a motion to keep the two divisions, but with a balanced schedule so that each team will play every other team four times, passes.

Within 24 hours, however, Covington, the league's most distant entry, has sent an e-mail to the league president voicing serious displeasure with this second version of the schedule, preferring instead the three-division format. More e-mails circulate, and it becomes apparent that a move may be afoot to "unapprove" the newly approved schedule at the next meeting.

In the meantime, Bruce has other messes to attend to, for along with the title "President and General Manager" goes the title "Co-Launderer." During the last weekend in October, Bruce and Lynne wash the uniforms that have been piled up in the Rebel office since the season's final game. It was not quite clear whether this was the first opportunity the Algers had to complete this task, or whether it was done at this time to prevent the uniforms from rising up and trick-or-treating throughout New Market on Halloween. In any case, washing, drying, and hanging up 42 home jerseys, 42 away jerseys, and 96 pair of pants is not something one does between running to the post office and cutting the grass; it takes some time.

Then, of course, there is the issue of paying for those uniforms. Just the two sets of shirts numbered 1 to 43 (with no #13 — baseball players are generally superstitious, Alex Rodriguez not withstanding) cost $6,000 and ensuring that the revenue stream is always running is a constant concern. The real-estate company that advertised atop the scoreboard has gone out of business, but the Virginia Farm Bureau Insurance has enthusiastically agreed to buy the spot, and when Bill Turner, owner of the Luray franchise and a car dealer with lots in Luray and New Market, proves ready and willing to pay in advance for his sign above the visitors' bullpen, the Rebels pay off the last of 2008's bills.

Nevertheless, an official Rebels board meeting is held that includes an agenda item for formalizing the process by which the team may accept a loan from an individual, something the Algers consider doing until the sign money comes through.

The week has involved more than the board meeting and a seemingly endless cycle of wash, rinse, and spin, however. Bruce also attends a meeting of the Shenandoah Valley Grandstand Managers' Club of New Market (SVGM), whose fundraising efforts on behalf of baseball in Shenandoah County are as impressive as their name. The money they raise goes to the Rebels, to the adult league team New Market Shockers, and to the Mt. Jackson/New Market, and Broadway/Timberville Little League. Money is raised through membership, the annual Rebels banquet, Rebels season ticket sales, and by parking cars at the Shenandoah Valley Music Festival at Orkney Springs. Bruce attends the meeting to thank them for their support.

By now, the ballpark itself has been cleaned and "put away" for winter. The bleachers have been hosed down, the trash has been picked up, the restrooms cleaned and locked, the bullpens and dugouts cleaned, the padding that runs along the wall from dugout to dugout has been removed and stored, and all the souvenirs and concession items have been inventoried and stored.

One week before Thanksgiving, Lucas Jones forwards to Bruce a tentative roster that includes 23 players, many of whom are from Virginia colleges, including James Madison, University of Richmond, George Mason, and Virginia Commonwealth University. A couple of players are from the

University of Maryland, while Carolina colleges supply several more. The one returning player from last year's squad is Steve Owens, the 6'9" right hander whose key hit fueled the Rebel rally that won the 2008 finale.

Mike Mooney, last year's shortstop from the University of Florida will not be returning, much to the disappointment of Melissa Dodge, his host mom, as he hopes to play in the Cape Cod League.[1]

Larry Heine begins the process of posting the biographies and player photos on the Rebels' website, www.rebelsbaseballonline.com. Larry is the webmaster, and he awaits the off-season updates as anxiously as anyone. He not only posts the photos that are returned with player contracts under "Meet the 2009 Rebels," he also updates the "Rebels in the Majors" and "Rebels in the News" pages, adds the new sponsors to the home page, and generally works to improve the site in any way possible. And given the latest league development, he will soon be able to post the 2009 schedule as well.

One week before Thanksgiving, the Valley Baseball League holds its monthly meeting and tops on the agenda is the approval of the specific schedule based on the two-division, balanced format that required so much discussion at October's meeting. Bruce believes that the desire to alter the format yet again has dissipated, but, to his surprise, Fauquier objects to the two division setup on economic grounds, stating that the three-division format makes the most sense. Fauquier's argument is reasoned and deferential, but quite firm. Haymarket is quick to agree with Fauquier and further raises the issue of the "process" by which the schedule has been determined. Haymarket is being quite polite by using the word "process." A sergeant-at-arms would need an entire platoon of parliamentarians to bring some kind of order to the process by which the scheduling decision was made. Indeed, the current discussion is taking place in the absence of any particular motion.

Fauquier joined the VBL in 2007; Haymarket's current ownership also took control of their franchise in 2007. The newer owners are relatively young, they are well spoken, and they are learning quickly how to wield influence and effect change. They have certainly figured out that *Roberts' Rules of Order* don't apply to the proceedings.

---

[1]Mooney would be drafted in June 2009 by the Baltimore Orioles in the 23rd round.

The owner of the Rockbridge Rapids, an expansion franchise that has yet to play a game, states at one point that "We're new, and everyone has the right to tell us we don't know what we're talking about," but goes on to articulate support for Fauquier and Haymarket.

A motion arises to give final approval to the two-division schedule, a motion that is defeated. New Market votes with the majority.

Again, with no motion on the table, an argument arises incredibly enough concerning which franchises would benefit the most from using three divisions. Fauquier points out that while some teams may benefit more than others, *everyone* will benefit more in a three division format because travel costs will be reduced, and the number of games against natural rivals will increase. At last, a motion is made to approve the three-division setup, and it passes 8-2, with two teams absent.

The next motion, unrelated to scheduling, is passed quickly and with enthusiasm. The Mid-Atlantic Sports Network (MASN) has invited the Valley League to send an all-star team to play a team of all-stars from the Cal Ripken, Sr. Collegiate Summer League (CRSCSL) in a game to be broadcast by the network on July 15, 2009. MASN, the Baltimore Orioles' cable network that also owns the broadcast rights to the Washington Nationals, is looking for programming on a night when both teams are off as a result of the Major League All-Star Game. The VBL quickly agrees to send a team, and Bruce is ecstatic. He is also named chairman of the MASN All-Star Game Committee.

After the meeting, Bruce and I head to Chili's in Harrisonburg, which is most appropriate, since Chili's is the largest single sponsor of the Valley Baseball League. We are both excited for the exposure that the MASN All-Star Game will provide the league and begin to design the league uniforms, not that anyone asked us to. Bruce makes a motion that we have a beer, and I quickly second. No one objects, and the motion carries unanimously and enthusiastically. An addendum of wings and nachos is added to the original motion, and the two of us get down to the serious business of stuffing ourselves silly.

Chapter 3
The Legend of the Valley

"No, you gotta do this," intones Mo Weber, as he indicates that I need to pivot on my back foot in order to clear my hips in order to drive the ball to left field. Maynard Jay "Mo" Weber, born June 24, 1923, in Trenton, New Jersey, is the batting instructor for the New Market Rebels. Nicknamed "The Legend of the Valley" by Bruce Alger, Mo's life is indeed the stuff of legends.

"No, you did this," says Mo, indicating that I lifted up on my right toe and slid my front foot forward.

"No, you're back to this."

"No ..."

"No ..."

"No ..."

Before the 2008 season ended, I asked Mo for a hitting lesson for my friend Al Smith and me. I wanted to get some idea of what it's like, not to *watch* Mo coach, but *to be* coached by Mo.

I'm concentrating hard on what Mo is telling me. It's three hours before a game against Covington. We've already spent 45 minutes sitting in the dugout listening to Mo discuss the most difficult art of hitting a baseball. Mo discusses the .4 seconds that a batter, on average, has to see the pitch, recognize it and its location, and then swing the bat. Calling it the "simultaneous moment of truth," Mo is adamant about the necessity to be quick, and with an almost evangelical fervor, he tells us to eliminate "any extraneous motion that inhibits the acceleration of the bat." Listening to

Mo discuss hitting is like listening to Sir Isaac Newton and Billy Graham all at the same time.

Mo mentions that hitters from Little League to college will often say that they hit a certain way — and he demonstrates a batter holding his hands up by his ears or waving it wildly — because they saw their favorite major league player hit that way. "'Joe Bonabonchuck plays in the majors and he swings like this,' says Mo, repeating a mantra he has heard for several decades now. "That's fine, but Joe's got 'Toronto' or 'Chicago' on the front of his jersey, and you've got the '10th Street Tigers' on yours.

"Major leaguers are so *good*!" he continues. "We don't realize how quick they are. They can watch the grass grow while waiting for the pitch, and the rest of us aren't even close."

Mo emphasizes four fundamentals, the first being to take no stride. "It's tough enough to see a moving ball; you want to compound that with a moving eye? Plus, you shorten the distance to the pitcher." Mo presses his fingertips together, his hands forming an upside down "V" as he says this. When the heel of his hand moves, his fingertips lower, of course, just as one's head must move when taking a step.

"Nipple to back foot" is Mo's second principle and his way of saying that a right-handed hitter should start with the bat over the right breast and take it back a mere 6 inches or so, as would a boxer when throwing a jab.

When the pitch is on the inside half of the plate, pull the ball by pivoting on the rear foot, thus clearing the hips. If done properly, the shin and rear foot will form an "L." Mo calls this "squashing the bug," and it is his third principle.

Mo's fourth principle is to drive the bat through the zone, transferring shoulders so that your back shoulder ends up where the front shoulder starts. If done properly, you may well hit yourself in the neck or shoulders with the bat on your follow-through.

Upon the conclusion of his dissertation, we head over to the netted batting cage where Al and I take turns tossing balls to each other from behind an L-screen.[1]

I manage an unenthusiastic "There" from Mo when I take a better swing, followed by "That's better" on the next swing. I am having trouble

---

[1]An L-screen is a net stretched across a metal frame with an upper corner cut away. This space allows room for the pitcher's arm to come through while still protecting him behind the screen.

pivoting on my back foot, having spent my entire adolescence keeping my back foot planted while striding toward the ball and, of course, Mo doesn't want us to stride at all.

"The ball's already moving. How are you going to see it if you're moving, too?" he asks rhetorically. He watches us intently through his glasses. He is wearing his navy blue Rebels hat with a red bill, a navy blue Rebels T-shirt, navy blue stirrups pulled up to just below his knee, and blue shorts. His legs are almost as white as the sanitaries that show through the stirrups, but his arms and face are tanned.

"No ..."

"No ..."

I swing and miss completely, but Mo sees something he likes. *"That's better!"* he yells enthusiastically, *"That's better!"*

We keep hitting until the Rebel players, who have gathered in the meantime, start looking longingly at the cage, no doubt wondering about the two old men who are receiving a personal clinic from their hitting coach. Finally, Mo says we better get out of the cage. It is a Friday night, and Al and I are on our annual baseball pilgrimage through the Shenandoah Valley. Tonight it's the Rebels, tomorrow night it's down to Salem to see the Salem Avalanche play a Carolina League contest, and then it's back to New Market on Sunday for another Rebels game.

"You guys are coming back here Sunday?" asks Mo, confirming what we've already told him.

"Then, get here at 4:00. We'll do some more hitting," he says.

At this moment, Al and I, excited to be swinging a bat again, are both 51 going on 12. Mo is 85 and ageless.

Sunday's batting practice goes much more smoothly, as Mo's instruction has had 48 hours to sink in. After the game, which the Rebels lose to Harrisonburg 8-3, we chat with Mo. He and I agree to keep in touch and that perhaps over lunch, we can talk about his life in baseball. I tell him that it would be helpful if he would jot down a timeline of all the places he's coached. He pauses, considering the immensity of the task and then deadpans, "I won't mention the time I played in Budapest. That's where I led the league in stolen gloves. We played in the winter, and they weren't baseball gloves, they were fur-lined." I ask whether he played for Kiev or Moscow, and he laughs hard and says, "No, but they're in the league" and that he met a girl named Petrol in Kiev. "She's a slick little number, isn't she?" I ask him, and Mo roars. Should vaudeville ever come back, Mo could embark on a second career, for he has not only kept his wits about him, he sharpens them on a daily basis.

In early October, Mo calls to tell me about an 18-day trip that he and his wife Dorothy have taken to Winona, Minnesota, the home of Winona University. Mo graduated from what was then Winona State Teachers College in 1950, and he is fiercely proud of his alma mater. And Winona is proud of Mo, for he was one of four alumni inducted into the school's Athletic Hall of Fame in 2008. This is just the latest tribute that Winona has bestowed upon Mo. A member of the Board of Trustees, Mo has also been honored with the Alumni Society's Distinguished Service Award, and he and Dorothy, his wife of 43 years, have been inducted into the WSU's Foundation Cornerstone Society. He also served as commencement speaker in 1998 and was named the Distinguished Alumnus of 2002.

"Austin, my talk you would have loved!" he says excitedly into the phone about his induction speech given after the dinner, and I can "see" his face alight on the other end of the line. "I started by telling them how much I enjoyed the honeymoon salad — lettuce alone and no dressing!"

I'm sure he's told this joke a couple hundred times, but he laughs at it as though he has just heard it himself for the first time. He tells me about how beautiful and clean the campus is and, as a true baseball man would, he notes a statistic, telling me that one fifth of the nurses at the nearby Mayo Clinic are Winona graduates.

We agree to get together sometime in November and, after another phone call, we settle on the date. We are to meet at Francesca's Restaurant in Harrisonburg for lunch at 1:00 p.m., and I arrive early and wait in the parking lot on what is a brisk, but sunny day. At 1:02, a silver Chrysler convertible pulls up with Virginia license plates that read "WINONA." Mo gets out of the car and, spotting me, apologizes immediately for being late. I assure him that he's not late, but Mo apologizes again, anyway.

We enter Francesca's, and Mo shows me the timeline of his coaching career that I had requested of him. It is eight pages long. Some entries are simple notations, while others are paragraph-

Mo Weber

length. After our first of three trips to the pizza and salad buffet, we return to the table, and Mo immediately asks me if I've heard anything about the upcoming Valley League schedule. I fill him in on what I know, and our conversation turns to Mo's recruiting strategy, the just concluded World Series, and more details about Mo's trip to Winona. After 20 minutes, I finally get to the first question that I want to ask, which is "Why baseball?"

"I don't know," answers Mo immediately, "I've often asked myself that same question." There is a long pause, and he tries to come up with an answer, noting that being little didn't preclude him from playing baseball, as it did other sports. "When I was in high school, I wrestled. They used to call me 'Rembrandt' because I was always on the canvas," he deadpans. "For some reason, I liked baseball better than the other sports. I just enjoyed it, and then I was lucky to have an ex-major leaguer as my high school coach."

This was Art Smith, who, as Mo tells it, was called up by the White Sox, made three starts, and was bombed in every one of them. The website www.Baseball-reference.com shows that Art Smith pitched in a total of three games, all in 1932.

Smith also served as a lifeguard at an area pool, and 16-year-old Mo Weber would stand outside the fence and ask him questions about the game. "I would stay there *for hours* on the other side of the fence asking, 'What do you do in this situation and what do you do there' ...and one day, when he was exasperated with me, he said, 'Mo, remember' — and I repeat this to the young managers every year — 'Let the game play itself.' Let the game play itself."

Mo elaborates on the idea of playing percentage baseball, and we agree that from little league to the major leagues, too many managers overmanage. He is fascinated when I quote him the statistic found in *Baseball Between the Numbers*[2] indicating that generally, you *lower* your chances of scoring by giving up an out to advance a runner to second. He is fascinated, but Mo hardly seems surprised, as if some internal baseball calculator that has been running numbers now for 75 years has already, instinctively told him this. In this sense, Mo is the most modern of baseball men who

---

[2]*Baseball Between the Numbers: Why Everything You Know About the Game is Wrong*, written by the staff at *Baseball Prospectus* and published in 2006 by Basic Books, applies rigid statistical analysis to a variety of baseball questions and is a fascinating read.

take a scientific approach to the game, yet when Mo talks about the *boys* who actually play the game, he sounds like one of the old bird-dog scouts who would traipse about the country looking for the kid whose heart more than made up for his lack of skills.

"I tell the players, 'I can measure your height and your weight and your pulse rate, how fast you run how heavy you are how big you are. I call those 'tangibles.' It's the intangibles that I can't measure. And they're in here some place; your determination, your desire, your intensity, your love of the game, the sacrifices you're willing to make. Are you going be the first one out there and the last one to leave and work on the things you need to work on?'"

I bring up the name of David Eckstein, a former Harrisonburg Turk, who has played for a number of big-league teams and was named the Most Valuable Player of the 2006 World Series as an example of a player whose heart took him further than his talent should have allowed him to go.

"He can't do anything!" intoned Mo ironically. "He's small, and he can't throw hard across the diamond, and he doesn't have the best foot-work in the league; yet somehow or another, he puts a lot of things together and becomes outstanding. You know who else was like that? Eddie Stanky. There wasn't anything he could do well, but he could beat you!" said Mo, referring to the three-time all-star infielder who also appeared in three World Series in the late 1940s and early 1950s.

I ask Mo exactly what it is about baseball that attracts so many people: "It's slow moving, it's not violent, and it has something to it that takes a long time to appreciate and understand; otherwise, you miss the significance of what's happening on the field." Mo recognizes that this isn't much of an answer, and he elaborates by joking about being old and having lunch in 1835 with Abner Doubleday and Alexander Cartwright, the men often credited with baseball's invention. "Doubleday said 'Let's make the bases 91 feet apart,' and Cartwright said '89'...and I said no, 91 is too far, and 89 isn't far enough!" He tells this joke in order to illustrate the intriguing nature of baseball, and then he adds seriously, "Don't you think it's remarkable how often someone is thrown out by just a step?"

I suggest to Mo that perhaps he inherited a certain artistic perspective on the world from his father, who it just so happens was Max Weber, the "dean of modern American art," according to the *New York Times* obituary that hangs on the wall in Mo's living room. Perhaps, he views baseball as an art to be appreciated as much as a science to be explained.[3]

"Maybe it is; maybe it is, because the happiest I am is when I see a replay and I watch the footwork and the handwork in a double play when it's done just right," says Mo intently. "I get more satisfaction watching a major league double play than I do with anything else, whether it's going to a ballet (and I haven't gone to that many) or reading something that they tell me is great literature...*nothing* gives me the feeling, the satisfaction, the feeling of warmth and good than watching that ball go from the shortstop to the second baseman — *bang! bang!* — and I can't believe it. To me that's the most satisfying; or to watch a hitter with his hands" — and at this point Mo holds his hands over his right breast, then takes them back just six inches or so and then suddenly they move forward — *"here, here!"*

Many a lifelong baseball man has expressed admiration for the beauty of a well-turned double play, but very few will use ballet and literature as a point of comparison. But then, not many make a point to attend the 2007 Picasso exhibit in New York or earn a Master's of Education degree from the College of William and Mary or essentially educate himself about stocks and become a successful broker.

Mo's journey is a unique one, to say the least, and it began with his induction into the United States Army in January 1943. He was a replacement in the 104th Infantry Division, and when he relates his time in the Army, he includes no funny stories, as he does when talking about his baseball experiences. He states simply that he "saw a lot of people killed" and saw others who suffered from "battle rattle," which now has the more scientific moniker of "post-traumatic stress disorder." Frozen feet kept him from crossing the Rhine with his outfit, and he recalls that he and his buddies had no food or sleep on a regular basis and were constantly cold, wet, and outside.

"It's not like when you see soldiers walking at home with spit-and-polish uniforms with the crease in their pants and all these ribbons and you're clean shaven ... It ain't like that at all," says Mo sternly, as if to indicate that I shouldn't ask what it *was* like. "It isn't like that at all ... *at*

---

[3]Max Weber's paintings hang in the National Gallery of Art and the Corcoran Gallery of Art, among many other galleries around the country. Max was often a guest of Leo and Gertrude Stein while studying in Paris, and it was he who brought the first Pablo Picasso painting to the United States. His October 5, 1961, obituary in the New York Times referred to him as the "dean of modern art in this country."

all," he adds, but then he does tell me about wearing the same underwear for days on end and having so much dirt on him that he couldn't find a clean spot on which to wipe his hands. He chuckles when he explains how they would try to pry food from a can that had frozen, using a bayonet or a trenching tool or "whatever the hell you had!"

It was while in training at Camp McCoy in Wisconsin (now Fort Mc-Coy) that Mo discovered nearby Winona State Teachers College while enjoying a weekend pass. Mo wrote to the president of the college while in Europe, and the president wrote back and told him to apply. Returning from the Army in 1946, Mo attended Winona on the G. I. Bill. Luther McCown, Winona's baseball coach, had heard that Mo had managed the Great Neck baseball team back in New York and asked him to be the assistant coach at Winona. Thus began a remarkable odyssey through college and semi-pro baseball that spans a dozen different Presidents, and included collegiate stops at Colorado State College of Education (now Northern Colorado University), St. Paul's College, Assumption College, Christopher Newport, two stints at the College of William and Mary, and most recently Eastern Mennonite University in Harrisonburg, where Mo served as a volunteer assistant.

Mo also managed in the semi-professional leagues in the 1940s and 1950s when semi-professional baseball was in its heyday. American towns were not yet connected by interstates, and American homes rarely contained a single television, much less one in every room. Baseball was by far the most popular sport in the land, and every town it seemed had a team that was comprised of local players and ex-professionals, mostly minor leaguers. This was Mo Weber's managerial heyday as well, and he skippered his share of clubs in the upper Midwest during this time. In 1948, he managed the Winona Merchants of the Bi-State League. In 1951, Mo managed the Schuyler, Nebraska entry in the Pioneer Night League. In 1952 and 1953, Mo guided the Huron Elks to consecutive championships in the South Dakota State League and added another title the following year when the league brought in other teams and formed the Basin League.

Like most baseball men, Mo can recall details of games as though they were played yesterday, and he can describe players as if he had seen them this morning. Clearly, Mo is still quite proud of that 1954 championship team, and he lingers on this subject, recalling his days in Huron, South Dakota with great fondness.

"I got $500 a month in 1954. *$500 a month in '54!* That would be like $5,000 today!" marvels Mo.

"I had the best looking girl in town ... she wasn't old enough to drink. She was a coed at the University of Indiana and sang with the Belles of Indiana," Mo laughed. "The general manager ran a bar in town; Bob Davis was his name. God, he was a good guy, *a good guy.* I'd go in there after the game and say 'hello' to all the fans — of course, we averaged 1,600 fans a game in '54. She'd wait out in the car until 12:00. Then, the bars all closed in town, but once you went out in the prairie and went outside the city limits, they had bars that would start to really open up and never close until people left ... 4:00 ... 5:00 ..." Mo laughed again as he continued, "you know, *6:00,* and the light would be coming up and people are still eating and dancing and yelling and screaming and having a ball!"

Mo paused and assured me that this all happened "way before" he met his wife Dorothy, then continued in a wistful way to describe the girl whose name he never reveals. "She was a typical Scandinavian: you know, blonde hair and really attractive. She became Miss Something-or-other and an airline stewardess. I don't know what happened to her." There was a pause: "Isn't that funny, I haven't mentioned that girl or thought of that girl in years." He laughs.

I tell Mo that he'll be seeing this girl in his dreams.

"She'd be number 26," he replies and then laughs again, heartily.

He tells me about his ballplayers from that 1954 team, all of whom were paid, including the college players and some of whom were ex-professionals, including a former major league pitcher with the Phillies named Jack Brittin.

"That's a sad case ... He was a little guy, maybe 5'9", 5'9½". He couldn't throw a curveball at the beginning of his career, but he learned and his curveball would go off a tabletop, truly it would go down that much. University of Illinois grad. A smart guy, well-educated. He'd be in the middle of the game, and the ball would end up right in front of him on the ground. The first game he pitched for us was in Chamberlain, and every one of those college kids got a hit or two. Next morning it was, 'Mo, we gotta let this guy go.' I said, 'No, they're hitting what they shouldn't be hitting. They're just fortunate,' so we kept him, and he was phenomenal. Some nights he would pitch as well as most major leaguers, but some nights that ball would go awry.

"The following year he came back to Huron and driving home he became ill — he had multiple sclerosis and nobody knew what that was at the time, and every now and then he just didn't have the ability — his nervous system wouldn't let him get the ball where it was supposed to go. He'd been sent to psychiatrists, to medical doctors, to specialists by the Phillies, and nobody could ever solve the problem for him. I think he ended up living for many years in Springfield, Illinois, that's where he was from. A sad story. Nice guy and could he throw hard, and a *curveball*, phuhf!" concluded Mo with the sound a baseball makes when it breaks sharply, as Mo gestured, down and away.

(After I got home, I checked www.baseball-almanac.com. In six games with the Phillies in 1950 and 1951, Jack Brittin totaled eight innings, giving up six runs while walking nine and uncorking two wild pitches. He died in Springfield, Illinois. But he was 5'11".)

As television grew and major league baseball expanded, semi-pro and independent leagues such as the Basin League vanished, and Mo became involved in running several different baseball camps in various parts of the country. He particularly enjoyed serving as the Supervisor of Instruction at the Art Gaines Baseball Camp in Hunnewell, Missouri.

"Our ball camp, well, if you didn't love baseball, it was purgatory! Hotter'n hell in Missouri. We installed an obstacle course for some running ... Lecture. Drills. Lunchtime. A little lecture, very short, then a baseball game in the afternoon. And we had these old buses. Gosh, they had wheels and an engine! We'd load up the kids and take them out and play doubleheaders against some of the teams in the surrounding towns.

Mo tells me that the camp housed players from 9 to 21 years of age. The showers were slow, and the bathroom was outdoors, "but at the end of the three-week curriculum that we had, hardly anybody would want to go home! The common denominator was baseball. You didn't know if the kid next to you was a millionaire's son or a poor kid who barely had enough money to get there.

"Some of those kids are still my friends, and they're 60 years old!" laughs Mo. He names some of "those kids," who are now working in professional or college baseball, including Lorenzo Bundy (the Arizona Diamondback's newly hired first-base coach) and Rick Smith (the Rebels' pitching coach).

"I used to work every day; day and night. I'd drive the bus! Sometimes, I'd be coaching third and fall asleep right on my feet!"

I tell Mo that he obviously enjoyed his camp experience because the joy still shows on his face.

"Oh yeah!" he exclaims. *"It was the best time of my life!"*

It was not difficult for Mo to work with players as young as 9 or 10 for, as one might expect of a graduate of Winona State Teachers College, Mo spent 20 years teaching elementary school everywhere from Winona, Minnesota, to Pennington, New Jersey. Indeed, Mo becomes as animated discussing education as he does discussing baseball, and a great deal of our conversation centers on the art of teaching.

There is one subject, however, for which Mo has no stories, and that is the subject of his famous father. "He didn't know if a ball was blown up or stuffed," says the son. Mo marvels at his father's intelligence: "the best command of the English language of anybody I ever heard," and he is proud, even fiercely so, of his father's achievements. Mo relates with disgust the art majors and artists to whom he has been introduced as "Max Weber's son" who do not recognize the name. "If you had said Mickey Mouse or Johnny Smith or Ralph Badoingdoing, it wouldn't have changed their expression a bit. There was no recognition at all."

Perhaps, because the world will not bestow upon Max Weber his just dues, Mo Weber protects him and keeps his private memories of his father private. Perhaps, as with many fathers and sons, they just didn't understand one another. (In a later conversation, I ask Mo if he had known that his dad was a famous artist. In the course of answering in the affirmative, he mentioned that he never "really knew him as a dad," because his father was so immersed in his art and in promoting modern art in this country. Mo says this, however, without a trace of bitterness.)

Mo finally married at the age of 42, wedding Dorothy Babbitt in February 1965. The year before, Mo had gone on sabbatical, ostensibly to attend graduate school at William and Mary, but his real motivation was the chance to coach the baseball team. Mo's best man was the football coach at William & Mary, one Marv Levy who went on to lead the Buffalo Bills to four consecutive Super Bowls.

Mo left William & Mary, but enjoyed a second stint there from 1978 until 1981. It was during this time that he first began coaching at New Market. He returned to the Valley to manage the Rebels in 1990 and 1991, and he has not missed a season with New Market since 1996 when his current tenure as hitting instructor began.

Mo had his own foray into the professional ranks when he served as general manager of the Peninsula Pilots of the Carolina League in 1987. The Pilots were a Chicago White Sox affiliate. The owner knew nothing about baseball, the White Sox management was non communicative, and Mo quite literally couldn't give the tickets away. The Pilots remained on the York–James River peninsula until 1992 when they were moved to Wilmington, Delaware.

"I've been a big fish in some very small ponds. Never made any money at the game ... but I've been fortunate just to be around the game. I've been fortunate to have a good mentor at the start, and I've been fortunate to end up in New Market. They've been good to me," says Mo, citing as an example the fact that, largely at the urging of Bruce Alger, the VBL created the Coach of the Year Award and named it in Mo's honor.

"It's been a great ride ... I've been a lucky guy," he adds.

I point out to him that it's not over yet.

"I hope not. As long as I can find my way to the ballpark," he laughs.

Our conversation that began at lunch is now at an end. It is dinnertime; we have been talking for four hours, and I recall one of Mo's signature stories that he related earlier in our conversation. A professor at William & Mary asked a question of a class of undergraduates, a class that Mo was taking as a 41-year-old graduate student.

"I put my hand up, and I said to myself, 'Hell, I'm experienced, I taught for years,' and I began to talk. And I realized after 30 seconds that I didn't really know the answer to the question, and the professor interrupted me and said, 'Weber, sit down, you're verbose!' And I smiled because I thought he said 'obese'!" Mo laughed heartily, adding, "I was a little heavier then," but, of course, this monologue is just part of Mo's comic repertoire.

We put on our coats and say goodbye to the wait staff at Francesca's, who have been most patient with us. A college coed behind the counter recognizes Mo from the time he spent as a volunteer coach at nearby Eastern Mennonite. She played softball and remarked that Mo would sometimes wander over to their field and offer tips. This is the second EMU student who has greeted Mo this day, and it pleases him.

The sun is hastening to set as we make our way across the parking lot, and after a moment's silence, Mo says of the coed, "She was not unattractive." He pauses, then adds wryly, "I think I'll go back and have dinner." His face does not change expression as he says this, but his eyes are sparkling, and he waits for me to laugh. I do, and then he breaks his straight face and guffaws at the merriment that he has made. I see him to his car and tell him that we'll have to get together for lunch again. After all, I think to myself, we haven't even covered half the questions that I wanted to ask.

Chapter 4
I Wish the Season Started Tomorrow

My wife Martha and I walk up the Algers' driveway on the first Saturday evening of December. Our way is lit by the myriad of Christmas lights that Bruce has strung on his house, including a red and green strand that winds its way to the top of a flagpole. An illuminated American flag is beginning to flap in a rising wind. A hand-lettered sign on the front door tells us to "Come on in" and we do so. Within 30 seconds, 12-year-old C. B. is giving us the official greeting, telling us to deposit our coats on the couch and that the food is straight ahead and, oh, that we should please make ourselves at home. I introduce him to Martha and, his welcoming duties fulfilled, he dashes back into a room filled with other kids.

We have arrived at 7:10 for a party that is scheduled to start at 7:00, but already the couch is piled high with coats and scarves. We no sooner make our way to the room containing a vast array of crackers and cheeses and finger sandwiches and desserts than we see Mo, a plate of food in hand, and Dorothy. We spy Larry and Sharon Smith as well. An hour earlier, Larry, in his role as New Market's mayor, officiated the lighting of the town Christmas tree while Sharon served as hostess, handing out cups of hot chocolate to everyone, including the eight or so members of the North Fork Middle School 8th grade choir who sang a few Christmas songs for the occasion.

Folks who have been watching the Florida–Alabama SEC championship football game on the Algers' big-screen television are buzzing over Riley Cooper's touchdown reception. A player may only spend one summer in New Market, but when you are adopted into the Rebel family, you are adopted for life.

We greet Lynne and wander into the kitchen where Jim Weissenborn is tending bar, that is to say, the Algers' breakfast table. Bruce is there talking to Lucas Jones and two of his new coaches: Corey Paluga, from Lynchburg College who will serve as Lucas' assistant; and Dan Rollins from Randolph Macon, who will intern on Lucas' staff. This is their first trip to New Market, and I assure them that they are in for a special experience this summer. They are all smiles, and it is clear that Corey and Dan understood that the experience for which they had signed up would be positive, but tonight they are beginning to sense just how positive it will be. We talk about Mo, and they are curious and excited about coaching with him. Dan laughs. "Everybody gets on me for talking non-stop, but I think I've met my match!" he says.

As this is the "official" Rebels' Christmas Party, there is official Rebel business that must be attended to and official Rebel traditions that must be followed. Therefore, after everyone has eaten, at least the first time around, Lynne shoos us into the great room, where her summer sons stay. Folks are seated on an enormous wraparound couch and on the floor and in a variety of chairs. Some are standing alongside a wooden Santa who is wearing a Rebels hat and jersey, while others stand in various corners and around the corners and into the next room.

Just as is done during the ballgames, 50-50 raffle tickets have been sold. Bruce holds the tub full of tickets and Katie Getz, the team liaison, pulls out the winning number, which nets the winner and the Rebels $134 each. Lynne then brings the meeting to order.

"Before I introduce the *assistant* general manager," she says to much laughter as she motions toward Bruce, "I have a few announcements."

"Hey, she writes the checks, so I don't argue with her!" hollers Bruce to more laughter.

Lynne becomes very serious, however, as she starts down a long list of thank-yous, including a special one for Dick and Nan Powell, longtime host parents who are contemplating a move to a smaller home in Harrisonburg. That would mean that they would be unable to house anyone this summer. As a token of thanks for having hosted players for 15 years, Lynne presents them with a poinsettia.

She notes some bad news: Richard's Pizza is closing in two weeks. The wooden Santa seems to be the only one in the room not dismayed by this news. Richard's often provided a great deal of pizza for many hungry ballplayers on very short notice, and Lynne wanted to recognize this contribution. She turns the program over to Bruce, who immediately asks Dick Powell the attendance at tonight's party. This makes everyone smile, for they know what's coming.

"14,523," says Dick, and the smiles turn to laughter. "I counted the ones who left already, too," adds Dick, and this keeps the laughter rolling.

One night several years ago at Rebel Park, Bruce shouted down from the press box to Dick, asking him what he thought the attendance might be. Dick shouted back a similarly ridiculous answer, and Bruce went ahead and announced it. A Rebel Park tradition was born and, without fail, the Rebels have always drawn exactly 1,000,000 fans each year, from that time to this. That's the unofficial figure, of course.

Bruce then acknowledges several other people in attendance, including Jerry Carter, a Luray businessman, so enamored with the Valley Baseball League that he ran his own promotion acknowledging fans who attended at least one game in every VBL park.[1] Kay Helsley, who "couldn't not go to games" easily qualified, but had not yet been recognized. Jerry presented an official "Around the Valley in 60 Days" jacket to Kay who, upon receiving it, did not do the Chicken Dance.

Like celebrity guests waiting in the green room, the coaches have been waiting in the next room with the food. Bruce introduces them one at a time, and the first, of course, is the "Legend of the Valley," who enters the room and waves amid applause and shouts of "Mo!" Bruce presents Mo with a team photo that I had found on the Internet of the 1954 Champion Huron Elks of the Basin League. Manager Mo Weber is seated in the front row at the far left, looking very serious, his right leg crossed over his left, his crossed arms resting on his legs. He is seated next to Jack Brittin.

Mo and Bruce immediately launch into an impromptu comic routine much to the amusement of their audience. Their timing is flawless, and if this routine is impromptu, it is clear that this isn't the first time they have worked together.

"Mo, this doesn't look anything like you," says Bruce, studying the photo.

"Well, I've lost about 80 pounds since then."

---

[1] Jerry Carter would soon purchase the majority interest in the Waynesboro Generals and make his interest in the league official.

"It must have been the war."

"It was. But I can't remember which war."

Mo is given the stage to himself, and he repeats his story about being told by his William and Mary professor that he is "verbose." He then sincerely thanks everyone for what they do for the Rebels and steps aside to applause. Bruce continues, noting that "as of now," Rick Smith is returning as pitching coach, news that is met with audible approval, and that John Combs from last year's staff will be returning as well. Bruce then introduces Corey and Dan and finally, "the guest of honor, new manager, Lucas Jones."

Lucas is greeted with applause. He stands before the crowd slightly embarrassed, but totally confident, and tells them that he's not much on talking, adding that he brought Dan along to talk. He thanks everyone profusely for giving him the opportunity to manage. He tells the Rebel faithful that he knows that the won–loss record hasn't been up to New Market standards and that he cannot guarantee a winning season, but that his team will play hard every night, and they will work hard to improve every day. It is a message eloquent in its simplicity, and it is much appreciated by the fans who smile at his words and applaud him at their conclusion. Martha tells me that he reminds her of Kyle Chandler from the television show, *Friday Night Lights*. Listening to him speak briefly, but sincerely, however, I am reminded of an actor from a couple of generations ago, Gary Cooper, who made a career playing this kind of man in movies such as *Sergeant York* and, appropriately enough, *The Pride of the Yankees*.

Bruce then informs the folks about the MASN All-Star Game, and a new ripple of excitement fills the room. Immediately, there are questions about taking a bus to the event. Bruce assures them that this can be done. The crowd also greets with firm approval the news that there will be three divisions and that New Market will play Luray, Woodstock, and Harrisonburg eight times each.

Finally, Bruce calls on Nan Powell to lead everyone in the singing of "Take Me Out to the Ballgame," thus concluding the meeting with another Rebel tradition, but she has an announcement of her own to make. Nan recognizes Becky Kipps, who is standing along the far wall with her husband Bruce, for taking over the responsibility of feeding the players after the games.

"I'm going to present this pointsettia to Becky because she deserves it," says Nan, referring to the plant that had earlier been presented to her.

Everyone applauds Becky, and Nan's gesture, and then Nan hits a note and the room erupts in song. No one thinks this is a corny exercise, and "Take Me Out to the Ballgame" is sung with the joy of a Christmas carol and the sincerity of a hymn, which, in effect, it is. Bruce is singing, the coaches are singing, Lucas is singing — even I am singing, but fortunately I am off in a corner where no one can hear me. The notes rise and fill the room, bouncing off the high ceiling, and fall back down upon us, transformed in their journey into summer sunshine.

"Folks, stay as long as you like. Talk and eat and drink, and if you're still here when I go to bed, turn the lights off when you leave," states Bruce, adding, "and if you're still here in the morning, then I'll just step over you like I do our Rebel players on my way out the door."

The crowd disperses throughout the house. Martha and I talk to Becky and Bruce Kipps and to Lucas, and finally we spot Mo. We talk about the photo of the Huron Elks. "Hard to believe that was 54 years ago," he muses.

While we talk, Lucas, Dan, and Corey are making their way out, shaking hands, and dispensing "thank yous" to everyone about. Lucas assures me that he has already written down some things that he will send me. They leave, and the room seems noticeably dimmer now that the three of them aren't standing in it and smiling so brightly.

Mo is seated on the coat couch, and he is tired. Though it is only a 12-mile drive to his home in Luray, the Webers must cross Massanutten Mountain. Route 211 is steep and winding and can be hard to navigate, especially in the dark. Mo decides it's time to leave and makes his way to the kitchen for goodbyes, but I ask him a quick question about the batting lesson that he gave us in July. The fatigue immediately falls from his face, and he enthusiastically launches into an answer to my question. He interrupts himself to say to me, "Here, hold this," and hands me the photo so that he can show me how my hands should look, depending on what pitch is thrown. He concludes his brief lecture and continues to the kitchen, hollering back to me to keep in touch.

Martha and I turn around and see Melissa and Charlie Dodge putting on their coats. We say goodbye, but not before discussing the revised schedule. We also discuss the potential that the Valley League has, what with 6 million people living off to the east, many of whom we are sure would want to sojourn in the Valley for a weekend to take in a game or two, if they only knew that the League was there.

The Dodges part after we talk for 15 minutes, and Martha and I make our way to the kitchen where sit Mo and Dorothy. He has his coat on and is wearing an Eastern Mennonite University baseball hat, but baseball is still being discussed, and he hasn't quite been able to pull himself away yet. Behind Mo is a large window from which one can see much of the outfield at Rebel Park and the entire scoreboard. The lights are on.

"The police called and asked me if I knew the lights were on at the ballpark," laughs Bruce. "I told them I was just showing the new coaches the field because they hadn't seen it before. I showed them the locker room, which is an absolute mess, but they thought it was great. I got 'em some Rebel gear out of the souvenir store, and they're real excited about coming here."

"It will be the greatest summer of their lives," pronounces Mo, with a look that suggests that he is not really seated in the Algers' kitchen, but is instead seated in the dugout in Huron, South Dakota, enjoying one of his great summers, when he was young and managing a championship team.

I look past Mo's shoulder to the field. The air is so cold and clear that it intensifies the glow of the lights, and I repeat to myself what has already been expressed out loud by many of the guests in the course of the evening: "I wish the season started tomorrow."

Chapter 5
The Long Winter

It has been a cold, cloudy, and windy winter in the Shenandoah Valley. The dark cloud that hangs over the economy is casting a shadow across the Rebel organization as well. Advertising money is not flowing in as readily as in the past, and Bruce Alger is anxious about the team's sponsors. A serious cold snap at the end of January causes first one and then another pipe in the New Market Community Building, where the Rebel offices are located, to burst. Such annoyances add to Alger's anxiety and subtract from the team's bank account.

In mid-February, Alger receives a notice from the Health Department that the paperwork for the concession stand is missing.

At the league meeting, board members consume over half an hour hammering out the wording of two sentences pertaining to the playoff format in the *Valley Baseball League 2009 Operating Policies and Procedures*. One half of the room cannot understand what the other half is talking about.

In spite of the gloomy weather and gloomier economy, there are a few warm and sunny days to be enjoyed. Two days after Christmas, the temperature reaches 60 degrees and, naturally, Bruce takes this opportunity to work on the bullpen fences and the gates at Rebel Park.

"Getting a chance to work at Rebel Park this time of year is just like receiving another Christmas gift. I wouldn't trade it for any other gift I received!" comments Bruce.

The league announces on February 7 that an agreement has been finalized with the Cal Ripken Sr. Collegiate Baseball League to play the all-star game on July 15. The game has been christened the "Mid-Atlantic Classic," and a photo of the signing appears on the league website. League President Dave Biery and a smiling Bruce Alger flank the Ripken League's Bob Douglas, who is putting his signature to the document as other officials from both leagues look on.

The Shenandoah Valley Herald, the county's weekly paper, runs an article on Riley Cooper's role on Florida's national championship team. The next month, the Algers receive a photo from Riley of himself and Tim Tebow. They have both signed the photo.

Melissa and Charlie Dodge are already scouting potential "summer sons." They attend a James Madison University–University of Maryland game in Harrisonburg to look over three Dukes and two Terps who will play for the Rebels this summer. While professional scouts look for five tools in a player — ability to hit, ability to hit with power, fielding ability, arm strength, and speed — the Dodges use four criteria to determine their selection:

#1 We're looking for a solid young man who not only plays like he means it, but has a good balance of academics and family values. Usually a young man that has siblings is a bit preferable, since we have two children of our own, and we're hoping that he'll be open to relating to our intelligent and artistic daughter, and our son who is athletic and musically inclined.

#2 Is he outgoing or introverted? We like a player who will fit into our family and be a part of it — not just some guy who sleeps at our house.

#3 Is he really tall? Since we have a three-bedroom house, we kick Noah out of his bedroom, and he is relegated to the futon in the den for the summer. Noah's bed is twin-size, so Gulliver may not fit so well in a Lilliputian bed!

#4 Is he a solid player, and what position does he play? This may seem like a shallow criterion, but we just feel that if we're going to spend our summer nights at the ballpark, we're hoping that we'll be able to see him play a fair amount. We had a pitcher two years ago, and it was agony waiting every 5th day to see him pitch!

Mo Weber's winter has been eventful in the extreme, as his wife Dorothy had emergency surgery. She recovers quickly, and I venture to their home in Luray for a visit. Our wide ranging conversation covers baseball and the Rebels prospective roster, as well as the economy, politics, getting older, the superiority of German equipment in World War II, and the crummy programming on television. Mo, who has no Internet and no desire to have the Internet, checks the business channel on TV from time to time. Otherwise, he watches sports and Turner Classic Movies. A few nights before, he watched *Witness for the Prosecution*, a 1957 Billy Wilder film with Charles Laughton and Marlene Dietrich, and enjoyed it thoroughly.

The Webers have a beautiful home, and the shelves to the left of the fireplace in the living room contain neatly displayed art books, several open to pages describing Max Weber's influence on American art. On the top shelf are two vases filled with brushes, and between the vases hangs an artist's pallet. Max's sketches are hung in groups in various spots throughout the house, and the only two sports paintings that he ever did are proudly displayed. One, a football scene, hangs to the left of the front entrance, while the other of a boxer in his corner with two attendants hangs in an office off the kitchen.

* * *

Throughout the winter, Rebel Park has sat as a silent reminder that summer and the summer game will eventually return. Baseball has been played on this site for a century or more, but the park itself was constructed in 1931 when the school, now community center, behind which it stands was built. It became known as Rebel Park no earlier than 1947, when New Market's town team adopted the name of *Rebels*.

Rebel Park is the perfect place in which to watch a baseball game, largely because there is nothing in or around the park to distract one from the game. There are no exploding scoreboards that tell fans when to cheer, no organs playing clever or insulting measures of themed music when certain batters come to the plate, no carousels or moon bounces to occupy bored children. The scoreboard that does exist shows the line score, the count, the outs, and the number of the player at bat. Above this information the message board displays the time, the name of the batter along with a non-color photo, and the pitch speed. This is all you really need to know to keep track of the game. Only the clock is superfluous, for the only time that may matter during a game remains unknown until the rhythm of the game itself makes it relevant:

"Time to strike this guy out."

"Time for a hit."

"Time for some nachos."

Rebel Park is not only a perfect place for a baseball fan, it is a perfect place for anyone who wants simply to relax, not mindlessly in front of a television, but reflectively in front of a summer evening. Perhaps, it is the color that promotes such relaxation, for all is green from the infield to the parking lot to the pastures that stretch out to Massanutten Mountain, to the mountain itself. The mountain, in fact, puts on a spectacular light show, if you are an observant spectator. Before the game, as Bruce Alger announces the starting lineups, the mountain is alight and green with the leaves of thousands of trees; the ones along the very top of the ridgeline even stand out singularly against the sky. As the sun begins to set, however, the dales at the mountain's base begin to take on a bluish hue, which gradually works its way to the crest. The color deepens, as does the blue background of the eastern sky. By the middle of the game, you begin to check between innings to see if Massanutten is still visible. Finally, it is not. If you are at Rebel Park at the right time, however, you may be fortunate enough to see the mountain illuminated once more when the full moon rises above the ridge. It's hard to say whether you will first notice the brilliant white tip of the moon or the audible acknowledgement of its rising by the crowd.

In major league parks, the moon is just another light.

As far back as 1965, Pulitzer Prize-winning author and baseball aficionado Roger Angell wrote about the insidious nature of the major league baseball stadium as an attraction in and of itself in his classic work, *The Summer Game*:

> *Baseball's clock ticks inwardly and silently, and a man absorbed in a ball game is caught in a slow, green place of removal and concentration and in a tension that is screwed up slowly and ever more tightly with each pitcher's windup and with the almost imperceptible forward lean and little half-step with which the fielders accompany each pitch. Whatever the pace of the particular baseball game we are watching, whatever its outcome, it holds us in its own continuum and mercifully releases us from our own. Any persistent effort to destroy this unique phenomenon, to "use up" baseball's time with planned distractions, will in fact transform the sport*

into another mere entertainment and thus hasten its descent to the status of a boring and stylized curiosity (Angell, 1972, p. 150).[1]

Angell has proven prophetic, as witnessed by the abysmal television ratings for the 2008 World Series, an interesting contest between two perennial losers, the Philadelphia Phillies and the Tampa Bay Rays. Tropicana Field, home of the Rays, actually has a tank full of stingrays beyond the outfield fence, which fans can visit and in which youngsters constantly stick their hands. Petting a fish has become more entertaining than watching the quickest swing on the planet in the person of the Rays' talented centerfielder, B. J. Upton. But then, no one has ever seen the moon rise above the artificial grass of domed Tropicana Field, either. If every city neighborhood had a Rebel Park, major league baseball might cease to exist altogether.

New Market's mayor Larry Smith and his wife Sharon have experienced both worlds, as they held season tickets to the Braves games when they lived in Atlanta, but now hold Rebels season tickets.

"It used to *drive us nuts!*" says Sharon of the "continual parade" of fans at major league games who wander up and down the aisles, oblivious to the action on the field. "This one would get up and that one would get up — sit down, for heaven's sake! You get all of your stuff, and you sit down and watch the game! That's why we came, to watch the game!" Sharon slaps the table for emphasis, and it occurs to me that I would love to sit between Roger Angell and Sharon at a Rebels game this summer.

"It doesn't happen in Rebel Park," adds Larry. "People come here to watch baseball, and they're serious about it."

So serious that in an era when every city, town, and village seems intent on building a shinier, artificially louder ballpark, overflowing with the local version of the Rays' tank, New Market is intent on preserving Rebel Park. Town officials recognize that they possess a most invaluable diamond, listing it as a "natural and cultural resource" in the *New Market Growth and Annexation Area Concept Plan*, a document that gives focus to future growth in the town. The plan notes that "it is also important that the views from the ball park into New Market Gap are considered in the location and design of neighborhoods" that will be built in the future.[2]

---

[1]Angell, R. (1972). *The Summer Game.* New York: Popular Library.
[2]New Market Growth and Annexation Area Concept Plan, November 2007, p. 25.

The park's dimensions are fairly standard: 322 feet down both the right-field and left field lines and 365 feet to dead center. The center-field dimension may seem a bit small, but few balls are hit out to dead center, a testament to the time it takes for college players to adjust to the less lively wooden bats. The deepest part of the park, at 385', is actually left-center, just to the right of the electronic scoreboard/messageboard.

An 8-foot high plywood fence, covered in advertising, runs from left center to right center. Local sponsors including the Southern Kitchen, Johnny Appleseed Restaurant, Pack's Ice Cream Stand, and Grubbs Chevrolet are featured on the plywood panels, as well as league sponsors Chili's and Shentel Communications.

The panels, like a lineup of old timers along a foul line, are bowed and bent. Like the old timers, however, what the fence lacks in rigidity and strength is made up for in character. To walk along the warning track and touch the peeling paint gives one the sense that, with a minimum of coaxing, it would tell plenty of stories about home runs that have sailed over it and of outfielders who have crashed into it.

The Rebels' bullpen lies beyond the left-field wall, which stands only four feet high so that the relief pitchers can view the game. A green rail fence runs from the foul pole by the bullpen all the way to the dugout. Cars are parked in the meadow beyond this bullpen. The dugouts themselves sit at ground level and contain a built-in wooden bench, painted green, of course. The dugouts seem to perpetually contain reminders of the baseball season even in winter: a ragged ball hidden in the corner, a dusty gum wrapper, an empty bottle of Gatorade resting where a summer someone left it; a small plastic monument to the season now past.

Word has begun to circulate on the collegiate circuit about Rebel Park's charm, and some colleges are now scheduling games in New Market when they make their Southern swings. Sunday, March 1st was to have seen the University of Pittsburgh–Bradford playing Lincoln College (Pennsylvania) in a doubleheader, but the game was canceled because of snow flurries, rain, and cold. Two weekends later, James Madison University (JMU) played a three-game series against Bryant University (Rhode Island) in a constant drizzle with a temperature that never rose above 46 degrees. The weekend in between was sunny, with temperatures in the low 70s. Such is March in the Valley.

A few parents from both James Madison and Bryant attend the games, as well as a few Rebel Park regulars, including the Dodges, Jim

Weissenborn, and "Front-Row" Fred Miller. Becky Kipps and her family are serving a meal to the JMU team after Saturday's doubleheader.

"You just can't stay away if there's a ballgame on, can you?" I ask Fred.

He laughs and replies, "It gets in your blood."

Early in the first game, the drizzle just about stops, and Bruce jokes that the sun will come out soon and "it'll be a beautiful day." We all laugh because everyone has seen the weather radar, and it shows more green than an Irish pub on St. Patrick's Day.

"Hey, we're watching a baseball game," says Charlie Dodge. "It *is* a beautiful day."

While standing under the concession stand overhang trying to keep dry, I meet Buddy Weiner, whose son James pitches for JMU and will pitch for New Market this summer. Bruce has opened the souvenir stand, and Buddy remarks that he'll have to get some Rebel gear to be ready for the summer. Bruce invites him in and tells him to pick out what he wants. Buddy tries on a hat and reaches for his wallet, but Bruce tells him, "We'll settle up later. We've got all summer."

Naturally, the first game takes slightly over three hours to play, especially since Bryant put up 22 runs in a 22-8 thrashing of JMU. The second game is postponed, and the Saturday doubleheader becomes a Sunday doubleheader. The teams split on Sunday, and everyone but the Bryant bus driver is happy that Bryant could stay long enough to get in both games before departing for Rhode Island.

* * *

April in the Shenandoah can take dramatic turns, with summerlike conditions one day and dustings of snow a couple of days later. The game of baseball endured three very dramatic turns during the first half of the month. Early in the morning of April 9th, Los Angeles Angels pitcher Nick Adenhart was killed when a drunk driver slammed into the car in which Nick was riding. On the following Monday, the 13th, longtime Philadelphia Phillies broadcaster Harry Kalas died in the visitors' broadcast booth in Washington. Former Detroit Tiger hurler and summer sensation of the bicentennial year Mark Fidrych was killed that same day when he became entangled in the power takeoff shaft of a truck on which he had been working.

Dying in the broadcast booth was a poetic end for Harry Kalas. Mark Fidrych, his baseball career long over, died, by all accounts, doing something he loved. Both were mourned and, in turn, saluted for what they had given the baseball community.

Nick Adenhart's death was a far different matter, however, for all of baseball and for my hometown of Williamsport, Maryland, for that was Nick's hometown, too.

I did not even realize that Nick had pitched the night before until I happened to catch the highlights of the game on *SportsCenter* the next morning. There was Nick, five years removed from Williamsport High School, throwing six shutout innings against the Oakland Athletics. And there was former Rebel Brad Ziegler, saving the game for Oakland, and I marveled at what a small world the baseball community truly is. Within minutes of the highlights, a "breaking news alert" came crawling across the bottom of the screen, followed quickly by the hosts solemnly informing the audience what had happened.

Willliamsport was devastated. With a population of approximately 2,300, it is slightly larger than New Market. Over 1,800 people turned out for Nick's memorial service in the high school gym.

It is interesting how particularly we are affected when such tragedies befall our athletes. I have no doubt that it's because they embody perhaps the most valuable commodity known to humankind: hope. They are actually living out their childhood dreams. As such, those young men out there on the diamond are proof that hope is real and that dreams do come true. We can't get enough of them, so we study how they bat and how they throw, and we collect their signatures as proof that we were in the presence of one who Made It. Our childhood dreams live on through their accomplishments, and when tragedy befalls them, we are reminded that, in fact, we are not children anymore. And when tragedy befalls one who came from our town, who was one of us, and therefore, who lived and validated our dreams, the grief is that much more intense.

When Mo Weber discovered that Nick was from Williamsport, he called immediately to check on us.

"Mo," I said, "at least Nick will always have his listing in the *Baseball Encyclopedia*, and no one can ever take away that final box score."

"That's right," said Mo almost fiercely, *"that's right."*

"Nick's death really hit me when I was watching [former Rebel] Brett Gardner come to bat for the Yankees," said Bruce, "All I could think of was Adenhart. I know all the hoops that Brett had to jump through to get this far, all the hard work he had to put in, and I'm sure it was the same for Nick. I can't imagine not being able to celebrate Brett's accomplishments ..."

I wonder if the baseball players who pass through our lives, whether in New Market or Los Angeles, truly realize what they represent to the rest of us. I'm sure that many do on some sort of intellectual basis, but how can they really know the emotions that we've invested in them? They've never had to look to someone else to live their dreams for them. They've *always* been able to play ball better than the rest of us, and I can imagine that they must wonder what all the fuss is about. Most people with a particular talent tend to take it for granted, because it comes naturally and seems, indeed, to have been granted as a matter of course. We fans, however, view that talent as a thing of wonder, and we stand in awe even of those who never made it for one reason or another, but who possessed the talent anyway. Real baseball fans talk in almost hushed tones about players that average baseball fans have never heard of.

In any case, baseball never forgets those who played the game because it is constantly erecting monuments in their memory. Some are literal, such as the plaques hanging in the hallowed halls at Cooperstown. Others are mere lines on a page, but they are monuments, nonetheless, and ageless:

Oakland Athletics at Los Angeles Angels of Anaheim,
April 8, 2009

LA Angels	IP	H	R	ER	BB	SO	HR	ERA
Adenhart	6.0	7	0	0	3	5	0	0.00

Chapter 6
You Can't Do It Any Other Way

May is a very busy month for members of the Rebel family. It begins with the annual Draft Day, when host families gather to select the players who will stay with them for the summer. It also includes the annual banquet, and many days of work at Rebel Park readying it for the players who will report on the month's final day.

Draft Day is an affair that is "decidedly less dramatic than the MLB version, but definitely better catered!" according to Melissa Dodge. It is held in the Algers' house in the same large room as was the Christmas party. Twenty-one people have gathered to determine who will host which player or players.

Different host families use different strategies for choosing players. Some consider the player's position, the school they're from, and some even take into account the player's size, the thinking being that this is some indication as to how much he will eat. Players' biographical profiles are also considered. Perhaps only one third of this year's players have submitted such information, but the ones who have are thoroughly scrutinized. These profiles list food preferences, role models, hobbies, goals, and even favorite books, which, much to schoolteacher Melissa Dodge's dismay are often left blank. Families with youngsters of their own in the house, such as Melissa's, check to see if the player has any siblings.

General questions are raised. Carol Lanham, who coordinates housing assignments and works with housing coordinator Lynne Alger, cautions families not to take only pitchers because "too many pitchers and they get crazy!" Four days between starts would, perhaps, result in some idle time in which boys may make mischief.

Problems and concerns are discussed, speeding tickets chief among them. The speed limit on Route 11 is 55 mph, but drops quickly to 25 mph in the towns. It is easy to cruise into a small town such as Tom's Brook and be halfway through it before you even realize that you are in the town. Some families want the players to call if they are not returning home for the night, while others do not. Some folks want to know whether it is wise to schedule a vacation during the season and leave their homes to relative strangers — and college-aged, testosterone-laced strangers at that. Offers were made to check on players or even take them in when host families leave for any period of time. As Carol's husband Bob points out, this was why taking at least two players was better than taking one because "If one sets the house on fire, the other one can put it out."

There is anxiety on the other end of the draft as well. Parents of players are sending them off to live with strangers for a summer in order to pursue a very elusive dream. They're parents; they worry.

Jill Lively, the mother of George Washington University southpaw Jay Lively from Atlanta, Georgia, freely admits that "sending my son off to 'strangers' did cause me some angst, but each person I spoke to reassured me more than the last. I was sold when Bruce Alger left me a voicemail and ended it with 'God bless.'"

By the end of the 2½-hour draft party, everyone seems to be satisfied. Dick and Nan Powell, who did not move to a smaller home and, therefore, continue to host, take returning pitcher Steve Owens because they have a big bed and because he is a big eater and Nan likes to cook. They also take Jeff Vigurs, the catcher from Bryant University. However, after a last-minute change in his plans, Vigurs will play in the Cape Cod League this year, so the Powells await another player. In addition to Jay Lively, the Lanhams take the University of Maryland players because Bob is a Terps alumnus. Richard Torovsky takes Eric Alessio, a senior pitcher from Marist and West Nyack, New York; and Brian Burgess, a sophomore pitcher from West Alabama University and Huntsville, Alabama, two players who have requested summer jobs. He will put them to work at Reveille Vineyard, which he co-owns in nearby Quicksburg. That works out well for Alessio, whose father is a winemaker.

The Algers had already selected their two players, Kenny Mickens from Los Angeles City College and San Francisco, and Seth Kivett, from UNC–Pembroke and Bearcreek, North Carolina. Kevin Dietrich who was honored in the 2008 final game also went to UNC–Pembroke and insisted that the Algers take third baseman Kivett, promising that his New Market "mom and dad" will love their "new son."

Kay Helsley takes three players from USC Sumter. As usual, Kay waits until everyone else has chosen. Her three players have sent no photos and no profiles. "They will be my mystery players," she says. Kay does not put much effort into her selections for one simple reason: With girlfriends, homesickness, summer school, injuries, and the major league draft held at the end of June, the roster is often in a state of flux. Only once in the seven years that she has hosted players has she ended the season with the same group with which she began the season. She'll take her chances with "pot luck," although given the fact that she will attend every game and that she goes through terrible withdrawal when her boys leave at the end of the year, it would seem that Kay is trying to minimize her sense of attachment from the very beginning. When she delivers to me a manila envelope with two old Rebel programs inside, it also contains an article on Brandon "Cotton" Dickson, a pitcher in the St. Louis Cardinals' system who was one of Kay's players some 3 years before.

Melissa Dodge and her family get their player, but only after the most painstaking research. Melissa selects "a very polite young man," junior shortstop Jordan Pegram from Greensboro, North Carolina and a collegiate teammate of Kivett's at UNC Pembroke. There is last-second hesitation, however, when she sees that he has listed "independent living" over "family living" on his profile. At Lynne Alger's suggestion, Melissa calls Jordan during the draft to clarify this comment.

Kay Helsley (standing) reviews potential "draft picks" with Carol Lanham (seated).

She is satisfied with his response, so Jordan Pegram is officially selected by Melissa and Charlie Dodge.

This is not Melissa's first contact with Jordan. She has already talked to him and texted him in order to have established something of a relationship before Jordan arrives in New Market. The fact that Jordan is a physical education major with a desire to coach factors into the Dodges' decision. Charlie is a coach and has served as an athletic dirctor, and this should give them plenty to talk about. Ever the mother, Melissa has already contacted Jordan's stepmother in order to provide "an idea about us, our home, and our commitment to providing a solid environment for their son." An immediate bond develops between the two moms when they discover that each is an elementary school teacher.

The following Friday on the 8th, Melissa speaks at the annual banquet, asking for volunteers to become host families. The Rebels are expecting three more players, and while there are beds available, Melissa's call is an attempt to involve new people. "You won't be sorry," she tells the audience, and notes that her 14-year-old son Noah feels that it is a great experience. This, in spite of the fact that he gives up his room and spends June and July on the futon in the den. Noah, seated at a table, nods and smiles to affirm his mother's assertion. It is a striking endorsement.

On behalf of the Kipps family, who cannot attend this evening, Melissa also asks for volunteers to help feed the players after games. She concludes her announcement by shouting "Let's go, Rebels!" which is met with applause and shouts.

The annual banquet is sponsored by the Shenandoah Valley Grandstand Managers' Club, which was formed in 1993 for the purpose of supporting amateur baseball in and around New Market, particularly the Rebels. The banquet is one of the club's fundraising activities and is held in early May each year at the Johnny Appleseed Restaurant just off I-81 in New Market. With an attendance of over 70 people, the 2009 affair has drawn more people than any previous banquet. Bruce's "right arm and left arm" Katie Getz, 24, has set the tables with the evening's program, a pocket schedule, and a red-white-and-blue pair of clappers, which are plastic hands on a stick with "Go Rebels" emblazoned across one palm. The clickety-clack of these mechanical clappers is heard at various points throughout the evening.

Katie has served as Bruce's assistant for 3 years, with the title of "team liaison." A lifelong baseball fan, she attended Harrisonburg Turks games until she was old enough to drive, at which time she started going to Rebels games.

"I absolutely love baseball. It's like my happy place. [My duties are] very stressful, but at the end of the day, I sit up in the press box and watch batting practice, and it's the life. I'd rather be stressed out at the ballpark than at the bank any day," relates Katie who works in member services at Park View Federal Credit Union.

Katie, who is also a volunteer, runs the scoreboard, the message center, and takes care of a multitude of details for Bruce and for the Rebels' organization. Scanning the Turks' website one day, she found an internship position advertised. While there was nothing similar on the New Market website, she "knew that's where I wanted to be." She called Bruce, and they talked it over. Katie soon had her internship with the Rebels.

"She's a real professional and I continue to marvel at her dedication," says Bruce.

The Grandstand Managers have business to attend at this meeting, as the officers for the upcoming year must be elected. Someone shouts that the current slate should stand, everyone agrees, and the business portion of the proceedings lasts about 45 seconds. Richard Orndorff, the current and now newly re-elected president urges non-members to join his organization, noting that by doing so one may help support the Rebels: "One of the great things that happens in this town during the summer." Introducing the master of ceremonies who will, of course, be Bruce Alger, Orndorff states that "without him there wouldn't be much of a [Rebel] organization."

Bruce welcomes everyone and has barely begun his opening remarks when Katie, seated behind him at the head table interrupts. Bruce has a call on his cell phone. Looking exasperated, he tells Katie to take a message, but she replies, "I think you better take it."

There is an uneasy moment in the audience as the worst flashes across most minds, but after greeting the caller and listening to what is said, Bruce looks at the audience and says, "Dick Powell is on the phone; he and Nan couldn't be here tonight, but he wanted everyone to know that from where he sits, the attendance appears to be 14,562 fans!"

Everyone laughs and claps. The Powells are in Indiana visiting Nan's mother for her 92nd birthday, but they missed being in New Market on this evening. For a moment, there is a palpable sense of reassurance, an unspoken acknowledgment that there *are* some things that you can count on in this life; and if it's only Dick Powell's overstated estimate on the evening's attendance, at least it is something.

Everyone is in full Rebel mode now.

Bruce introduces Mo, who is seated in the audience, noting that he will turn 86 in June.

"That's a lie," deadpans Mo.

But Bruce never breaks stride, "and he looks 86."

Bruce introduces Katie and the appropriately named Marvin Diamond, who is Rebel Park's unofficial caretaker. It is at this point that Melissa speaks and then the Valley League officers who have been specially invited this year are introduced. A special presentation is made to Dave and Ardis Beaver, who had no idea they were going to be recognized. A plaque acknowledging their 20 years of service to the Rebels is presented by Bruce with "love, admiration, and respect."

The Beavers are moved, and Dave thanks Bruce and the audience, saying that he and Ardis are involved "because we love our community." Dave notes that they are able to "travel the U.S. through our ballplayers," but concludes by saying, "there's no place like Rebel Park." This is met with great applause.

Bruce announces the new schedule and a murmur of approval is heard. Rebel fans like the idea of eight cracks at archrivals Luray and Harrisonburg and in-county competitor Woodstock. Indeed, New Market has an in-season trophy competition with both Luray and Woodstock. The Battle of the Mountain Trophy marks the rivalry with Luray, while the Grubbs Chevrolet Shenandoah County Championship Trophy marks the rivalry with Woodstock. The respective trophies are presented to the winner of each game, and ultimately, the winner of the season series keeps the trophy over the winter.

"Lucas," Bruce intones with mock seriousness to manager Lucas Jones, who will soon address the crowd, "You will notice that we are not in possession of either of those trophies."

Bruce also announces that the season has been dedicated to the memory of two "longtime, loyal Rebel fans" who died in the past year, Barbara Zuspan and Bessie Nonnemacher. Such dedications are a Rebel tradition.

The featured speaker follows, and he is none other than Bob Douglas, the Commissioner of the Cal Ripken Senior College Baseball League, the Valley League's opponent in the Mid-Atlantic Classic All-Star Game. Bruce has invited him to speak so that Rebel fans (and the League officials in attendance) will have an increased sense of what a momentous occasion — and opportunity — it will be for an all-star team from the Valley League to appear on a regional sports network. Douglas, a polished, middle-aged gentleman wearing a black pullover with the league name stitched across the left breast, relates the story of how the game came about. He waxes enthusiastic, not only about the game, but also about the banquet itself and the number of fans in attendance, calling the affair "a model" for their own league. He is received enthusiastically.

At the conclusion of Douglas' speech, Bruce introduces the evening's final speaker, Head Coach Lucas Jones. At 26 years of age, he is a contrast to Douglas, and he approaches the podium as though he is not quite sure that anyone really wants to hear from him. He is very sure of his message, however, and he delivers it with grace and sincerity. In his introduction, Bruce has reviewed Lucas' many on-field accomplishments, including the fact that as part of Randolph Macon's coaching staff, he has helped guide the team to its first league championship since 1987 and its first NCAA tournament appearance since 1977. Immediately, Lucas turns the spotlight away from himself.

After making a joke about jotting down some notes that will do him no good because he can't read his own handwriting, he tells the audience, "Those accolades were only done because of the people around me," adding, "both from a playing standpoint and the coaches I played for."

After introducing his staff, Jones tells the audience that he has sought players who know how to play the game, who have good skills, and who will play with the proper attitude, the trait that he deems the most important of all. He informs everyone that he laid out a highly detailed 61-day plan for the upcoming season with a theme for each day, "and then last week ... it's a very tragic story," continues Jones, who proceeds to tell the crowd about Jeff Taylor, Sr., a professor at Liberty University whose son plays baseball for Jones' alma mater, Lynchburg College.

Only the week before, the father was throwing batting practice to his son who hit a line drive back up the middle. Taylor turned his head, but the ball struck him in the neck and killed him.

"He was a baseball guy," said Jones, "and when I think of this organization and I think of what the New Market Rebels have done, I think of Jeff Taylor, Sr., and I lump him into this group because he is all about baseball, he's all about relationships, and he's all about the positive things within the community."

Jones then reads the congratulatory e-mail that Taylor had sent him upon hearing the news that he had become the Rebels' head coach. Lucas tells his audience that he tore up his 61-day plan.

"We're going to play it in the moment. We're going to play it pitch to pitch. You live the present moment, and you live the present life, and you don't worry about the other things. You just enjoy the time that you have, and you work from pitch to pitch, and if we can do that, we're going to have a successful year. Like I told you at the Christmas party, it's all about these young men; it's about their experiences. It has nothing to do with me. It has nothing to do with me furthering my career. It's all about their experience, and it's because of things like this and because of people like you that create those experiences."

Lucas' speech concludes the banquet and people mingle briefly.

I spy Mo, who is most impressed with Lucas' talk: "We've got a good skipper," he says "he's going to command a lot of respect in that dugout."

Later that night, on his way back to Baltimore, Bob Douglas calls Bruce to thank him for the invitation and to reiterate how impressed he was by the banquet and the enthusiasm of the fans who gathered there.

I stay over at Bruce's this night, as I will help him install a piece of synthetic turf that has been donated for use in the batting cage. While it is a sunny Saturday morning, rains earlier in the week have rendered the ground too wet to work, a precursor of the season to come. We walk down to the Southern Kitchen for breakfast and, upon being seated, Bruce immediately jokes with the waitress about how much of a tip he should leave. We eat our fill and then some. Bruce grabs the check in a flash and will let me contribute nothing. His tip is very generous.

On our way back, we pass a building that housed the Midway Market, a grocery store at which Bruce worked as a teenager. It reminds him of a story very similar to the one he told me last fall about stealing a rubber ball and then feeling guilty, ultimately confessing and paying for it. This time, his employers, Henry and Betty Tusing, overpaid him by $5 — earnings at that time were paid cash in an envelope — and Bruce never said a word about it. Until 18 years had passed. An adult now, something made him think of the $5 one day. When the incident came to mind again a couple of days later, he was instantly determined to "make it right." Bruce called the now retired Mr. Tusing and told him what had happened, insisting that he would pay back the $5 with interest. Naturally, Mr. Tusing told him that his call was worth more than any amount of money, and that, in itself, made it right.

"'If it would make you feel better, Bruce, you can pay me the $5,'" recalled Alger, relating Mr. Tusing's response. "I sent him $10," added Bruce, who relates this story in a totally unassuming way.

Continually driven to do right, perhaps an ever-maturing Bruce Alger examined a stretch of youthful selfishness and became determined to turn thoughtless disregard for others — not an unusual attitude in young men — into a thoughtless *regard* for others. Perhaps, if the latter became as automatic as the former, it would somehow balance the scales in Alger's life; as if Bruce judged his past transgressions and sentenced himself to a lifetime of community service, discovering in the process something that makes him truly happy.

This thoughtless regard is applied even in the tough economic times of 2009, when sponsorship money is hard to come by. Grubbs Chevrolet in Woodstock has been a longtime Rebel sponsor, but owner Bobby Grubbs has no idea how long he will be able to keep his dealership, given the fact that General Motors will close 1,100 of them. Bruce has left a message with Grubbs, who finally returns his call saying, "I know why you called, but I just can't do anything this year."

"Then you don't know why I called," laughs Bruce, who tells Grubbs that he will keep his outfield sign, his passes, his name on the "Dash for Cash," and all the other benefits of his usual sponsorship package and that it won't cost him a thing.

Needless to say, Grubbs is appreciative, but not surprised.

"That's just our way of saying thanks for your support over the years and for helping us out when times were tough for us," says Bruce.

Bruce pauses after telling me this story and then adds matter-of-factly, "You can't do it any other way."

Of course, "it is done" in other ways, but not in New Market and not by Bruce Alger.

Chapter 7
A Gathering of Rebels

L ucas Jones will earn $3,500 for his summer in the Shenandoah. Not bad money for two months of managing a ballclub. It's not as if, however, he can simply show up just before the game, fill out the lineup card, send in a pinch hitter, give a postgame interview, and then go home for the night. For his $3,500, and in addition to his actual on-field management of the team, Jones is responsible for maintaining the field and the bullpens, cleaning the dugouts, picking up trash around the park, hosing and wiping down the bleachers once a week, cleaning the rest rooms after each game, sweeping the concessions area, keeping track of and maintaining the baseball and field equipment, and preparing the field for the local adult league team. He is also expected to ensure the participation of the team in all planned community service events, such as "Reading With the Rebels Day," which is sponsored by the New Market Library. Most importantly, he is responsible for the conduct and discipline of the coaches and the players. This last responsibility was emphasized heavily during Lucas' pre-hire interview.

Jones has two opportunities to earn additional income over the summer. First, for organizing and conducting the Rebel Baseball Camps, he will receive half the registration fees. Second, Jones earns a $100 bonus for reaching the first round of the playoffs, $200 for reaching the second round, and $300 for reaching the third round.

Lucas is given a budget of $2,500 with which to hire coaches. Corey Paluga from Lynchburg College, Daniel Rollins from Randolph Macon, and John Combs from the University of Rio Grande, along with Mo Weber, round out the Rebels' coaching staff.

Paluga, who played with Lucas at Lynchburg College, serves as Lucas' top assistant. "Basically, I wanted a friend, somebody I knew and could trust. I want somebody that I know I can get along with," said Jones. "Hopefully, this opportunity will open a door for him in the future."

With a B.S. in math and having just completed a master's in education administration, Paluga, 25, would like to serve one day as a college athletic administrator. The former catcher, who plans to pursue a Ph.D. at some point, will coach first base.

Rollins, whom Lucas describes as being "very passionate about the game," will throw batting practice and hit fungoes and "do all the things you have to do as a young guy in this business and, hopefully, it will open a door for him, too." Rollins also has a reputation as a talker about anything in general and about baseball in particular. The youngest coach on the staff at age 22, Dan graduated with his bachelor's degree the day before he reported to New Market to begin what he hopes will be a lifelong career in baseball.

"Both those guys are young, they're energetic, they're passionate about the game, and that's all I can really ask for, and I trust them both. I know that they'll give me their honest opinion."

Combs will work with the outfielders as well as serve as the strength and conditioning coach. Already in possession of a master's degree in business management, the 25-year-old Combs is working on a master's degree in special education. He is a graduate assistant at the University of Rio Grande. Pronounced with a long "I," as in "Rye-o Grande," the school is located in the southeast corner of Ohio, and not in the southwestern United States. This is John's second season in New Market, giving him more experience with the town and the team than anyone except Mo Weber, who is in his 16th season as a Rebels' coach. Mo states that Lucas and his staff are "the brightest young coaches I've ever been around."

Paluga, Rollins, Combs, and Jones live in basement quarters at the Cross Roads Inn Bed and Breakfast, one block south of the ballpark. A spacious home built in 1925, the inn is owned by New Market's mayor, Larry Smith and his wife Sharon. Hosting the coaches is their contribution to the Rebel cause.

"We enjoy keeping the coaches, we truly do," says Sharon who serves them breakfast, tends their laundry, and opens her kitchen to the

2009 Rebels staf (from l. to r.): Mo Weber, John Combs, Lucas Jones, Corey Paluga, and Dan Rollins.

young men who are charged with looking after younger men. "I tell them the rules, which are simple: If you come in and a door is shut, shut it behind you; and if it's open, leave it open! Don't feed the dogs, and bring up your laundry every night. If you've got family that want to come and stay, give me plenty of notice so that I can set a room aside, and that's about it."

Past coaches have held dinners and other team functions at the inn. "They can use the house however, as long as we know ahead of time," says Larry. "We try to support the coaches as much as we can. Their job is to coach."

"It doesn't get much better than that," says Combs of the accommodations that the Smiths provide.

"I'm enjoying it; I'm *loving* it," echoes Paluga.

"It's a fantastic setup, and the Smiths are great people," adds Jones.

Both Jones and Paluga remark on the fascinating dinner conversations that take place around the Smiths' table and that they are gaining a depth of knowledge about the world just by listening to Larry and Sharon speak about their travels and experiences.

The Inn's proximity to the ballpark is a definite advantage for coaches who are charged with field upkeep. "We'll see our lawn mower heading over to the field, and they're welcome to use it," chuckles Larry.

Adds Sharon, "And they do become good friends; they become very good friends."

It does not take long for the coaching staff to begin referring to Larry and Sharon as "Ma" and "Pa."

The Smiths have resided in New Market only since June 2003 when they bought the bed and breakfast. Former professors at Northern Virginia Community College, the couple became involved in their new community immediately, first by hosting the coaches beginning in 2004, and most recently in July 2008 when Larry ran for mayor and won. In fact, the dedication to their new community on the part of the Smiths is every bit as strong as Bruce Alger's.

And no native New Marketer is a bigger fan of the Rebels than are the Smiths. "We were baseball fans before we moved, so we were thrilled that first year we were here to go over and watch games, and we felt like, 'This is so cool!'" says Sharon. "So, it was easy for us to become involved," adding, "we have been known to tell guests that we have plans for a given evening because it's an away game. Check-in is between 4:00 and 6:00 p.m., and we won't be back here until maybe 10:30 or 11:00 p.m. If you don't make it, too bad because it's baseball season! We leave notes on our door with Larry's cell phone number, saying we'll be at the game. We'll come from Rebel Park, because Larry will hop over the back fence, but we're not coming from Harrisonburg!"

The Smiths — and the rest of New Market — are hopeful that Lucas Jones' squad will enjoy a successful season. Jones adheres to a strategy of recruiting experienced players from top Division II schools, as well as Division I players from teams not likely to qualify for the NCAA World Series tournament. This is because by the time players from those teams arrive in the Shenandoah, the VBL season is well under way.

"We don't have many ACC guys or any SEC guys or guys from any of those big name conferences, but at the same time, we've got solid players from solid programs. I wanted guys who played. I think that's the biggest stat: games played. Our strength is our experience. Most of these kids are going to aspire to play some type of pro ball. They understand that every night's a show for people, and every night's a show for scouts. I've tried to find good kids who play hard, and I think we've found that."

Lucas discusses his expectations for the team clearly and in great detail. He appears to have prepared as well as possible, so much so that it is hard to remember that this will be his first year as a head coach at any level. He is quick to acknowledge the help that he has received along the way, particularly from Shawn Stiffler, friend and pitching coach at Virginia Commonwealth University, a Division I school with an outstanding baseball program.

"I've just been blessed to be around good baseball people who have opened some doors for me, and I just kinda want to serve as that for my own coaches, to try to open those doors for them. They're great guys, and they're going to do well if they get a chance once they leave New Market," concludes Lucas, who is beginning to sound a great deal like Bruce Alger.

As for the team itself, Jones expects that the 2009 Rebels will not necessarily hit for much power. "What I envision is a gap-to-gap type of team; just a team that will hit, that will get the singles and get the doubles."

Just as Lucas Jones did when he played at Lynchburg. Aside from being an outstanding hitter with a .426 career batting average, Jones also earned the Old Dominion Athletic Conference, State, and Regional Player of the Year Awards. He was a conference baseball Scholar-Athlete of the Year and was a first-team academic All-American.

Jones has expectations for his team that go beyond what's accomplished between the lines at Rebel Park, however, as he delineated so well at the banquet. "I want to make it fun for the players and for them to enjoy their experience and enjoy each other."

The players do have some idea what to expect. All have talked to Lucas and Bruce, who sent out a three-page letter detailing various dates, information on the Mid-Atlantic Classic, the need for players to bring their own bats (although maple bats are prohibited, "for safety reasons"), the fact that the Southern Kitchen gives a 10% discount to all players on the roster, and various other pieces of information. The letter concludes with "It will be a summer where you will establish relationships and create fond memories that will last each of us a lifetime. We look forward to your arrival at Rebel Park on Sunday, May 31. GO REBELS!"

* * *

Finally, after 10 months of planning, it is May 31st, and the players are due by 6:00 p.m. this day. Every Rebel fan — in other words, most of New Market — is excited. The McDonald's and Burger King on the short stretch of Route 211 between the interstate and Congress Street display

"Welcome 2009 Rebels" on their marquees, a touch that Dan Rollins finds noteworthy. He is as excited as any of the players to be in New Market this summer and is determined to soak up and enjoy every minute of his experience.

Slowly, but surely the players trickle in throughout Sunday afternoon. Bruce, the coaches, and Abbie Hansberger, in her 6th season as the Rebels trainer, await their arrival in the Rebel office. C. B. Alger is directing traffic, both automotive and human, out in the parking lot. C. B. is slightly built, but it is impossible to miss so much energy swirling about, so everyone finds where he or she needs to be.

As each player arrives, he must fill out a medical profile, have his insurance card copied, and be fitted for his uniform. Abbie takes care of the former, while Bruce takes care of the latter. The coaches introduce themselves to each player and banter with each other. Mo is engaged in a conversation about the state of pitching "before the war."

"The Civil War, Mo?" deadpans John Combs. "Weren't you here for the Battle of New Market?"

Everyone laughs, especially Mo, who proceeds to repeat the story that it was he, and not Abner Doubleday or Alexander Cartwright who decided that the bases should be 90 feet apart.

Some of the players have sent word that they will be arriving later in the week. Bruce receives a call from Kenny Mickens, who is taking a redeye flight from Los Angeles to Reagan National Airport in Washington. He is due in at 6:52 a.m., and Dan Rollins is immediately designated as the person who will pick up Kenny. Dan does not protest because he is not present. Later on, he receives a bit of a break when Kenny's arrival time is pushed back until 8:52 a.m.

Kay Helsley has already proven prophetic. She has chosen three Fire Ants from the University of South Carolina at Sumter, including outfielders Sanchez Gartman and Kevin Rufus, as well as pitcher Tom Garner. The latter, however, had surgery on an ailing right shoulder only the day before, so he is out for the summer, leaving Kay to house a yet to be determined player.

The Powells, who live some 18 miles from Rebel Park, have also lost Steve Owens, who asked to be housed closer to town, a request that was granted. Meanwhile, the Algers had picked up catcher Steve Cochrane from Spartanburg Methodist and would have housed three players. Only Cochrane can't make it, either, because he needs to attend summer school, so Bruce and Lucas are already scrambling to find another catcher.

All expected players have arrived by 6:00 p.m., but processing the medical paperwork takes longer than anticipated, and the meeting of players and host families does not begin until 6:40. The players sit on one side of the "luxury" seats behind home plate, while their parents and host families sit on the other. As I look over the 2009 Rebels, it occurs to me for the first time that this is a frightening experience for many of them, and it shows in their faces. Some may already be missing home or girlfriends or the lazy summers that they enjoyed before their talent blossomed. All are facing stiffer competition than they have ever seen in their lives, and every one of them is wondering how he will measure up against that competition and wondering even more so how he will measure up against his teammates.

Bruce calls on Lynne to speak first, and while thanking the host families, she reminds the players that "without these folks, you wouldn't be here!" She urges the players' respect for the efforts of the host families and explains that the players are, indeed, role models and that if there are children in the house, they must be aware of how they act.

"Those kids will idolize you," she says.

Lynne adds one more caution. "Don't say, 'I don't care' when you're asked what you want to eat. I hate that. Be very specific and say, 'I like spaghetti with Prego mushroom sauce, if that's what you like!'"

Bruce rises with his own set of reminders. He cautions the players about speeding on Route 11 and tells them to call their host families if they are staying somewhere else for the night. He reminds them that they are in a small town and that "being a New Market Rebel means something here." He tells them "If you do something wrong, I'll know about it before you tell me." He also reassures them that they will eat well and points to Steve Owens, the one returning Rebel.

"Steve was 6'0" and 150 pounds last year when he came to the Rebels, and now look at him!" His teammates have had no time to get to know him, but they laugh because no one can help but notice the 6'9", 255-pounder from the University of Richmond.

Spying Front-Row Fred in the crowd, Bruce introduces him, tells the players that they may expect to find him in the front row, of course, for every home game and that he will get on them if they don't perform well. It is with mock seriousness that Bruce says this, but he becomes very serious when he adds, "Fred is here every night cheering for *you*."

Bruce next calls upon Lucas to address the team. The new skipper reiterates points that he made to the fans at the banquet: He tells everyone how much he appreciates the opportunity to be the head coach, he thanks the host families, and he assures the players that he will "do everything in my power to see that you get better over the summer." Lucas tells them that they will make relationships that will last a lifetime; that for the first two weeks they won't talk to anybody, but after that, they'll never shut up. He is self-deprecating in his humor, but much smoother when addressing the players than when he addressed the attendees at the banquet.

After introducing the coaches, Lucas distributes the practice schedule for the week, reminds the players of the community service that is expected of them, and then hammers away at his most important rule: being on time. He assures the players that the team bus will leave at the scheduled time, whether they're on it or not.

Abbie addresses the players next and says simply that her philosophy as a trainer is to keep them playing, not to prevent them from playing, but if she is to do that, she must know about injuries as soon as they occur.

I am then introduced to the group, and I explain this project. I tell the players that whenever they see me, they should know that they are "on the record," unless they tell me otherwise.

Before Bruce dismisses the players to join their host families and head to their new homes, he addresses what is an obvious issue whenever a group of college men are assembled.

"Boys, let me remind you that every girl whom you see in the stands here in New Market is under 16 and, therefore, off limits!"

Everyone laughs, but a little bit of humor has emphasized a point far better than a long lecture would have.

The players and their new temporary families, anxious to acquaint themselves with one another, quickly scatter, and in no time, Rebel Park empties out.

Chapter 8
All Hail Breaks Loose

The next day dawns cool, and the sky above Rebel Park is a cloudless royal blue. The first official practice will take place at 10:00 a.m., right after the first team meeting. I wish Bruce Alger a "Merry Christmas," and he smiles broadly.

"I have two Christmases," he had said to me several weeks before, "the real one, of course, and the first day of practice. That's when I get to see what the baseball gods brought me this year!"

Bruce looks tired, though, and I remark upon that fact.

"I always have trouble falling asleep on Christmas Eve," he replies.

After breakfast at the Southern Kitchen with Mo, we attend the first team meeting. For 40 minutes, Lucas addresses the players about a myriad of subjects, from wearing folded hat brims on the field to the NCAA rules governing tobacco use. He talks about playing time, a subject certainly on the minds of most players, and urges them to talk to him if they have any problems.

"I'm an adult, you're an adult. We'll sit down and have a man-to-man," he says.

Lucas also addresses the grind of playing 44 games in 50 days, telling the players that they should view it as four 11-game seasons, the most important being the first 11 games and the last 11. Jones assures the squad that he will do what he can to keep it fun, including holding a Kangaroo Court, with fines ranging from 25¢ to $1.00. He will serve as judge. He will also put out a suggestion box.

"I'm here for you," he tells them. "I'm here to make you better."

Before concluding, however, Lucas goes back to his expectations, imploring players to do what they see needs to be done, even such trivial things as keeping the bullpens clean. Having to tell them such things makes him "uncomfortable," and he doesn't like feeling that way. It is part plea and part threat.

Lucas turns to his other coaches, who have nothing to add until he comes to Mo, who steps forward and intones, "Let me have your attention, please," even though everyone had given it already.

He tells the players that he is known to be "verbose," and I expect him to launch into his story about the professor at William and Mary who accused him of just that. He doesn't. Instead, he says, "I like to talk baseball. Some people say that I'm a fanatic about baseball — *and I am,*" he says pointedly. Every eye is riveted on Mo, whose voice is now strong and clear, his expression one of utmost seriousness; he is even standing straighter. I feel as Moses' neighbor must have felt, seeing the guy next door suddenly transformed into a prophet.

He tells the players that they don't have much time in which to learn, in which to break old habits, and that to make progress, "you must be receptive."

Mo reminds them that there are high school ballplayers who will be drafted in three weeks and that by the time those players reach 21 or 22 years of age, they will have already had three or four years of professional experience. "If you don't give 100 percent, there will be someone else out there who will," he adds for emphasis.

"Try to realize how hard it is to be a ballplayer," he tells them. "Repetition is the law of learning! You must work at it constantly. In a stressful situation, you will revert to old habits, and *the game itself* is a stressful situation."

Mo tells them what he has told me — that he can measure their heart rate, their speed to first and all the tangibles, but he cannot measure their intangibles.

"I cannot measure your willingness to work, your willingness to sacrifice, your perseverance, *your love of the game!*" His voice rises as he reaches this last note, and there is no doubt in the minds of any of the players that this old man is not just full of stories about the old days. Just as the dew on the outfield grass is becoming ever brighter in the morning sun, so, too, is it dawning on these young men that this man — who is four times as old as they are — has forgotten more about hitting than all of them combined have ever known.

With his voice now lower, Mo addresses directly their fears about belonging and succeeding. The boys seem relieved that someone is willing to confront the thought that every athlete dreads: *"I'm not good enough."*

Mo briefly introduces them to their first lesson on hitting. He acknowledges that many great hitters have had unorthodox stances, but adds, "Don't tell me about the exceptions; practice the accepted."

Mo tells them that they will make progress if they're receptive, that they will have a great experience, and that they should learn from each other.

"Talk to one another about baseball," he says and then thanks them for their attention and sits down.

There is a moment of silence. This group of boys, as most groups of boys, is too self-conscious to applaud, but their body language and their silence indicate that they know that they have been listening to a real baseball man. For some, Mo's speech marks *the* moment when they begin to wear the Rebel *R* in their hearts as well as on their caps.

Lucas dismisses the players to the locker room where they don gray Rebel T-shirts, their away pin-striped game pants, and their spikes. The players do not spend a great deal of time in the locker room, not this day nor any day for the rest of the season, for the simple reason that it is not the most pleasant place to be. Which is to say that it is cramped, smells like a goat covered in stale beer, and contains one bathroom, the door to which is barely wide enough for the goat to fit through. There are no lockers in this locker room. The players have open cubicles mounted on the walls, in which to hang their uniforms and place their equipment. A couple of wooden benches and several green plastic chairs provide seating. Three of the walls are cinderblock and either painted white or blue-green, while the fourth wall is constructed of old-fashioned wooden siding, as it used to be an outside wall. They exit in a hurry to stretch as a team on the field.

As they do so, Bruce and I head to the press box to take in the morning practice.

There is something special about baseball in the morning. The vast majority of games are played at night, of course, so perhaps it is the idea that the ballpark is getting *brighter* as the morning goes by, and not receding into darkness. For those watching baseball in the morning, the feeling is not that of having nothing better to do; it is the knowledge that there *is* nothing better that one could do. It is a regal feeling and, indeed, Bruce and I sit in the press box surveying an emerald-green kingdom. The players below take grounders and fly balls; they work on bunt plays and cutoff plays and, all the while, the robins, who hurriedly abandoned the outfield once the players took the field are perched in the trees beyond the outfield fence and harmonizing with the meadowlarks. Later in the practice, their singing is accompanied by the repeated *crack!* of the fungo bat hitting balls to the outfield, followed by the distant *pop* of the cutoff man's glove and then the near pop of the third baseman's glove.

Our regal revelry is occasionally disturbed by the realities of running a baseball team. Bob Douglas calls to say that he needs the Valley League's insurance papers and the League logo before he can proceed with any further arrangements for the Mid-Atlantic Classic. Bruce immediately places two calls to get that information moving. He also takes a call from a company who has been hired to fix the scoreboard. The "pitch speed" area is randomly flashing lights, an effect that would certainly prove a distraction to any hitter.

Upon the conclusion of practice, I find Mo and begin discussing one of the infielders who fielded every ground ball hit to him with one hand and off to the side. Handing me his jacket, Mo begins to demonstrate the proper setup for fielding a grounder, but we are quickly interrupted by two excited Rebels.

First baseman Zack Helgeson, a freshman from the University of Maryland and Roanoke, Virginia, and catcher Jake Pierce, a freshman from Louisburg Junior College and Chesapeake, Virginia have found stirrup socks in the uniform pile, and they want to tell Mo that they "liked his look" and want to go "old school," too. Mo is a classic stirrups man; he wears them high, and he even had me check his pant legs before practice began to make sure that each leg was bloused evenly. They were, of course. "Blousing one's pants" is the art of rolling the top of the stirrups and the sanitary socks, which are worn underneath, into the bottom of the pants leg. This makes for an excellent sliding pad and good protection from flying spikes. Ever the instructor, Mo promptly delivers a talk on sanitaries and blousing the pants.

Helgeson and Pierce are especially excited to see that the stirrups that they had found were indeed high stirrups, just like Mo's. Soon, southpaw pitcher Jay Lively joins the discussion and ponders grabbing a pair of stirrups as well. Armed now with the stirrups and the instructions in wearing them, Helgeson and Pierce return to the locker room.

"I heard about Mo before I got here," said the 6'4", 225-pound Helgeson after emerging once again from the clubhouse. "I heard about him being a legend and all, and I'll tell you—anybody who has that much passion for the game is a man worth listening to!"

I find Lucas, Corey, and John relaxing in the office after practice. Lucas is not sure how the day went, but confesses that he didn't really know what to expect in his first day as a head coach. He seems daunted by the task of putting together a lineup in four days, lamenting that "Everybody loves you until game one," after which someone is already upset at being on the bench.

The second practice of the day begins at 7:00 p.m. and consists almost entirely of hitting. Making the adjustment from the aluminum bat that is used in college to the wooden bats of the summer and professional leagues is not an easy transition. A player may hit a ball on the thin part of an aluminum bat near his hands and the metal will still impart enough energy to the ball to carry it over the infielders' heads for a base hit. Likewise, a fly ball off a wooden bat may be a home run when hit with an aluminum bat. Bruce Alger estimates that the difference in bats spells a 75-point difference in a player's batting average. Indeed, this is a prime reason for the existence of the college summer leagues, for it gives professional scouts an opportunity to obtain a true reading of a player's bat speed and his ability to "square up" the baseball; that is, to hit it on the "sweet spot" or the biggest part of the bat.

During this first session of batting practice, the players seem to be making the transition quickly, and Corey Paluga is "very pleased" by the results, as is Mo.

Tuesday brings another morning practice and another evening practice. The latter is not held, however, until after the "Meet the Rebels" night at the local Burger King. The affair lasts three hours, and Katie Getz notes that the players sat in their booths, in uniform, and talked to any kids who came in. She described them as "real troopers."

"Yes, they were real troopers," noted Lucas, adding, "the team chemistry seems to be really good."

Wednesday afternoon saw the Rebels take a round of batting practice before the annual "Meet the Rebels" picnic held in the pavilion at Rebel Park. The entire town is invited, admission being a covered dish, and the picnic is followed by a scrimmage with the New Market Shockers, the local entrant in the Rockingham County Baseball League.

Before batting practice begins, catcher Jake Pierce and first baseman Zack Helgeson negotiate a trade of pants. Zack has been searching for 3 days now for a pair that would fit.

Helgeson, an intelligent and articulate kid, is all business in the batting cage, and on his final swing, which produces a line drive to left, he declares to no one in particular, *"That's* the stroke I'm looking for!"* Returning to the cage for his next round, he floats a weak line drive over the third-base bag and promptly boos himself.

Upon the conclusion of BP, as the players refer to batting practice, they are disappointed to hear that they still must wait an hour until 6:00 before the picnic will start. Bruce Alger cannot be here this night, as Trey is graduating from 8th grade, and there is a ceremony at the middle school. He calls, however, and leaves instructions for the field to be covered. Thunderstorms are predicted for the region and, indeed, the clouds are gathering on this humid day in June. The players begin unrolling the tarp and pulling it across the infield, a task that is not as easy as it looks.

C. B. Alger is not attending his older brother's graduation. Ever the needler, he spies shortstop Jordan Pegram pulling on the heavy tarp. "C'mon, Jordan," yells C. B. "put some back into it!" Jordan smiles and pulls.

It is finally time for the picnic to begin and, as usual at Rebel functions, there is food aplenty. An entire table is covered with nothing but desserts. The team has provided fried chicken. Over 60 people plus the Rebels and the Shockers line up to pile their plates high with baked beans, deviled eggs, chicken, and a host of other dishes. The line has barely formed, however, when thunder is heard off to the west and, indeed, the skies have darkened over Rebel Park. A late spring thunderstorm appears imminent, but no one is concerned. In the Shenandoah Valley, such a storm might last only five minutes as it moves through an area.

Still, there are wispy swirling clouds below the main cloudbank, a fact noticed by pitcher Joe Hammond, a junior from Presbyterian University and Lilburn, Georgia.

A dozen or more people are still in the line that snakes outside the pavilion when the storm breaks. It is a real downpour, but soon intermittent plinking on the tin roof is heard, and it feels as if the backs of my legs are being pelted by windblown pieces of gravel from the parking lot. It is hail. Within two minutes, there is nothing but hail falling from the sky, although "falling" is too gentle a word. Ranging from the size of a quarter up to the size of a golf ball and with a westerly wind blowing it directly into the open pavilion, we are being assaulted by the hail. The outfield grass is soon a sheet of white, and visibility is as limited as it would be had a blizzard suddenly descended upon us.

Hail pours down on Rebel Park.

We endure the storm without speaking. It is impossible to hear anyone shout over the barrage of hail on the tin roof, even if standing next to the shouter.

At one point, the wind swirls around and blows the hail into the center of the pavilion from the east, and at that moment, I could sense a common thought: "Is it time to make a run for it, before this gets any *worse*?"

The hailstorm lasts for some 12 minutes, which is a long time, by hailstorm standards in the Valley. So much vegetation is cut from the trees throughout New Market and up the western side of Massanutten Mountain that the odor of rotting leaves could be smelled when ascending the mountain some three days later.

"You know, there's a fine line between an adventure and an ordeal, and *that* quickly became an ordeal!" says Sharon Smith, who along with husband Larry had their legs cut by the flying, bouncing hail. They finally resorted to turning over the table at which they were sitting in order to protect themselves.

Others were cut as well, including Mo's wife Dorothy, despite the fact that Jordan Pegram took it upon himself to shield her as best he could.

"How did you hear about that?" asked the reserved Pegram, somewhat embarrassed to talk about himself as he always seems to be.

"It's just like Bruce told you," I answered, "this is New Market, and I heard about it before I left the pavilion!"

Jordan's batting practice jersey showed signs of two flying dinners. When it was all over, his UNC–Pembroke teammate Seth Kivett asked, "Any food left? Mine's out in center!" Not only did Kivett lose his plate, but he was also hit by a blowing table.

Cars were covered in leaves, as was the team bus, and a full can of Coke that had been left in a cooler outside the pavilion was sliced open by the hail.

Utility infielder Zak Messer, a junior from Walters State Community College and Bristol, Tennessee freely admitted, "I was terrified," a sentiment that was shared by many.

Joe Hammond and Zack Helgeson were among a group of about nine players who had gone to rescue gloves and equipment from what they thought was going to be a thunderstorm, but ended up being trapped in the dugout. At first, they tried hiding under the bat rack. Then they broke out the batting helmets and put them on. Hammond grabbed a bag of lime and covered his head with that as he huddled in the corner.

"I got sniped in the head, and my hat got knocked off," reported Helgeson, "and when I went to get my hat, I got bombarded in the shoulders!"

Kenny Mickens spent the hailstorm huddled under the pavilion. Fresh from Los Angeles, Mickens said that he had never seen the kind of intense rain that followed the hail, much less that kind of hailstorm itself.

Not even during his days managing in the upper Midwest, where fierce storms are not uncommon, had Mo experienced anything like that storm: "I have never seen hail like that!" he said, adding for emphasis, *"Never!"*

Second baseman Richard Gonzalez, a junior at Virginia Commonwealth University, who three days before had been at his home in Laguas, Puerto Rico said, "The only time we see ice in Puerto Rico is in the drinks!"

As the hailstorm abated, the outfield, which had been basking in 85-degree heat only an hour before was steaming from the ice now covering it. We were all soaked and growing cold, but we were happy that the worst was over. Corey Paluga called to me and asked if I had "taken notes on *that!*" I assured him that I would need no notes.

"Now you have a first chapter for the book," laughed Paluga.

"All I know is I'm going to need a few beers after this," replied Lucas Jones.

On his way back from Trey's graduation, Bruce called Katie Getz to find out how the picnic was going.

"It was a disaster!" replied Katie.

"That's all she could say," said Bruce, laughing, "'It was a disaster!'"

Indeed, the Algers returned at 7:25 p.m. to find their neighbor's tree limb across their fence, missing third baseman Seth Kivett's car by about three inches.

Andrew Kipps arrived at home to change out of his wet clothes and found hail in his pockets.

Two days later, players are still talking about the storm.

"Hey, the hailstorm has to make the book!" they yell to me. Unfortunately, two days later, it is still raining, having never stopped since Wednesday's hailstorm. Opening night against Woodstock is canceled, as is the rest of the Valley League schedule.

It is a portent of the season to come.

Chapter 9
Opening Week

By 5:00 on Friday evening, June 5th, the time when the Rebels should be starting batting practice, they are watching the last few drops of rain fall. It soon stops, and the boys, in shorts and sneakers, line up to remove the tarp. When they do, a vast, muddy lake with a grassy island in the middle appears.

Mo Weber is shocked. "I have never seen that much water gather under a tarp!"

New Market's tarp is 12 years old, and besides the wear and tear from age, it now has punctures from the hailstorm. Some players sink into the infield mud almost up to their ankles and leave large, ugly footprints on both sides of second base when they pull the leaking cover off the infield.

Fortunately, the next day's game is at James Madison University's Long Field at Mauck Stadium against the Harrisonburg Turks. Long Field has synthetic grass on the infield, and there is no doubt that the game will be played. It has no lights, however, forcing the start time of all games to be moved up to 5:00 p.m. Except for Harrisonburg, virtually all games in the VBL start between 7:00 p.m. and 7:30 p.m. in order to draw the greatest number of people.

We board the school bus that has been painted white and emblazoned with "New Market Rebels Baseball." The first letter in each word is painted red, while the other letters are blue. A solid blue stripe outlined in red shoots out from both sides of the printing.

Harrisonburg is a short trip down I-81. Junior Nate Furry, the replacement catcher from Virginia Commonwealth University and Salem, Virginia, has arrived only that morning. He has had just enough time to take his belongings out to the Powells, his host family, before returning to Rebel Park to catch the bus. As we ride along, Nate reviews the pickoff signs with Dan Rollins and compares notes with fellow catcher Jake Pierce. Though in competition for playing time, they share a bond by playing baseball's most demanding position.

Pierce jokingly complains that he will be the first to crack a wooden bat. He looks out the window at the refreshingly sunny sky, however, and says to no one in particular, "Great day for baseball."

Lucas Jones tells me that he is not nervous before his first game as head coach, and he certainly doesn't appear to be. "It's baseball," he says simply, implying that the game doesn't change just because he is now the head coach. He soon turns his attention to a book on pitching that he has brought along. Lucas is not only the head coach, but he will also fill the role of pitching coach, as former pitching coach Rick Smith has not returned. Lucas had said in his interview back in the fall that pitching represented his most limited area of baseball knowledge, so he studies up.

Jones has given the honor of the Opening Day start to Steve Owens. Owens is not nervous either, saying that there is "no point" in getting nervous. Owens, from Sykesville, Maryland, is soft spoken, but matter of fact. He had a good year at the University of Richmond, and he is hoping to be selected in the upcoming major league draft. His parents, Carla and John, who are in attendance, have draft hopes for their son as well. Jones certainly believes that he has a good chance of at least being signed as a non-drafted free agent.

"I told him, 'I hope you're not here by the end of the year,'" relates Jones.

We arrive at Long Field, which is hidden from I-81 by a row of tall evergreens that tower beyond the right-field fence. The outfield is natural grass, and right field runs uphill toward the foul line. The synthetic infield has been overfilled with crumb rubber, however, and the spongy turf quickly absorbs the energy of any batted ball.

A red "Valley Baseball League" flag flies on one side of the press box, while a blue flag flies on the other. Three American flags are flapping lazily in the breeze to either side of the league flags. Long Field holds perhaps 1,000 people, and the seats by and large sit above both dugouts. The hot dogs are excellent, the programs are free, and this day of June

6th is "Dairy Month Booster Night." Cartons of milk, string cheese, and ice cream sandwiches are passed out to anyone in the crowd who desires any of these dairy products. This afternoon, the scoreboard appears to be having a psychotic breakdown, as lights and numbers flash furiously and continuously across the board.

The Rebels are dressed in road gray, of course, with "New Market" printed across the jersey in block letters that are navy blue and outlined in white. "Johnny Reb," a cartoon Confederate soldier leaning on a bat, tossing a ball in the air, and scowling at any onlooker, adorns the right sleeve. Blue pinstripes highlight the pants, a mismatch with the solid gray shirts. Many players are wearing solid blue socks and all sport a navy blue hat with a white R outlined in red on the front and the Valley Baseball League logo on the left side.

A large contingent of New Market fans has made their way to Harrisonburg, as usual. Front-Row Fred and his daughter Melissa, the Smiths, the Lanhams, the Powells, the Dodges, the Beavers, and Kay Helsley, among other fans, sit above the Rebels dugout on the first-base side, armed with cowbells and barbs for the umpires.

Owens begins the game by retiring eight straight Turks, but gives up a walk, a single, a hit batsman, and another walk, forcing in a run in the 3rd inning. In the 4th inning, Owens gives up a three-run homer to Turk second baseman Raymond Quinones, then strikes out cleanup hitter Garret May to end the inning, but he is done for the day. A fantastic diving catch by Turk centerfielder Ryan Eden in the 2nd inning saves two runs, and the Rebels are frustrated by an even better catch in foul territory by right fielder Nathan Weglarz to begin the 8th inning. New Market loses the contest by a final score of 8-2.

"It was just one of those days [for me], I guess," said Steve Owens the next day, with half a shrug. Nevertheless, Lucas Jones is encouraged and tells his squad after the game that he "saw more positives than negatives" and that but

Steve Owens

for one swing of the bat either way, the game could have been much different. Indeed, trailing 6-2 in the top of the 8th inning, Seth Kivett came to the plate with the bases loaded. He worked the count to 3-2 and fouled off two pitches before taking a healthy cut at a high fastball and striking out. Such is baseball.

Midnight found Bruce Alger placing the "Rebels Baseball Tonight" signs at strategic spots around town. After 10 months and one rainout, Rebels baseball is indeed returning to New Market. The attitude of the town toward this event is best summarized by Larry Smith's final paragraph in "The Mayor's Corner," appearing in the June issue of *Our Town*, the monthly New Market newsletter:

> *Enough for now as the sounds of "Take Me Out to the Ballgame" are beckoning—I've got to go! Hope to see y'all at Rebel Park and all the other ballparks throughout the Valley where the New Market Rebels or our hometown Shockers play. There will be no "Mayor's Forum" during baseball season, so if you want to talk to me, you can always find me at the ballpark!*

Lucas and his staff work virtually all day on Sunday to get a still tacky infield ready for the home opener against Luray that night. Bruce has his own troubles in the press box, in the form of a scoreboard control box that is completely dead. He finally calls, Todd Fannin, the athletic director at Stonewall Jackson High and the AD brings the school's control box to Rebel Park, and this solves the problem.

Lynne has her volunteers in place, which means that Tim Loman, a student at JMU, and his friends from the honor society at his alma mater Stonewall Jackson High School, stand with spatulas ready inside the General Lee Concession Stand, while Tammy Barb and her daughter Leslie man the Rebel Yell Souvenir Stand. Tammy's husband, David Barb, has several responsibilities, particularly in the area of security. Being head of security at Rebel Park means standing ready to prevent would-be foul ball chasers from swarming into the back yards of those homes that border the park behind the first-base side of the field.

Official scorers Dave Beaver and Mike Ritchie are ready.

The scoreboard now alive and kicking, Katie Getz is ready at her post.

All of New Market is ready.

Both the Wranglers and the Rebels are introduced to the crowd, and the latter line up along the third-base line in their home uniforms. They wear the same blue hat as with the away uniforms, but the home jerseys are navy blue button-down with *Rebels* printed in white and outlined in red across the chest. White piping runs down the front on either side of the buttons. The home white pants feature blue pinstripes, which, with the blue top, are not mismatched, as are the away shirts and pants.

A large crowd is on hand, and many Wrangler fans have made the trip over the mountain. Bruce is on the field coordinating events, as Lynne takes his place in the press box and introduces the players. It is June 7, and after saying a few words about the 65th anniversary of D-Day, which was the day before, Lynne asks any veterans present to please stand. About 6 do so. Mo, who is lined up with the players along the third-base line, does not step forward and later tells me with his usual humor, "I was already standing."

Tacy Hawkins, a grandmother, sings the National Anthem, as she has done at virtually every Rebel home game for the last four years. She explains that she often recruited Bruce to sing in the choir at church when it was short a few members, especially during the Christmas Eve services: "I must have twisted Bruce's arm once too often, so he twisted back!" she says. Tacy and her husband Dan are Rebel fans, and it is during the games that she knits sweaters and receiving blankets for Reformation Lutheran Church's "Yarn Angels."

"I can knit about two sweaters a week, as long as there are home games!" says Tacy, who attends quite a few away games as well.

Back in the press box, Bruce plays a CD of Michael Buffer, the wrestling announcer, half-singing, half-yelling, "LET'S GET READY TO RUMBLE!!!" and then music plays and the Rebels take the field.

And immediately surrender two unearned runs. Starter Brett Harman, a sophomore from the University of Maryland and Westminster, Maryland, pitches well for two innings and then surrenders single runs in each of the next three innings. Zach Helgeson smashes a two-run homer in the 4th inning. Trailing 5-4 going into the bottom of the 9th, the Rebels tie the game when center fielder Kevin Rufus, a sophomore from USC-Sumter and Andrews, South Carolina, reaches on an error by the Wrangler first baseman, steals second, advances to third on the play when the catcher heaves the ball into center field, and scores on a wild pitch. It is a gift run, perhaps the work of the full moon, which has risen above Massanutten on this night. If so, the moonlight magic switches sides in the 12th inning, and Luray explodes for 4 runs. After 4 hours and 12 minutes of some of the sloppiest baseball possible — the two teams combine for nine errors while leaving 25 men on base — New Market suffers its second defeat of the season.

Around midnight, the Rebels enjoy their first postgame meal, which happens to be Heavenly Ham, served by Bruce and Becky Kipps. The Kippses are in their second year as the Rebels postgame meal coordinators, after taking over the position from Nan Powell. They are assisted by their three adult children: Anna, 26; Liz, 21; and Andrew, 17. The Kippses will sometimes prepare meals themselves, as they have this night; sometimes purchase food, such as fried chicken and side dishes; and sometimes recruit organizations or other families around New Market and Mt. Jackson to feed the players after all home games, as well as after games against nearby Luray and Woodstock. A lifelong baseball fan, Becky seems to regard as strange the question of why she would volunteer to make sure that a group of hungry ballplayers are fed.

"Nan just asked me if I'd do it. I would help Nan a few times ... and it was fun and the kids enjoyed it. We could do it, so we did it. There are things we can't do. We can't really be a host family because of the way our house is set up," says Becky.

"It's a way to be involved," adds Anna.

"There was one night last year," continues Becky, "[when] Bruce Alger looked at us and said, 'You've got it, don't you?' I'm like 'Yeah, we have it, whatever it is.'"

But Becky immediately adds, "*It* has something to do with you just really care about the Rebels, and you're going to be a part of it."

* * *

More rain descends on the Valley, and both Tuesday's game against Haymarket and Wednesday's game at Woodstock are rescheduled. On Thursday, the rain lets up, but the losing doesn't stop. Brought on in the 7th inning of a scoreless game against Fauquier, Jay Lively surrenders a 3-run homer to Gator designated hitter Kevin Deese. Again, the Rebels rally in the 9th, when Kenny Mickens rips a two-run double to center, but right fielder Matt Townsend, a senior from James Madison University and Lorton, Virginia, strikes out, as does Zach Helgeson, ending the game.

Helgeson would have his revenge the next evening, however. Facing the Rockbridge Rapids, the VBL's newest franchise, he smokes two two-run homers — one to right and one to left — and the Rebels defeat the Rapids

9-2 for their first victory. Helgeson's performance is matched by starter Eric Alessio's. The 6'2", 215-pound right hander goes seven strong innings, while surrendering only one run.

"I gave up one run too many," he says later, adding, "I don't like giving up hits."

Still, the victory is somewhat deceiving. The Rebels managed only six hits, but were the beneficiaries of 10 walks, two hit batsmen, and two errors in the field. They cannot count on 14 free base runners per game.

Nevertheless, with a win under their belts and decidedly more relaxed, the Rebels venture to Covington, the southernmost town in the Valley League. Two players — Matt Townsend and his JMU teammate, junior McKinnon Langston from Tallahassee, Florida — have missed the bus, however, and never show up at Covington's Casey Field. They have violated Lucas' primary directive to be on time.

Of course, if you were going to miss a bus trip, the 2 hour and 15 minute ride to Covington would be a good one to miss. To reach Covington, we must travel 73 miles to Exit 191 and then venture another 40 miles west on I-64. One can always take in the scenery, and there is a great deal of it on this trip. John Combs and Corey Paluga are especially impressed by the distant vistas of rolling blue hills. I spy a flock of turkeys in one field and a few deer running in the very next field just south of New Market. Sophomore reliever Spencer Clifft from the University of Tennessee and Huntingdon, Tennessee, is the only other person who seems to notice the turkeys, while a few players comment upon the deer. We pass wildflower areas of purple and white lupine and red poppies and, of course, this year, everyone is keeping an eye on the haze and the large clouds that dot most of the sky.

We actually cross a river named the "Cowpasture River," and I wonder if any of the city kids believe that they are close to the capital of Nowhere. About nine miles from Covington, we pass the unimaginatively named "Mountain View Elementary School." It would appear to me that every school and park from here to central Kentucky could be so named.

Sleeping is a favorite activity on this trip, and even on the short rides. Some place their heads on the back rest in front of them, and I wonder if anybody can truly fall asleep this way. Kenny Mickens is very adept at sleeping on the bus. Even on this drive, with the bus chugging up several steep hills, and with his head bouncing this way, that way, and occasionally into the window, Kenny does not wake up.

Playing handheld video games and listening to iPods is another favorite way to pass the time. I look back to see Seth Kivett and Jordan Pegram sitting across the aisle from each other, each with an earbud from the same iPod.

We finally reach Covington, and at about 4:30 p.m., we immediately disperse in the direction of Wendy's, Subway, Kentucky Fried Chicken, and all the other food joints that are within walking distance of Casey Field. This ballpark presents two contrasting views beyond the chain-link outfield fence from which hang a regiment of advertising banners. Beyond the left-field fence lies a beautiful view of the mountains, as well as of the commercial outskirts of town, while beyond the right-field fence lies a rock crusher and a large gravel pile. Towering football bleachers lie beyond center field and divide the opposing views. No dimensions are listed on the fence, but the grass is lush and weed-free. This night, the crowd is sparse as is, once again, the Rebels' ability to score runs.

Making his second start, Brett Harmon gives up an unearned run through the first five innings, but a run-scoring single by Seth Kivett following Jordan Pegram's triple ties the score. In the bottom of the 6th inning, Harmon promptly gives up back-to-back home runs to Sherman Johnson and J. J. Muse that begin a five-run inning. The Rebels manage two more runs, but lose by a final score of 9-3.

As do most college teams, the Rebels gather in the outfield after each game, for a debriefing of sorts. With the loss to Covington and the schedule now more than 10% complete, Lucas can't just say "We'll get 'em tomorrow," clap his hands, and send everyone off for the postgame meal.

"We had some good AB's [at bats] tonight," he begins, and notes that there were several "loud outs," but he adds that the pitching staff has given up a big inning in each of the four losses, and that the pitchers "have to make pitches" in certain situations. Then he quickly gets to a problem that has become evident, even to those of us in the stands:

"Here's the discouraging part, guys: Our body language is terrible. You make an out, and you throw your helmet or the bat, and you look like children. Look, if you make an out, you make an out. You represent the people of New Market, you represent your schools, and you're going to conduct yourselves like adults. If you don't want to be here, go home; if you want to be somewhere else, then leave. That's not a threat, that's just the way it is. Go do whatever it is you want to do, but while you're here, you're going to conduct yourselves in a professional manner. We're not going to have any more of this hissy-pissy bullshit."

The squad is silent as Lucas talks. He has never changed his low-key demeanor or raised his voice, but there is no doubt that he means what he says. Again, were such cursing allowed in films 60 years ago, I can see and hear Gary Cooper delivering this admonition. Lucas assures his players that he wants them there, or they wouldn't have been recruited to play in New Market, but he reminds them that "the way you play the game is noticed."

There is no smiling or giggling, and no clowning glances are exchanged. The players gather tightly together, shout "Rebels!" after a 1-2-3 count, and then grab their gear from the dugout. They make their way to a picnic area beyond the right-field fence and sit down to a meal of chips and subs that Lynne Alger has procured.

When we arrive back in New Market, Zak Messer, who had one hit in three at bats, asks Dan Rollins if he would come out early and throw some extra batting practice at 1:00 the next afternoon. I have no doubt that Rollins would have come out at 1:00 in the morning to help someone improve at the game he loves. Between his fervent desire to talk baseball and his passion for the game, he reminds me of what I imagine Mo Weber must have been like at the same age.

The next day, Zak and Dan are joined by Jordan Pegram, Seth Kivett, Kevin Rufus, and Kenny Mickens. They work hard in the batting cage, but neither their efforts nor Lucas' talk produces a win, and the Rebels fall to the Waynesboro Generals on Sunday evening in Waynesboro.

Reaching Waynesboro takes only half the time as does traveling to Covington. Fishburne Military School Park at Kate Collins Field — yes, naming rights are even sold in the VBL — is located on the edge of town at Kate Collins Middle School. The field is well kept, and a low brick wall runs from dugout to dugout. Evergreens stand behind the outfield fence to form a solid green background for the hitters. It is 389' to center field, where the American flag hangs from a pole just behind the fence, which is spotted with various billboards. Relatively new houses can be seen beyond the left-field fence, where the pines are thinner and shorter. Lots of folks are in lawn chairs behind the low brick wall, which is topped by a net some 25' or so high. A large grassy hill rises behind the first-base dugout up to the level of the middle school. Throughout the game, children can be seen staking out sections of the hill in order to catch — or pick up, as the case may be — any foul ball hit into their respective sections. The first foul finds everyone abandoning his or her territory in a mad scramble to retrieve the prized baseball from the territory in which it landed. At the top of the hill are additional lines of lawn chairs.

Waynesboro has its own resident character, "Generals Sign Guy Mike," a 31-year-old fan who makes a new sign for almost every game. Most of the signs are designed to attract the attention of WHSV TV-3 in Waynesboro, should they send out a camera crew to capture a portion of that night's action. This night, Mike has a sign that reads "Waynesboro Generals Spells Victory: TV-3."

The Rebels fall behind 6-0 after only three innings, and every miscue is magnified. Starter Ryan Stauffer picks off the Generals' Robert Kral in the third, only to have Kral slide safely into second. First baseman Zach Helgeson, showing excellent fundamentals, has properly moved to the inside of the baseline so that his throw will not hit the runner, but he cannot get the ball out of his glove quickly enough. The play seems to summarize the season so far.

The Rebels scratch out three runs, largely on Rich Gonzalez's three hits. Joe Hammond throws 4²/₃ innings of stellar relief, but the Rebels lose the game 6-3. Helgeson's bad night continues when, representing the tying run in the top of the 9th, he strikes out looking. A boy's frustration flashes across his face, but Zach almost visibly wills himself to be an adult, as Lucas has urged his players to be, and he returns to the dugout, bat in hand and helmet firmly planted on his head.

New Market has shown character in this game, rallying for three runs when they could have given up early, but moral victories count for nothing, and the team falls to a record of one win and five losses. The team batting average stands at .179, while the team earned run average stands at 5.17. For the first time in the young season, a sense of discouragement permeates the team, and the bus ride back to New Market is a quiet one.

Chapter 10
Pointed in One Direction

Like New Market itself, baseball is a tightly knit community, and there are not many degrees of separation between any two players.

This explains how someone playing for Los Angeles City College ends up flying across the continent to play summer baseball in New Market. Mike Easler, the former Pittsburgh Pirate outfielder, who currently runs his own business as a private hitting instructor, was hired by the Mickenses to tutor Kenny. Rick Smith, the Rebel pitching coach for the past 4 years until this season, coached for the Nashua Pride, a team formerly in the independent Atlantic League that Easler managed. Smith eventually became the Rebels' pitching coach because he knew Mo Weber as a young camper at Mo's Art Gaines Baseball Camp. Much later, in 1990, Rick, became the head coach at Assumption College, and hired Mo to be his assistant coach. Rick did not return to New Market as pitching coach this year because he and Easler are writing Internet instruction manuals on playing the game of baseball. Therefore, when Kenny Mickens was looking for a summer league team on which to play, he turned to the man who was now his mentor and family friend Mike Easler, who asked his writing partner, who directed him to the team for which he had coached, which in turn, had been introduced to him by Mo Weber, who at different times served both as Rick's instructor and as his assistant. In other words, Kenny knew Mike who knew Rick who knew Mo. Small world, indeed.

Then, there is the case of Richard Gonzalez and Zak Messer, who played against each other in a 62-team USSSA (United States Sports Specialty

Association) World Series at the Houston Astros' complex in Florida when each was 15 years old: Zak for the East Tennessee River Dogs, and Richard for the Puerto Rico Reds. "They made it further than we did," says Messer in his East Tennessee drawl. Neither had any idea that the other was playing for the Rebels until they saw one another at Rebel Park on report day.

Upon arriving at Harrisonburg for the Opener, Gonzalez spied fellow Puerto Rican, pitcher Ramon Lancara, and began a lengthy conversation in Spanish. Now a rival with Harrisonburg, Lancara and Gonzalez have played against each other since high school. Gonzalez and Covington's Samuel Rodriguez used to "hang out together."

Steve Owens, the Opening Day starter against Harrisonburg, faced his former battery mate from the University of Richmond, Evan Stehle, who is playing for the Turks.

Shortly after boarding the bus for the opener in Harrisonburg, catcher Nate Furry, who had just arrived that morning and who hails from Salem, Virginia, looks across the aisle and spies Zack Helgeson sitting by the window. Helgeson attended Hidden Valley High School in nearby Roanoke, and they greet each other warmly.

"Hey, Helgeson! How ya doin'?" asks Furry, as they engage in a power handshake. "We used to pitch around him!" Furry tells me.

Dan Rollins from Middlesex, Virginia, and Furry played on Team Richmond in the Blue–Gray Classic tournament, when both were in high school. In fact, Furry was behind the plate catching Rollins, who was pitching.

Shortly after Rockbridge arrives at Rebel Park, Furry strikes up a conversation with Matt "Lefty" Flora, a former tee-ball teammate from Roanoke; as well as Mike Cheatham, a teammate at VCU. At Covington, Furry finds Lumberjack Brandon Lower, who played with Helgeson at Hidden Valley High, and they immediately become engrossed in conversation.

Given the interconnectedness of the baseball world, it comes as no surprise that Bruce Alger receives a call from former Rebel, Riley Cooper, who is looking for a place to play. Cooper was signed as a temporary player by a team in the Cape Cod League and, as such, he was released when his short-term contract expired and his permanent replacement arrived. Cooper was selected in the 25th round of the draft the week before by Texas, and the Rangers wanted him to play every day throughout the summer before deciding what kind of money to offer. That meant, of course, that Cooper needed a place to play. New Market has no openings on its 28 man roster, however, and so Cooper will not be returning to the Rebels.

In any case, if at all possible, the coaches do not want to disrupt the personality of the 2009 Rebels, a personality that is a delicate blend of quiet, yet witty young men who are both determined and relaxed.

The concept of team chemistry is often debated in baseball; whether it produces winning or whether winning produces team chemistry or whether it even matters one way or the other.

"I think chemistry is very important," says Zack Helgeson, as we sit in the dugout in Woodstock. "They did a great job putting this team together. Everybody fits together well —"

"Except him," interrupts Jordan Pegram, who happens to be strolling by and points at Helgeson.

Zach laughs, and a wonderful example of chemistry takes place, as if on cue. On a baseball team, *chemistry* may best be defined as the situation in which nothing is sacred and anything from one's appearance to one's performance is fair game for a joke, while at the same time players support each other through times of failure, of which there are many.

Catcher Nate Furry goes so far as to say that players don't even have to like each other, but because "baseball is so failure-oriented," it is very important "to have 9 guys on the field all pointed in one direction. If they're not oriented toward one goal, then they're not going to be successful."

Certainly the coaches are pleased with the way the team has come together.

"We've bonded very quickly," says Mo, who has been part of over 100 teams.

Lucas Jones describes the chemistry as "awesome. We have a great group of character guys who haven't been frustrated with each other. They haven't pointed fingers, and they've battled."

"They're starting to joke with each other about being 0-for-4," observes Corey Paluga. "I don't see any other teams exhibit the camaraderie that we show, and I watch them all in BP and pregame warm-ups. They're starting to believe."

Nate Furry

Furry notes that losing is "not that taxing" when it's only one bad inning or one bad play. "Most of us are juniors or seniors, so we understand that it's a process. We're doing good things, like the coaches keep telling us; we all know there's a lot of ball to be played."

Indeed, there is. Undeterred by their 1-5 start, the Rebel bats come alive as they defeat Woodstock 7-2 in the makeup game of the home opener that was rained out. One of the runs scores when center fielder Kevin Rufus bowls over River Bandit catcher Shawn Ablett in a collision at home plate, knocking the ball loose. Rufus, listed at 5'8", is the shortest Rebel, but he is more fearless than anyone on the team and thinks nothing of running into walls — or catchers.

The next night in Woodstock, Rufus makes a headlong dive in center, snaring the ball with what Mo describes the next day behind the batting cage as "a big-league catch." This elicits a big-league smile from Rufus, who says, "If there's one thing I'm cocky about, it's my glove." Neither the catch nor four leadoff doubles do the Rebels any good, however, as they lose 1-0 on a controversial home run by Woodstock's Stephen Hunt.

"It bounced over the fence," said Melissa Dodge, who, unfortunately for New Market was not umpiring the game, so the call stood.

In what has become a weekly occurrence, the next night's contest with Harrisonburg is rained out, but the Rebels show their resiliency by shrugging off the tough loss and the rainout and defeat Luray 8-1. In the middle of the 7th inning, the lights suddenly go out, not just at Rebel Park, but all over town. In about 10 minutes, they begin to blink back on, and in another 10 minutes after that, the game is resumed. The highlight of the game, not counting the time when there was no light, occurs when USC-Sumter Junior College sophomore Sanchez Gartman sends a mammoth home run sailing through the trees beyond the visitors' bullpen in right field. Eric Alessio pitches six strong innings, allowing only one run and picking up the win.

The next night, before a game in Haymarket, I talk to Gartman, from Newberry, South Carolina, about the homer, and he informs me that he is making some adjustments to using a wooden bat. "That little light bulb came on," he says with a laugh. Gartman is an amiable, funny guy who is "not afraid to chirp in a guy's ear" about playing the game right, according to Lucas. As we chat, we are interrupted by freshman reliever Jake Guengerich from Florida Southern and Sarasota, Florida, who happens to stroll by while Gartman is describing how he turned on the home-run pitch.

"He just closed his eyes and ran into one," says the reliever casually. Gartman laughs and Guengerich proceeds to tell the right fielder about one of his most embarrassing mound appearances: After coming on in relief and proclaiming to his coach that there was no longer anything to worry about, he promptly gave up several hits, including a home run to the first batter.

The Haymarket Senators play their games at Battlefield High School, a park with short dimensions. There are so many chain-link fences around which to navigate to get to the bleachers that one has the sense that the game is actually being held at the Haymarket Corrections Facility. Once in, however, it is a pleasant place in which to watch the game; that is, if you don't sit too high in the bleachers so that the top of the chain link fence that separates the fans from the field is directly in your line of vision.

The most notable feature of Battlefield Park is Haymarket Joe, the team photographer and number-one fan. With his hat on backward, kneepads, and ever-present camera on a tripod, Haymarket Joe can be spotted all over the park, snapping photos of the action. He is especially noted for yelling, "LET'S GO HAYMARKET!" in a booming voice that seems to resonate to New Market and back at random times throughout the game.[1] He enjoys talking to the Rebel fans and banters with Front-Row Fred.

Haymarket Joe will go home unhappy this night, however, as the Rebels defeat his Senators 3-2, improving their record to 4-6. The game is a perfect example of the team chemistry that has been building. Newly arrived sophomore Derrick Kline from Millersville State and Lleona, Pennsylvania, pitches five strong innings, and the Rebels cling to a 3-2 lead heading into the 6th when Lucas Jones calls on his bullpen. Joe Hammond promptly walks the first two batters, records two outs, and then loads the bases with another walk. At no time during the inning, however, do Hammond's infielders show their disapproval by walking around with their gloves off and their hands on their hips, visibly wondering if Joe is ever going to throw a strike. They stand ready to bail him out on every pitch and, indeed, third baseman McKinnon Langston fields a groundball off the bat of Senators' leadoff hitter Zeth Stone and calmly steps on third for the force to end the inning.

The very next inning, sophomore lefty James Weiner from JMU and Charlottesville, Virginia, loads the bases with none out, but strikes out

---

[1] "Haymarket Joe," aka Joe Cashwell, maintains a website (www.haymarketjoephotography.com) from which he sells photos of VBL action.

Pete Onorato. Lucas Jones then turns to his bullpen once more and calls on Guengerich, who induces a slick 6-4-3 double play, the kind that can only be turned when the infielders are alert and ready. Guengerich promptly walks the leadoff batter in the 8th, but the runner is erased while trying to steal by a strong throw from catcher Jake Pierce. With two outs in the 9th, closer Brian Burgess allows a two-out triple, putting the tying run only 90 feet away, but Burgess induces a groundball to the ever-reliable Jordan Pegram at short, who throws to first for the final out and his first save of the season.

The relief corps made pitches when they had to and the team clearly believed that they would. And when they did, the infielders calmly converted batted balls into outs. No one stood in the field pawing the dirt with his spikes and silently blaming the pitching staff for creating a mess. They stood ready to bail out their teammate on the mound, knowing that the next night, one of them might create a mess with an untimely error, and it would be up to Hammond or Weiner or Guengerich to bail them out. That's team chemistry.

"An outstanding win," Lucas tells the players after the game. "Night in and night out, if we play a certain way, we're going to have an outstanding summer. We have the talent."

"A win like that is the most important win of the season so far," says Eric Alessio the next night. "It breeds confidence.

"The chemistry on this team is good," he continues. "It's better than a lot of teams I played on. It's important for the players to like each other, or they won't play hard for one another. Respect for each other is the important thing."

Saturday night sees the Rebels in Woodstock once more for their third contest in 6 days against their division opponent. The River Bandits play their home games at Central High School's football field, and the arrangement is not conducive to baseball.

Home plate is perched on the edge of a hill that marks the far end of the football field, so when the batter stares out at the pitcher, he is also staring at the lights reflecting off the windows in the football press box.

The concrete football bleachers are closest to center field, rendering it the shallowest part of the park at 338'. The lines are a healthy 340', and the left- and right-field power alleys are a major league 376' and 372', respectively.

On this night, we can hear the roar from a tractor pull taking place a half mile or so from the field at the Shenandoah County Fairgrounds.

Some sit in the football bleachers, while the rest of us, including a host of usual Rebel fans, sit in the small section of bleachers that are perched on what little room there is behind the backstop.

A one-run Rebel lead is quickly erased when Woodstock scores four runs in the 4th, including one on a Nate Furry throwing error on a double steal. Trailing 6-2 after 5 innings, the Rebels add a run in the 6th, when with two on and two out, leadoff hitter Kevin Rufus steps to the plate.

Rufus swings, and the ball rises swiftly into the twilight toward deep right field. Rebel fans rise in unison. A couple of steps in front of the 372' sign, however, Woodstock's right fielder catches the ball for the final out of the inning. With a groan, we sit down. Rufus shakes his head and heads to center field in disbelief.

In the 8th, Richie Gonzalez, Matt Townsend, and Sanchez Gartman try to conjure up a rally with a musical interlude. Gonzalez thumps out a beat on the bottom of an empty bubble-gum tub, while Townsend enhances the rhythm by rubbing his keys over the ridges of an empty water bottle. Meanwhile, Gartman emits a noise that is somewhere between singing and screeching, depending on whom you ask. The combo with the Latin flavor can work no magic, however, and the Rebels go down 1-2-3.

In the 9th, McKinnon Langston leads off for the Rebels, and with the count 2-2, he takes a beautiful curveball from Woodstock reliever Guido Knudson. Langston is frozen by the pitch, as is the home plate umpire, apparently, who somehow does not raise his right arm and instead, calls the pitch a ball. The next pitch is above the letters and is clearly out of the strike zone, but the ump's right arm rises and Langston is rung up. The groans and hollering that had come from the Woodstock dugout the pitch before now emanate from the New Market dugout, and the home-plate umpire promptly ejects someone, but we in the stands cannot tell who.

John Combs immediately pops out of the dugout waving his arms and asking — rhetorically, of course — how in this wide, wide world the umpire had ever been allowed to work in the Valley League. John mutters something else, but nothing profane, as he leaves the field.

Coach Combs has done what any good coach does: He protected his players.

"McKinnon can thank John for saving his butt on that one," says trainer Abbie Hansberger.

It was McKinnon who was yelling at the home-plate umpire, but before the ump could find Langston in the dugout, John jumped up and took the blame, playing his part by hollering and waving as he exited the field.

"I took one for the team," he says matter-of-factly after the game, regarding his ejection, which indeed ends in a 6-4 loss. By taking the blame, he kept Langston in the game, which could have been an important development, had New Market forced extra innings.

It is a tough loss, but one thing is clear: Everyone is pointed in one direction.

Chapter 11
Father's Day

Father's Day is bright and beautiful. A parade of white clouds blows from the northwest across what is now officially a summer sky. The mountain is clear, and the breeze is strong; downright windy at times. I have been hitting balls off a tee in the batting cage at Rebel Park. I am alone in the sunny park, which will start swirling with players soon enough. The batting cage is behind the visitors' dugout along the first-base line and next to the Algers' backyard. I spy Bruce cleaning his van and chat with him for awhile, but soon make my way back to the cage to pick up my bucket of baseballs. In the far dugout, I spy a solitary figure, sitting on the back of the bench, half swinging a bat. It appears to be Zak Messer. It is an interesting fact that every ballplayer, professional and amateur alike, possesses unique mannerisms in the field and at the plate; and even from this distance, I am sure that it is Zak. I get my ball bucket and walk across the field. Dressed in his BP white shirt, blue shorts, and Rebel hat, he greets me.

"I thought that was you, Zak," I holler.

"I didn't feel like waiting around the house," he says, "so I thought I'd come out here."

It is only 1:00, and players do not need to report today until 4:30 when the Kangaroo Court will be held. I sense that he is worried about his play and that by hanging around the park, an answer will somehow come; that if he replays last night's at-bats in his mind, or if he holds the bat he has in his hands long enough, or if he just sits and contemplates inside this

Temple of The Game, that an unseen oracle will whisper the right words ("Hold your hands lower!"; "Exchange your shoulders!") and he will hit as he once did in high school.

"That was a nice single to center last night," I tell him.

"Thanks, but now I can't bunt," replies Zak, who popped up a bunt attempt when he tried to lay one down for a hit the previous night in Woodstock. "That's three bunts in a row I've popped up. I used to be a good bunter, but now I suck."

I reassure him that he can still bunt, and I offer him some tips. I am not a coach, but I am a father, and I know that whatever I say about bunting mechanics and strategy does not matter nearly as much as getting him in a frame of mind that will move him forward. I tell him that he's jumping at the ball while bunting, just as hitters often do when taking a regular swing. I tell him to stay back and to pick a spot in the grass, a target toward which he should aim his bunt. This will get him thinking about something besides his mechanics.

"That makes sense," he says.

In any case, I know that he can't just sit in the dugout for 3 more hours, so I offer him my bucket of balls to use in the batting cage. He takes me up on the offer.

As he makes his way across the diamond, I holler to him while pointing to the bucket, "And if you go three for four tonight, I'm taking all the credit!"

"If I go three for four tonight," he replies, "I'm keeping your baseballs."

I tell him that's a deal, and I head to the Southern Kitchen for lunch.

Baseball is such a hard game to play. "It's so failure-oriented," as Nate Furry put it. Zak's frustration was visible to us all the night before, after he failed to drop that bunt. The River Bandit catcher had no sooner caught the ball than Zak walked briskly to the dugout and angrily swung at the empty air.

As any good teacher does, Lucas Jones does not lie in wait for his charges to do something unprofessional, such as taking angry cuts at imaginary baseballs. He does not see half of what he sees, nor does he hear half of what he hears. In Haymarket, Jake Pierce drove a ball deep to center field, but the center fielder had no trouble making the catch and Jake, in his frustration, punted his helmet about 15 feet into the dugout. Lucas promptly removed him from the game. Immediately after doing so, Lucas stood in the dugout with Jake, a hand on each of his shoulders, scolding and reassuring at the same time. Jake's face showed that he knew he deserved the former and also that he was grateful for the latter.

"I worry about Pierce," says Mo to me. "He's a good kid, and I don't want him to lose his confidence."

He and Zak and Zach Helgeson seem so intent on improving, on trying to prove themselves first and foremost to themselves that they think and analyze and try to figure out everything that they are doing wrong. There is a fine line, however, in life and in baseball between analyzing and worrying. You cannot throw strikes when you are thinking about your mechanics. You cannot hit a baseball when you are thinking about the components of your swing. It is a compliment to a ballplayer to say that he is empty-headed, for only when his head is devoid of thought can his natural ability take over and allow his body to do what he has trained it to do.

"You have to be a little bit arrogant and a little bit stupid to play this game," reliever James Weiner put it so eloquently. "You have to be both, *knowing* you're going to go up there and fail seven out of 10 times."

"Every year, I talk to these kids who are having trouble hitting the ball," relates Mo, "and I'll say, 'You played shortstop and pitched in Little League, right?'

"And they'll say, 'Yeah.'

"And I'll say, 'And you were All-District in Pony League, right?'

"And they'll say, 'Yeah.'

"And I'll say, 'And you were the best player on your high school team and you made All-County,' and they'll say, 'Mo, how do you know all this?!'

"And I'll say, 'Because everyone who comes through here has the same story.'

"They're competing against nothing but All-County guys, and for some of them, they've reached as far as they're going to go. To realize that can be devastating."

Warming to his subject, Mo continues, "We're all *human!* A machine can punch out a hole in the exact same spot thousands of times in a row without making a mistake, but you *can't* put the same swing on the ball every time. It's not humanly possible!"

And yet, in New Market, and in towns all across North and South America, young men will leave home for the summer, and instead of hanging out by the pool or in the mall, they will work and work and work, just as Zak Messer is doing, in a solitary batting cage, in the early afternoon sun, placing balls on a tee, seeking to teach their muscles to repeat the perfect swing; or at least learn to repeat a swing that is good enough, often enough to advance to the next level and keep alive their hopes of moving from the Valley League or its equivalent to the big leagues.

Zak Messer at bat.

After lunch, I head to the New Market Library to type up some notes, and upon my return to Rebel Park, I find that Zak is still there, but he has been joined by Zach Helgeson and Dan Rollins. They have been hitting baseballs, and I join Messer, who is collecting them in the outfield. I throw a few into the infield, and Dan comments on my good form. For a moment, I am not 30 years Dan's senior; I am 12 and basking in the glow of praise from a coach. I saw my own dream to play in the big leagues again for a moment, as I saw it when I was 12. I touch the sky ever so briefly, but my wings don't melt, and I glide back to Earth easily. Age does have a few rewards.

Helgeson wants to work on his fielding at first base. Rollins has Messer soft-toss balls to him and he hits them to Helgeson, allowing Zach to read the ball off the bat. I run to get my glove out of the trunk of my car so that Helgeson can throw the balls back in, rather than having to bounce them gently to Rollins and Messer. He practices holding an imaginary runner, then coming off the bag, fielding a ball, and mimicking a throw to second.

"You want me to cover second, so you can actually make those throws?" I ask. Helgeson says "sure" or some word to that effect and begins to field some more grounders. On some throws, I am anchored at the bag, while on others, I try to come across it as the shortstop would and give Zach a moving target.

When he is finished, Messer takes a dozen more swings, and I track down a fly ball and catch it. Rollins cheers. Messer jogs into the outfield to pick up baseballs and thanks me for helping him do it. Helgeson thanks me for taking throws at second.

"*Any* time," I reply. I tell Helgeson that if he turns a nifty 3-6-3 double play tonight that I'm going to take all the credit.

He laughs and says, "Hey, I'm real superstitious, so if I do that, you're going to be taking a lot of throws at second base!"

I leave, hoping that Zach turns several double plays, just so I have an excuse to return to the field.

"It's always a thrill to be on the field doing something baseball-related," Bruce Alger had said to me during our chat earlier in the day, and it is. W. P. Kinsella, the author of *Shoeless Joe*, wrote a short story called "The Thrill of the Grass" about people who break into a big league park during the major league players' strike to replace the artificial turf with real sod. Kinsella writes that when the old-timers on the team finally return from the strike, they will "raise their heads like ponies, as far away as the parking lot, when the thrill of the grass reaches their nostrils. And as they dress, they'll recall sprawling in the lush fields of childhood, the grass as cool as a mother's hand on a forehead."

It is like the reverse of the scene from *Field of Dreams*, the movie based on *Shoeless Joe*, in which Moonlight Graham must step off the field to rescue a little girl who is choking. The young ballplayer steps across the line dividing the field of play from the stands and reverts to the old doctor he has become. The difference for Bruce and me and millions (I think that it *is* millions) like us, is that when we step onto the field, we revert to the dreaming children we were.

Even Mo, who will turn 86 in three days, tells me after the game this night, "I don't get it, Austin. I'm up late, and I'm not tired! Six months ago, I had to sit down and rest while I was doing the dishes at 8:00 at night. But now, I feel great!"

"We weren't playing ball six months ago, Mo," I tell him.

He is silent for a moment. "You're right," he replies.

The Kangaroo Court seems rather subdued today, and when it breaks up, several players inform me that Nate Furry has quit the team. I am stunned. Nate was always happy to talk to me and always had an intelligent perspective on the game. I had seen him earlier in the day, even spoke to him, only to find out now that he had been there to turn in his uniform to Lucas, telling his coach that he was "burned out."

Nate had many intelligent thoughts about team chemistry in general, and so much good to say about the chemistry on the Rebels in particular and, yet, here he was leaving. I have no doubt that he was sincere when he shared that perspective with me, but something had happened to Nate the night before. In the 4th inning, he threw a ball into left field on a steal attempt at third. He tried to throw over the right-handed batter at the plate, instead of stepping out to throw around him. Sitting as close to home plate as I was, I could easily see the disgust on his face. He knew how to make that play, and he didn't do it. He went 0-for-4, and even had trouble handling a warm-up pitch from Spencer Clifft late in the game.

"Burned out" is a phrase that is often used to explain feelings that a person can't explain, and I wonder, last night in Woodstock, did the end of Nate's dream flash before his eyes? I wonder if I witnessed the moment when he *admitted to himself* that this was as far as he was going to go with his baseball talent. It is the hardest moment in any ballplayer's career. We all know that the odds of making the big leagues are astronomically slim, but knowing it in your head and accepting it in your heart are vastly different acts. I am only speculating, but if that were the case with Nate, I wish that I could have told him that he will get past that moment, that he can be proud that he got much further than most of us. I would have told him to stick around and just play for the thrill of the grass.

Furry's departure is not the only topic of conversation in the dugout. Tonight's scheduled starter, Steve Owens, is nowhere to be found. Lucas is unhappy, to say the least.

Nothing has gone as planned for Steve Owens. Hoping to get selected by a major league organization during the June 9-11 draft, he watched with increasing "embarrassment" as the draft ended, and his name was not called. Upon the conclusion of the draft on Thursday, June 11, Owens packed up his personal belongings at his host house, then proceeded to Rebel Park, where he gathered up his baseball gear. He was heading for home, but he didn't get very far before he returned and asked to be reinstated.

Baseball is so failure-oriented that it can push you over the edge sometimes, just as it did with Nate Furry. Sometimes, it can push you way over the edge. One of Owens' short-lived Rebel teammates arrived just before the draft, threw one bullpen session, was not drafted, and quit baseball on the spot, declaring that he would never play again. He went home without ever playing in a single game.

"At 21 or 22 years of age, you go from prospect to suspect in a matter of months," states Mo Weber.

On the other hand, baseball is an enchantress and, once smitten, no matter how much it has hurt you, it can lure you back with the most improbable of promises. Though he has already graduated, Owens has a year of college eligibility left because of Tommy John surgery performed early in his college career that forced him to miss a season. He tells me that he might enroll somewhere — Kings' College or UNC–Pembroke — in order to play one more year. Maybe then, the scouts will see him. As he talks, however, I sense that there is something more profound at work than his dream of playing professionally.

"Is it too corny to say that it's the love of the game that brought you back?" I ask him.

"Nah, it's not corny at all. It is the love of the game," he says, and I ask him no more questions about it. I don't have to.

Finally, shortly after 5:30 p.m., Owens wanders into Rebel Park. He tells Lucas that he's always done it this way, that when he is the scheduled starter, he has always been on his own schedule.

Lucas has none of it and pulls him from the start.

"You think those JMU boys who missed the bus wouldn't be in my office first thing in the morning, telling me they couldn't play for me if we left without them, but I let Steve pitch tonight? *I* wouldn't want to play for me if I let Steve pitch tonight," he tells me later.

Joe Hammond gets the emergency start against Waynesboro, a team he dominated in relief just the Sunday before. He struggles with his command, however, walking two batters, both of whom score on a two-out double by the Generals' Ryan Mathews. The Rebels, however, undaunted by Joe's command issues or Owens' late arrival or Furry's departure, score five runs in the bottom of the first and never look back. Hammond guts out two more innings, allowing one more run before coming out with bicep tendinitis.

In a reverse of their roles from the week before, Ryan Stauffer who started and lost to Waynesboro, relieves Joe and tosses four innings of one-hit ball to record the victory. It is a breakthrough performance for Stauffer, who entered the game with an 11.25 ERA. New Market tacks on five more runs throughout the contest and wins by a final score of 10-3. Jake Pierce is 3-for-4 with a double and two RBIs.

"I haven't been to first base in about a year," he laughs, after the game. He can afford to laugh now.

I can't help but think about Furry's assessment of his now former team when he said that the Rebels were "a solid group of guys. We have some real character guys." They certainly rose to the occasion on what could have been a very distracting day.

The victory was thoroughly enjoyed by their families, many of whom had ventured to Rebel Park on this Father's Day. I spoke with Buddy Weiner, James' dad, who introduced me to Frank Langston, McKinnon's dad. Jordan Pegram's stepmom Amy, dad Eddie, and sisters Morgan, Ashton, and Katlin traveled the four hours from Greensboro, North Carolina to Rebel Park. During the game, Melissa Dodge, Jordan's host mom, brought the Pegrams up to the broadcast booth, where I have been helping Charlie Dodge, Jay Hafner, and Kevin Barb with some of the webcasts. We interview them, and the three younger sisters say little, but the pride on their faces speaks volumes. Later on, Eddie says to me, "Jordan doesn't say much, does he?"

"Absolutely not!" I reply.

Eddie laughs and says, "That's Jordan."

The players have enjoyed a great deal of support from their families in general so far this season. I have chatted with Seth Kivett's parents everywhere from Covington to Haymarket, which means that they have attended games literally from one end of the Valley League to the other. Occasionally, Seth's sister visits as well. Zach Helgeson's mom and dad take turns driving the 2 1/4 hours from Roanoke to New Market to watch Zach. I sit with Zach's dad, Steve, in Woodstock, and he faithfully records each at-bat and phones home with an update on Zach's every move. Jake Pierce's dad, Mike, drives three or more hours from Chesapeake, Virginia, to see the Rebels play. He attends many games, and it is hard to tell which boy is his, he roots so hard for each and every one of the players on the field and at the plate.

Before the game, I receive my own show of support when Becky and her fiancé, Jesse Dice, surprise me by showing up at the park, just to be with me on Father's Day. I invite them into our broadcast "booth," which in actuality is a second-story deck adjacent to the press box. There is plenty of room, as only Charlie and I occupy any of the four plastic chairs on this night. Becky and I don't have much opportunity to talk, but I look over occasionally and she smiles at me, and I think about how seven seasons earlier we had ventured to our first game at Rebel Park. Now, here she sits with her fiancé.

Slowly but surely, the pavilion empties out after the postgame meal, and a certain quiet settles over Rebel Park, the merriment of victory and of families reunited for an evening having faded into the night.

Zach Helgeson turned no 3-6-3 double plays this evening, much to my disappointment. In the bottom of the 8th, Zak Messer appeared on deck to pinch hit for Seth Kivett. There are two outs in the inning, and I desperately root for Kenny Bryant to reach base so that Zak will have a chance to hit. As he loosens up in the on deck circle, I imagine Zak stepping into the batter's box and dropping a bunt. I can see him running to first, being called "Safe!" and then taking his lead with a big, relieved smile on his face. Such a play would have been a meaningless little single on the score sheet and to almost everyone in the stands, but it would have had a great deal of meaning to Zak — and to me. But it was not to be. Bryant strikes out swinging, and Zak returns his bat to the rack, grabs his glove, and takes Seth's place at third. This night, Zak Messer is left stranded in the on-deck circle.

Chapter 12
That's Court Material

The average fan does not give much thought to the time that ballplayers must fill during the day when they are not playing or while passing the time waiting for the game to start.

Some of the Rebels have jobs. Jay Lively, for example, runs the zip line at Bryce Resort from 10:00 to 3:00 during the week, for which he receives $8.00 an hour. Eric Alessio, Brian Burgess, Joe Hammond, Spencer Clifft, Ryan Stauffer, Kenny Bryant, and Sanchez Gartman work at Richard Tovorsky's vineyard. From about 8:00 a.m. to noon during the week, they weed around the vines and trim suckers. All but Gartman have poison ivy after the first week of the season.

When he is not working at the vineyard, Hammond spends his time plinking tin cans and bottles and shooting the ground hogs that infest the farm of a relative of host dad Bill Harlow. A hunter and fisherman, Hammond also spends time riding four-wheelers around the farm. Hammond, from Lilburn, Georgia, which is some 20 miles northeast of Atlanta, is happy to be in New Market.

"Too many people [in Atlanta]," says Hammond. "I love it up here. There's a nice, slow pace to life."

While Jake Pierce is enjoying his new surroundings, it has taken some time to get used to the rural environment. "I miss people," he says. "Where I'm from, there's like, a house. I saw a *cow run* for the first time in my life! I've seen more livestock than in like ... ever."

When not working, Alessio and Burgess spend a great deal of time playing X-Box and watching movies, since the room in which they are staying has no cable or satellite. They have also embarked on a summer-long golf game at The Shenvalee. They continually add up their scores and will determine the grand champion at the end of the summer. A "chauffeur penalty" is applied, which is to say that whoever loses the hole must drive the cart. While the War Between the States may be very much alive in New Market, Alessio, from West Nyack, New York, and Burgess, from Huntsville, Alabama, have no difficulty getting along.

The two pitchers find other interesting things to do as well. Alessio arrives at Rebel Park one day sans his goatee and most of his hair. Burgess, however, shows up with a lightning bolt shaved into his head, courtesy of Alessio, who traced the image with a Sharpie before he started barbering.

"Just trying to keep it interesting," says Burgess.

Pitcher Brett Harman is actually taking a summer school class. He rushes to New Market from his home in Westminster, Maryland, where he attends Carroll Community College after class on Thursdays, and then departs New Market for home after the game on Sunday night.

Seth Kivett and Jordan Pegram fill some mornings by wandering through the mall in Harrisonburg. Kivett and Pegram, as well as most of the other Rebels, spend a great deal of time working out at the Body Oasis in Mt. Jackson.

"Every night," says Kivett.

Zack Helgeson works out in order to become "faster and stronger," a goal of his this summer that he feels he must accomplish in order to improve his game.

For $45.00, each player is given an access code, which allows entry to the workout center 24 hours a day for their entire two-month stay. The players often work out after home games.

All Rebels are expected to perform three community service events. Kenny Mickens spends an hour one Saturday morning calling bingo numbers for about two dozen residents at the Life Care Center of New Market. A lady to Kenny's right had a wonderful time simply making sure that Kenny shuffled the deck properly.

Lucas and his coaches spend the week of June 15th teaching local youngsters some fundamentals of the game. Thirty-nine aspiring ballplayers, both boys and girls, pay $60 each to attend the "2009 Coach Jones Baseball Camp at Rebel Park" from 9:00 to 12:00 each day. Kevin Rufus and Nate Furry take turns running the concession stand.

Kids also have the option to attend a couple of two-day camps the following week: one for pitchers and catchers, and one for advanced hitting.

"I think they had fun," recounts Jones, adding, "Out of all the camps I've done, this has been the best behaved group of kids." Not only were they well behaved, they were eager to learn the game, some wanting to know why there was no camp on a day when it was pouring—yet again. Lucas likes to work out himself, and also spends a great deal of time during the day reviewing statistics for that night's game.

The four young coaches and 24 players spent an hour reading to over 70 kids during the annual Reading With the Rebels Day, sponsored by the New Market Library, the chairperson of which is Becky Kipps. Players selected their favorite books from childhood and read to small groups in the pavilion at Rebel Park.

"As we kept going through the Dr. Seuss books, it reminded me of my younger days," said Gartman, who explained that he was leery of reading to little kids, based on previous experience with such events. "But these were good kids, who were paying attention and interested. They watch your every step."

Richie Gonzalez shares a book with a very interested party on Reading With the Rebels Day.

"If [the players] haven't already, they're starting to realize that kids here do look up to them," said Corey Paluga, who noted that the players were "engaged with the kids; not just reading to them, but hanging out afterward."

Indeed, Reading With the Rebels was scheduled to last for one hour, but lasted twice that long when the players took on the kids in game of wiffle ball.

Paluga has even been seen reading on his own, as he has spent time perusing *Baseball Between the Numbers.*

* * *

Naturally, there is the business of assigning nicknames, but this is an informal and natural process. Some players' nicknames are derivations of their given names. Matt Townsend becomes "Townie," and Steve Owens becomes "SteveO." Richie Gonzalez is increasingly known as "Chi Chi" because, well, because he is Hispanic and in baseball, "Chi Chi" is a typical nickname for Hispanic players. Some nicknames are simply givens: All Lous are "Sweet," most Bills are "Wild," and lots of guys named Rhodes are nicknamed "Dusty." McKinnon Langston has acquired the moniker "Nugget." At 5'9" and 185 pounds, "he just looks like a chicken nugget," and with the shortened handle of Mac, he has become McNugget or just Nugget. The knobs of his bats are even labeled Nug. The fans have taken to calling Brian Burgess "Lightning," thanks to his new haircut.

Then there are the bus rides, which can consume as little as 25 minutes to Woodstock or as much as the two hours and 15 minutes to Covington. There is usually lots of interesting conversation on a bus ride. Early in the season there are arguments over who is the "filthiest" player in the College World Series; "filthiest" meaning the best, as in "FSU's centerfielder is filth, man."

"The Louisville third baseman is better than *he* is."

"No, the Virginia centerfielder is the best player I've seen."

"Guy from Arkansas was filth."

Of course, there is general conversation, too, and it is usually punctuated with humor. Dan Rollins tells me about his Bachelor of Arts degree in political science, but adds, "That BA really stands for 'bad ass.'"

"Well, I know what it would have meant if they gave you a BS," I reply.

In general, there are moments of quiet on a bus ride, some short and others long, which are almost always broken by raucous laughter. This evolves into many conversations liberally laced with the most graphic and colorful cursing that only ballplayers on a bus can string together. It takes me back 35 years, and I find that even profanity can be restorative in the right context.

Indeed, some things never change, although the technology that delivers them certainly has. No longer must someone sneak a *Playboy* onto the bus. Now, all someone must do is dial it up on his Blackberry and a naked woman appears on the tiny screen. And as with all boys in all times, even a tiny photo of a naked woman elicits a large amount of boisterous commentary. Perhaps out of respect or perhaps because they think that I'm too old to care, the players don't pass the Blackberry to me. I hope it is out of respect.

Sleeping is a favorite pastime, not only on the bus, but in general. Spencer Clifft explained to me that at one point in the season, he slept 26 out of the past 48 hours; a feat — if one can call it that — that seems almost impossible.

A baseball team will spend two to three hours prior to every game taking batting practice and fielding practice and hanging out in the dugout or locker room. This is why ballplayers know all the words to certain songs, because these songs are played continuously from ballpark to ballpark during pregame activities. Various Rebels are only too happy to sing a wide variety of genres, from country tunes such as "Don't Mess With Texas" and "She Thinks My Tractor's Sexy" to oldies such as "Sweet Caroline" and "Runaround Sue" to ballpark favorites such as "Glory Days." Uninhibited performers — you have to be uninhibited to stand in the batter's box or on the pitcher's mound and invite everyone to scrutinize your performance — do not let an inability to sing keep them from belting out their favorite tunes once they start playing over the public address system.

Another favorite pastime is practicing the art of ragging on one another. All ballplayers seem to have the same sense of humor in that they delight in insulting one another in subtle, or not so subtle, ways.

Jordan Pegram hits two balls to the warning track in left field, and John Combs immediately yells, "Weight room!"

Jordan hits the next pitch out of the park.

Mo has been going around amusing everyone, especially himself, by sidling up to anyone at hand and saying, "Hey, there are a couple of girls in the stands...and yours isn't so hot." We've all heard this before, but Mo laughs so hard and so genuinely each time he says it that the joke always elicits at least a chuckle from everyone.

Baseball's humor is often formalized in an exercise that fills the long hours between games and lessens the grind of a season. This exercise is known as the "Kangaroo Court." For the uninitiated, if a player or coach does something dumb or clumsy, or if he misses a sign during the game, or hits a teammate during batting practice with a batted or thrown ball, he is usually taken to court. Instituted on the first day of practice by Lucas, cases are brought before a three-judge panel of one's peers, with Lucas as the presiding judge. Fines in the New Market Court range from $0.25 to $1.00, with the accumulated funds going toward an end-of-year party. Charges may be brought against anyone at any time for anything, and all cases are heard before Sunday's game. Court is not open to the public, but it is easy to discern when it is in session, for raucous laughter routinely emanates from the open clubhouse door.

During the first session, Dan Rollins was charged with abandoning his teammates, because he had sense enough to run for the office just before the hailstorm hit. Compounding his troubles, he proceeded to "throw two of his teammates under the bus," according to John Combs, when, in his defense, he stated that Matt Leskiw and Jake Pierce were in there with him. Rollins was fined the $1.00 maximum, and the two players were then also fined a lesser amount.

Zak Messer was fined for declaring that the Haymarket game was over after Brian Burgess recorded the first *two* outs in the 9th inning. After the ensuing triple, Paluga turned on Zak and said, "I hate you right now." Burgess closed out the game, but Messer was taken to court for almost jinxing his pitcher.

In fact, a player does not even have to do anything dumb to be taken to court. Just *say* something dumb, and a player is likely to be hauled up on charges. During the bus trip to Waynesboro, the conversation had turned to the best kinds of sandwiches. When peanut butter and bananas was mentioned, the conversation naturally turned to Elvis Presley, since that was the King's favorite sandwich. Someone asked if Elvis was from "Graceland."

I tell him that yes, "Graceland" was the name of Elvis' home, which is in Memphis.

"Yeah, but where was he from?" asked Kevin Rufus.

"Memphis," some of us answer in unison.

"I *know* he's from Memphis," retorted Rufus. "I just didn't know what city he was from."

"Dude," said Dan Rollins, "Memphis *is* a city."

"That's court material," stated Zak Messer.

"The sad thing," said Rufus, laughing as hard as anyone, "is that I have a 3.8 GPA."

Chapter 13
It's Not That I'm Tired

Before the start of the 4th inning of the June 24th game against the Staunton Braves, Mo Weber was called to home plate and was presented with a birthday cake. On this day, he turned 86. Bruce called on the crowd to sing "Happy Birthday," which they did enthusiastically, and both dugouts emptied, the players and coaches applauding "the Legend of the Valley." Even the Rebel relief pitchers ran in from the bullpen to join in the salute to Mo. Weber knew this was coming because every year he is honored at the ballpark. This year, he joked as he always does about receiving a car.

The applause from the crowd lingers, and Bruce allows the moment to speak for itself. There is no doubt from the expression on his face that Mo is pleased.

While Mo marvels at the fact that he is keeping late hours and not feeling tired, he is, in fact, tired; something that Mo will admit after the rush of the game has worn off.

For the first time, Mo is telling his hitters *not* to incorporate his teachings into their swings until they get home and have time to practice.

"It's a law of learning," says Mo constantly. "You must have enough repetitions to break old habits, but with 44 games in 55 days, there simply isn't time to shed old habits and learn a new way of hitting."

John Combs, the one returning member of the coaching staff never heard this last year, and Bruce has *never* heard Mo express this sentiment. Both agree that it is a sign that Mo no longer has the energy to corral two or three players at a time and work on them and talk to them and stand by the batting cage and *drive* them until they drop their bad habits and begin to form new ones.

Mo is certainly tired of some of the changes that have taken place in the game, changes that pass for progress.

"These pitchers can't find the plate because they don't throw enough innings!" he says, noting that some pitchers log only 20 innings in a three-month college season. "How in the hell can you learn your craft pitching two innings a week?" he asks.

He does not understand the benefit of pitching batting practice from behind an L-screen from 45 feet. "You can't get a ball to break from only 45 feet! Do they lower the basket to nine feet in pregame warm-ups for basketball or do Olympic swimmers swim 80 meters to practice for a 100 meter race? We're the only sport that practices differently from what the game conditions will be."

The Rebels do not fulfill any poetic destiny by defeating Staunton in dramatic style to reward Mo with a birthday victory. Instead, they play their worst game of the season, committing three errors and a series of base-running blunders that takes them out of one promising inning after another, and they lose 11-3.

New Market had begun the game having returned to .500 after defeating both Haymarket and Covington at home. Both games were sloppy affairs, however. The Rebels overcame a whopping six errors to defeat the Senators 5-4 on a single by designated hitter McKinnon Langston, who had begun the season ice cold, but, as will happen in baseball, had suddenly turned white hot. The game was also noteworthy for Lucas Jones' first ejection of the season when Zach Helgeson, trying to score what would have been the go-ahead run at the time, was ruled out at the plate.

Helgeson thought that he had been ejected, for he was yelling at the umpire on his way back to the dugout. It was, in fact, Lucas who was ejected after running to the home-plate umpire from his position in the third-base coach's box.

"I played against their catcher in high school," related Zach, after the game, "and he got down to first base and says to me, 'Yeah, you were totally safe'!"

Langston was impressed by Coach Jones' ejection, describing it as "a good one! He didn't back down, and he got his money's worth."

Lucas had been planning his first ejection for some time, as he and Corey Paluga had discussed it at the postgame meal the week before. An ejection is an important tool that a baseball manager uses to communicate a message; not so much to the umpire, as to his players. He must pick the right moment in the right game, and Lucas timed his perfectly. Noting that the crowd was dead and that the bench was lifeless, he seized on the opportunity presented by a terrible call to wake up both.

"It was planned, but it was also a good opportunity to shake things up," noted Paluga.

Joe Hammond deadpanned that Lucas' ejection was "weak," referring to the fact that there was no helmet tossing or dirt kicking or wild gesticulations. "Classiest ejection I ever saw," laughed Bruce Alger.

"He got his point across to us," continued Joe, in a serious vein.

"Which was?" I ask.

"That he's behind us and he's going to sacrifice for us, and he expects us to do the same for one another," said Hammond.

While writing down Joe's statement, I make a mental note that the team chemistry continues to evolve in a most positive direction.

The next night, the Rebels knock off Covington 8-5 in a game that features the ejection of mild mannered shortstop Jordan Pegram. Mild-mannered, but highly competitive, Jordan is thrown out at first on what first-base coach Corey Paluga described as a bang-bang play.

"I was just about to argue when Jordan went by and yelled, 'That's @#$% terrible!' and I thought, well, you're on your own, Jordan!" laughed Paluga.

I ask Jordan the next night if he cared to tell me what he said to the umpire. He smiled and replied, "No," ever reluctant to talk about himself, especially under the circumstances.

The real play of the game occurs in the very first inning when Kevin Rufus makes a sensational running catch an instant before crashing into the wall just to the right of straightaway center.

"I've never heard a child hit the wall that hard," said Abbie Hansberger who rose from her seat as the play unfolded, anticipating the crash. "He really scared me." Rufus, who was unconscious for a few moments, was mad about being pulled from the game. The next day, his ribs and neck were sore, and he was bruised from the top of his shoulder to his elbow. Still, he came into the office to see if he should "sit out everything today." The coaches told him that he obviously should, but when Head Coach Jones walked in, he asked again. He refused to give *himself* permission to take a day off, just as he refused to allow the ball to drop in.

"What did you think when you looked up and saw Abbie and Lucas standing over you?" I ask him.

Kevin turned to Jones and said, "You were out there?"

Eric Alessio picked up his 3rd win, Brian Burgess his 3rd save, and Zak Messer had two of the Rebels 14 hits against Covington, but the team also committed three more errors.

There's an old saying in baseball that you're never as good as you look when you're winning, and you're never as bad as you look when you're losing. These three games certainly illustrate the point and, indeed, the Rebels could not possibly be as bad as they looked against Staunton.

The next night saw the Rebels in Front Royal to play the Cardinals at Bing Crosby Stadium. "The Bing" as it's known, was built in 1950 and refurbished in 2006. The famous singer had served as the Grand Marshal of Winchester's Apple Blossom Festival in 1949 and had friends in Front Royal. Asked to make a benefit appearance to help raise $10,000 for a new ballpark, Crosby graciously consented, and when the fundraiser came up short, he wrote a personal check for the difference. Hence, a grateful town named its stadium in his honor.

A beautiful little ballpark on the outside, on the inside it has its problems. Center field lies a mere 349' from home plate, and the outfield wall is cinderblock, which is painted the same color as a game-used baseball. Directly beyond the centerfield wall is another diamond with lights, rendering the hitting background even worse than Woodstock's. Not half a dozen advertising banners hang inside the park, and the noise from the sparse crowd is drowned out by a public address announcer who draws out almost every syllable of a player's name so long and pronounces each name with so much guttural intonation that it sounds as if he is suffering severely from stomach cramps.

Again, the Rebels fall behind early and enter the 9th inning trailing 6-3. They load the bases, however, with none out. Richie Gonzalez drives in one run with a single to right, and Kenny Mickens drives in another with a single to left. The Rebel faithful are optimistic, but a shallow fly to left by junior centerfielder Matt Leskiw, from Virginia Commonwealth and Plains, Pennsylvania, and a pop fly to right by Messer temper the fans' enthusiasm. Sanchez Gartman, who doubled in the first, steps to the plate and laces a shot to center field. It is right at the center fielder, but it is hit so hard that for a second, everyone senses that the ball will sail over his head before he can react to it. He recovers, however, and the bases are left loaded as the Rebels fall back to two games under .500.

After the game, as tough a loss as any the Rebels have suffered, Lucas tells his squad simply, that next time they should "hit 'em where they ain't." He adds, "We're going to build off the positives. We looked tired tonight, but all in all, it was a heck of an effort."

Lucas knows that his squad has struggled to put together a string of wins, but it hasn't been for a lack of effort or passion. Yelling at them certainly won't make them hit or pitch or field any better. Indeed, this team increasingly reflects the low-key but determined personality of its head coach. There is another old saying in baseball: Never get too high when you win, and never get too low when you lose. The Rebels are illustrating many of baseball's old sayings this week.

* * *

Jake Guengerich's night was eventful far beyond the 3²/₃ innings of one-run relief that he pitched. After arriving back at Rebel Park, he realizes that he had set his wallet on the concession-stand counter at Front Royal and was without any identification. As fate would have it, and as Bruce had warned the players, Jake was pulled over by the police for speeding in Mt. Jackson. He explained the situation, leaning hard on the fact that he was a Rebel, and he was released without even receiving a warning. As for the wallet, it was found — minus the cash — and the Cardinals stopped by Rebel Park on their way to Harrisonburg the next night to return it to Jake.

* * *

After two weeks of unusual rain, followed by a week of clear, beautiful days, the Valley's usual summer weather pattern has finally appeared, at least temporarily. It is hot as the Rebel bus travels down I-81 for the next day's contest in Lexington against the Rockbridge Rapids. Humidity is on the rise, increasing the chances of pop-up thunderstorms, and for four miles we ride through a downpour. By the time we arrive at Cap'n Dick Smith Field on the campus of Washington & Lee University, however, the sun has returned, and the players are sweating profusely during pregame warm-ups.

Cap'n Dick Smith Field is set in a bowl and is surrounded by tall pines. The grass is as meticulously kept as any golf course green, and I marvel at the lack of a single weed. With huge dugouts that actually contain a water fountain and a bathroom, the facilities are luxurious, by Valley League standards. So, too, are the bleachers, which feature backrests, and the concessions include a smoothie bar. I balance my diet this evening by following a chili dog with a pina colada smoothie. A good crowd is on hand.

Before the game, Mo and I are discussing Sanchez Gartman. A powerfully built left-handed slugger, Gartman has been crushing the ball when he stays back, but he has trouble doing just that. "Staying back" is a difficult thing for hitters to do. A hitter is naturally anxious to strike the ball, and in that anxiety, he will tend to move toward it by stepping toward the pitcher. It is a natural reaction, but completely counterproductive. Such a step cuts down on the time a hitter has to react to the ball. As it is, he has only about .4 seconds to see the ball, decide whether it's a hittable pitch, and then swing. If a hitter has even a slight hitch that might slow his swing by even 1/20th of a second or so, it could mean the difference between a pop fly to center and a line drive to left.

Furthermore, if a hitter does not stay back—that is, if he "jumps" at the ball — it dissipates the energy that exists in his coiled body. If the energy stored in his hands, shoulders, hips, and legs is unleashed in one smooth, short swing, he will impart maximum force to the ball. If any of these moving parts does not work in perfect partnership with the others, a hitter will often find himself jammed and hitting the ball down on the label of the bat, rather than on the sweet spot.

Gartman has been tapping his front toe while the pitcher is in the windup and then taking a second short stride while the pitch is on the way.

In the course of our discussion behind the cage, Gartman wanders by, waiting to hit in the next group.

"Hey, we're talking about you!" yells Mo.

Sanchez comes over to us, and Mo grabs him by the shoulder and tells him that he has real potential, to advance to the next level if — Gartman interrupts — "I just stay back."

Mo beams, "That's right!" he exclaims, and I laugh and say, "You've heard this before, haven't you?!"

"I'm working on it," he says, and he proves it in the 7th inning by launching a rocket over the right-field fence toward the tall pines with what Mo describes later as "a perfect swing." It is the beginning of a four-run inning that increases the Rebel run total to 13. They have begun this night with two runs in the first inning, and they bookend it with two more in the 9th for a 15-5 victory over the Rapids. The Rebels amass an incredible 28 base

Mo Weber gives a tip to Zach Helgeson.

runners, and everyone contributes offensively; Richie Gonzalez strokes a single, double, and triple, and drives in five runs. New catcher, senior George Carroll, who was signed to replace Nate Furry, singles and scores after replacing starter Jake Pierce. Carroll, from New York Tech and Bayside, New York, arrives in New Market from New York about 30 minutes before the bus leaves for Lexington.

Kevin Rufus singles, triples, walks twice, scores three runs, and in the 6th demonstrates what a hard nosed player he is when he is hit squarely in the helmet by an errant curveball. The ball ricochets a good five feet into the air, but Rufus merely flips the bat toward the Rebel batboy and hustles to first.

"Way to keep your head in the game," yells C. B. Alger from the stands to Rufus, who has been taking shots of one kind or another since arriving at the park. Before the game, Rufus laments the ball he hit at Woodstock that was just short of being a game-tying home run.

"If you were a real man, you'd have hit it out anyway," Seth Kivett tells him. Rufus, ignoring this, adds that today he will, indeed, hit the top of the wall. "With your body, or are you talking about hitting a ball?" replies Kivett.

The game takes over 3½ hours to play, and it is after 11:00 when the players find the bus and receive their postgame meal from the rear of the

Algers' van. There are 16 medium pizza boxes, one for every two players, and a cooler of bottled waters and Pepsis. Mo shares his pizza with me on the darkened bus.

He tells me once more that he feels energized. For the first 30 miles, lightning flashes far off to the east, and we talk baseball. I ask him why pitchers no longer throw batting practice from the mound, which would help them practice their craft and allow batters see a real windup, at least.

"Don't get me started," he says disgustedly, although getting Mo started about any baseball subject is never a problem. Stopping him can be hard, however, and we talk about how there are so many sore arms now, compared to 60 years ago.

As the clouds light up from the distant storm, the conversation takes a turn, and Mo tells me that this year may be his last hurrah in coaching, and then the conversation takes an even more serious turn. He says that he doesn't want to "linger in a bed" and adds, with earnestness, "I'd like to die on a baseball field."

We roll into New Market around 1:00 a.m. I am staying with Mo this night, and we drive over the mountain to his house. At 2:00 a.m. we're still talking baseball, even though I am more than ready for bed, and Mo has yet to shower. He pauses before heading to the shower and says, "This might be the end of the 'Legend of the Valley' business," hastening to add. "It's not that I'm tired, it's just that there is not enough time to get these kids the repetitions they need."

Chapter 14

We Had a Little Heart-to-Heart

The Rebels cannot put together any kind of winning streak. They follow their demolition of Rockbridge with a clunker of a loss at Fauquier, then defeat Woodstock 6-5 with an 8th-inning rally, only to lose the next night to the River Bandits 9-4.

They are banged up and hurting for arms. Brett Harman has been shut down with a sore arm by the University of Maryland team doctor. Joe Hammond has been suffering from bicep tendinitis. Steve Owens has a sore arm. Derrick Kline has gone home after only two starts. Outfielder Matt Leskiw returned home with a torn anterior cruciate ligament (ACL); freshman first baseman Kenny Bryant from Presbyterian and Goose Creek, South Carolina, has a sore left shoulder that affects his swing; McKinnon Langston has a bad elbow that limits him to DH duty. Shortstop Jordan Pegram had to come out of the game at Front Royal in the middle of an at-bat when he swung at a pitch and aggravated his left hand, which Abbie Hansberger described as a "bone contusion to his carpals and metacarpals."

"He's got a bad bruise on the back of his hand," translated Joe Hammond.

Hansberger, 25, has definitely been busy treating the many injured Rebels, but notes with humor that her first two years with the team were "painful for me and the team!

"I knew nothing about baseball. Absolutely nothing. I mean I knew that there were three outs. That's what I had for you. And I still sometimes will catch myself being really confused and [the players] don't mind explaining it to me. A balk? What the heck was a balk?"

While being considered one of the boys is a compliment to Abbie, she adds that "some days I wish I had a little extra estrogen in the dugout.

"They have no shame, stripping down to their jock straps in front of me. Sometimes, I'm like, 'Oh, I didn't need to see that today!' but they take me in as one of the boys."

* * *

Sophomore Steve Thiele, who started the Rockbridge game but did not qualify for the win because he was removed in the 5th, has joined the Rebels. Thiele, from Belmont Abbey and Miami, Florida, is a quiet, thoughtful right hander whose demeanor fits right in with the team. In spite of the addition of Thiele, Lucas Jones continues to burn up minutes on his cell phone, calling friends and friends of friends, trying to find some pitching.

Lefty freshman Garrett Baker from Western Carolina and Rome, New York, started the game at Fauquier, having only allowed one earned run so far on the season. He allowed only two earned runs to the Gators, but New Market collected only two hits after collecting 16 against Rockbridge.

"That was the first night this season that we weren't ready to play," said Bruce Alger of the 6-1 loss to Fauquier, "and it showed."

If they weren't ready to play on Saturday night, they were certainly ready to help on Sunday afternoon. Bruce who, not surprisingly, is the coach of son Trey's 14-16-year-old all-star team, organized a practice at Rebel Park. Kenny Mickens and Seth Kivett wandered over from the Algers' to the park and worked with the younger ballplayers. Kevin Rufus showed up, and without being asked, ran to the outfield to work with the outfielders. When Zach Helgeson arrived early to work on his swing in the batting cage, he was more than happy to work with Bruce's first basemen on fielding their position. George Carroll came over and spent an hour and a half working with the young catchers. Bruce has told me that this is the nicest, most attentive group of young men that he can ever recall coming to New Market, a sentiment that has been echoed by Vic Moyers, who, as the bus driver, sees these guys in their most unguarded moments.

Vic is the only paid member of the Rebel staff, making $10.00 per hour, but considering the odd hours and the responsibility of delivering 30 ballplayers and coaches safely all over the Valley, it seems at best a token sum. In addition to driving, Vic also maintains the bus, washing it and having it inspected, and this is done on a voluntary basis. Vic finds his real compensation in his association with the team.

"I enjoy it," says Vic. "It's priceless when you get to spend time with the players and the coaches, and this bunch here is a real good bunch."

Moyers, who drives a school bus in Rockingham County, also has his own lawn and landscape business. As if that isn't enough to keep him busy, he repairs and refinishes furniture.

Vic rarely misses a home game, either, and he was part of the largest and most enthusiastic crowd of the season to date that Sunday evening when the Rebels took on Woodstock at Rebel Park. The Mt. Jackson/New Market Little League was in attendance, as were camp counselors from the Shrine Mont Church Camp in Orkney Springs. Admission for Shenandoah County senior citizens was only $1.00, and it was Shenandoah Dairy Club Night to boot. As if that weren't enough, Mo Weber arranged for a between-innings fashion show by Casual Fridays, a clothing store in New Market, and Casual Fridays in turn agreed to donate 10% of all sales generated that night to the Rebels.[1]

"There was so much going on, I didn't even play any between-innings music until the 8th," exclaimed Bruce Alger, who was thrilled with the $1,000 in business that the concession stand did. The official attendance was 687, "but I think we miscounted too low," added Alger.

Bruce did manage to squeeze in the nightly Dash for Cash, sponsored by Grubbs Chevrolet in Woodstock in the middle of the 5th inning. A lucky fan is selected from the crowd and is given a shovel, with which he must run to a tub full of $1 bills some 30 feet away, take a scoop of money, and run back to a bucket placed at the starting line and dump it in. The contestant gets to keep any of the money that makes it into the bucket, and the night's contestant walked away with $90.00.

The Shrine Mont counselors — all girls — formed a loud and ardent cheering section, and they had much to cheer about.

Eric Alessio gave another strong performance, yielding only two runs (one earned) in six innings. The Rebels fell behind 5-4 in the top of the 7th, however, when Jake Guengerich, pitching in relief of Alessio yielded three runs in only 1/3 of an inning. The Rebel bullpen did its best to create

---

[1]The Rebels received a check for $100.00, so it was a good night for everyone!

a rally, however, when each member donned a clear plastic rain bonnet: the kind that your grandmother — or at least mine — always kept folded in her purse should the skies suddenly open. The July 3rd edition of the *Shenandoah Valley Herald* would feature a photo of several relievers in their unusual headwear.

"We wanted it to rain hits," said Jay Lively, matter-of factly.

"Saw 'em in the BP station at five for a dollar," said Steve Owens, who provided the rain bonnets, "and I knew I had to have 'em."

While hits did not pour from the sky, enough fell to garner the win. With two outs in the bottom of the 8th, Richie Gonzalez singled home Jake Pierce, who had doubled, to tie the score. After loading the bases, New Market pushed ahead what would prove to be the winning run when Sanchez Gartman walked. Brian Burgess came on in the 9th to pick up his 4th save of the season, and everyone from the Little Leaguers to the senior citizens went home happy with the 6-5 New Market victory.

Joe Hammond

Then came another clunker at Woodstock. Joe Hammond, who had returned from a weekend wedding in Atlanta, the timing of which was perfect, as it gave his ailing arm some rest, threw five gritty innings and left with the score tied at three. A series of relief pitchers surrendered six runs over the final four innings and New Market fell by a final score of 9-4, failing to get back to the .500 mark for the third time in a week.

Lucas Jones had seen enough.

"I was disappointed in the loss ... the last two losses we've had, I've been very disappointed. I was very disappointed with our effort at Fauquier. I was disappointed with the fact that we just weren't there. The Fauquier pitcher didn't have overpowering stuff; he just kept pounding the zone, and we just weren't attacking, we weren't doing anything offensively, bad body language, 'Hey, how am I getting screwed today?' I'm tired of hearing that."

And so, the next day, Lucas called a meeting before boarding the bus to Luray.

"I knew it was a matter of time," said Vic about the scolding that the team received.

Jones told his players that they had done things their way for the first 20 games, and now "It's our way. We're going to do it the right way and make sure that we're paying attention to detail; that we're doing the minor things that need to be done for 3½ to 4 hours a night, and if not, then you're going to go home. I'm not putting up with it. You've been told directly. We're communicating with you. You've been told directly. This experience is about you, but if you're not going to get out of it what the expectations are, then you need to just go. No bad wishes upon you, but you just need to go."

Lucas maintains his low-key demeanor, even as he relates to me what he said to the team, but his passion for playing the game the right way borders on fierce. No story about Lucas illustrates this point better than the one his father, Roger, told about Lucas when he first began to play baseball. After playing tee-ball for one year, Jones refused to play again until he was old enough to play in Little League where the regulation nine took the field and no tees were used.

"It wasn't right," he says of the tee-ball setup. He says it with a smile, but clearly, it *still* annoys him that anyone would play the game at all if it wasn't going to be played the right way.

Jones is guilty of assuming that every player will bring the same passionate, fastidious approach to playing the game that he had. In his first year as head coach, he is finding that even the most talented college players do not necessarily approach the game the same way that he did. He is learning quickly, however, and admits that if he had it to do over, he may have imposed a stricter regimen from the beginning.

Lucas' disappointment does not turn to disgust, however, but to determination. His love of the game is such that he will not allow his players to give any less than their best. He will not let them set their sights on going home and merely playing out the string. And no one wants to.

Furthermore, help has arrived. Matt Burnside, a sophomore lefty from Southern Union State Community College drove 11 hours from his home in Montgomery, Alabama, and arrived in the 4th inning of the game at Woodstock. Righty Mike Roth from Rockville Centre, New York, a senior and teammate of George Cooper from New York Tech arrived just before the bus left Rebel Park for Luray. He had departed Athens, Georgia, where he had been playing in the Great South League, at 3:00 a.m., and 11 hours later arrived in New Market.

Steve Owens has also returned from a tryout in Baltimore and will make the start tonight against the Wranglers. It is extremely rare for anyone to be signed to a professional contract at one of these tryouts, and I am concerned about his outlook after his disappointment at not being drafted. The dream of playing in the major leagues may be the hardest dream of any to give up.

"It's a participatory thing," explains Mo. "When you're little and dream of being a fireman, you never get to put out a fire, but you *play* baseball, and whether it's not making the high school team or the college team or being drafted when you thought you would, it's very hard. It's demoralizing."

Nevertheless, SteveO has always been forthright, and upon spying him alone in the bullpen, I ask him about the tryout.

"A waste of time," he says, almost with a smile. "I threw about 7 pitches, and that's all they looked at."

Owens elaborates on the tryout, laughing about the fact that of the 200 or so guys who showed up, 100 had no business being there, participating in street clothes or softball uniforms.

I ask him if he is simply looking forward to a good rest of the summer, and he says wholeheartedly that he is.

I make my way from the bullpen across the outfield where I find Kevin Rufus patrolling center by himself. He has chased out all the pitchers, who usually shag fly balls during batting practice.

"Working on reading the ball off the bat?" I ask.

"Yeah, I like to read balls off the bat."

A fielder who can "read the ball off the bat" means that he can react to the ball, even as the hitter is swinging and before contact is actually made. This allows the outfielder to "get a good jump" on the ball and run to the spot where it will come down, rather than running to intersect the path of the ball and then either in or back. Most fans see an outstanding catch such as any of the several that Kevin has made this year and simply say, "He's a good outfielder." They don't see the work that takes place at 5:30, two hours before the game even starts. They don't see that an outfielder such as Rufus takes off after a ball *expecting* to catch it, no matter where it is hit, and this is why he catches so many. Other outfielders don't get a good jump; they *hope* to get to the ball, and then catch it if they get there.

On such details are games won and lost, and such details are what Lucas has said must be attended to in order for his 9-11 team to get better.

There is one particular fly ball, however, that Kevin cannot track down, and it nails Joe Hammond right in the leg above the knee as he is running on the warning track.

"I yelled, 'Heads up,'" Rufus explains to Joe back in the dugout after batting practice.

"Yeah," said Joe laughing, as Abbie tapes an ice bag to his leg, "but you're so damned fast that I thought you'd catch it!"

They're loose and they're laughing, and there is no doubt that the Rebels are ready to play tonight. That is a good thing for Rebel fans, for if there is one team to whom they hate losing, it is the Luray Wranglers. This is explained in part by the fact that the Wranglers have won two of the last three VBL championships. Furthermore, the Wranglers currently sport the best record in the VBL at 12-5. In addition, Luray manager Mike Bocock managed New Market at one time and has been known to do a fine Lou Piniella imitation. Last year, after tossing more than a few choice words in the direction of the umpire, he hurled an armful of bats and a bucket of balls onto the field.

Luray, pronounced *Lu*-ray by natives and New Marketers alike, rather than Lu-*ray*, as one might suppose, plays its games at Bulldog Field, the local high school diamond. A chain-link fence covered in advertising banners runs the length of the outfield, which is 310' down each line and 368' to center. A truck trailer with *Wrangler* painted on its side sits behind the left-field fence. There used to be a Wrangler jeans plant in Luray; hence, the team name and the trailer.

The game has an auspicious beginning. With two out and Kenny Mickens on first, Sanchez Gartman hits a screaming one-hopper to first, which skims off the glove of first baseman D. J. Hicks and nails him directly above his left eye. He remains on the ground for some time, attended to by Abbie and the Luray Rescue Squad, who are on duty for the game. Finally, he rises from the grass, holding a bandage to a wound that Abbie estimates will take 10 stitches to close. The game is resumed, and Zach Helgeson smacks the very first pitch he sees well over the left-field fence and the truck trailer for a three-run homer.

In the bottom of the first, with two out and two on, Steve Owens hangs a curveball to Dan Bowman, who drives the ball to the right of the trailer and over the fence for a three-run homer, and the game is immediately tied. Owens, however, has little trouble in the next three innings, and the Rebels tack on runs in the third and fourth for a 5-3 lead. Mike Bocock is not happy with his squad and gathers them all at the entrance of the dugout for an intense chat.

Helgeson leads off the top of the 5th, and again hits the first pitch he sees even deeper to the same spot for a solo homer. Carol Lanham, Zach's host mom, tells me that her husband Bob had given Zach the advice earlier in the day to swing at the first pitch. She is beaming.

Owens throws better in the 5th than he has the entire game; the entire season for that matter. Standing atop a pitching mound that appears to be far higher than the regulation 10", Steve appears almost as tall as nearby Massanutten Mountain.

In the top of the 6th, Helgeson is hit by a pitch and takes a couple of steps toward the mound. He has no doubt that it was intentional, after hitting two home runs, but the umpires keep order, and the inning resumes. The Rebels score four more times before it concludes. SteveO dominates the Wranglers in the 6th and 7th, giving way to the bullpen after having only surrendered two hits, both homers.

The Rebel faithful, which include Fred and Melissa Miller, Melissa Dodge, the Lanhams, the Smiths, Tacy Hawkins, and other fans and parents are having a rollicking good time. Early in the game, Bruce has called Vic on his cell phone for his usual updates. Bruce is on the phone when Bowman hits his home run, and the Rebel fans declare that Bruce is a jinx.

"Bruce hasn't called again, has he?" asked Melissa Miller later in the game.

"No, and I ain't gonna answer the phone if he does!" declares Vic.

Bruce does call again, but the fans implore Vic to ignore the call. Reluctantly, he answers by saying, "They told me not to answer this!"

Vic pauses a moment and then relates to us, "He said to call *him*, then," which Vic faithfully does. No hex ensues, and this satisfies the crowd.

We sit extremely close to home plate, and when Kenny Mickens walks by, Front-Row Fred calls to him, "Kenny, hit a home run, and I'll buy you a Popsicle!"

Vic looks at Fred with mock disgust, "Well, if he hits a home run," he tells Fred, "you oughta buy him more than a Popsicle, you tight-ass!"

The Rebel stands rock with laughter. And no one enjoys a good laugh, even at his own expense, more than Front-Row Fred Miller. A baseball hat firmly perched atop his head, he always wears long pants and long-sleeved shirts, as older farmers are wont to do. Clothing was the only protection from the sun when out working cattle or cutting hay before the days of sunscreen. You'll also recognize Fred if you should happen to walk past him with a plate of nachos or the like, for he will invariably ask if some of those are for him. And, of course, there's the fact that Fred will be the one razzing the umpires from his seat in the first row of the bleachers where he is closer to home plate than anyone on the field, except the batter and the catcher.

Famous around the league for tossing good-natured barbs the umpires' way, he shows no mercy toward home-plate ump Dwight Godwin when Godwin absentmindedly puts a second ball in play during the opener against Harrisonburg. After the game, Fred tells Godwin that he has done a good job. Godwin smiles and thanks Fred, adding, however, "But, you're not going to follow me all summer are you?"

Fred and his daughter Melissa have season tickets to Rebel Park and attend about half of the away games as well. Sitting on the visiting side of the bleachers does not deter Fred from his umpire baiting. At Haymarket one night, following a questionable strike call, Fred yells, "C'mon ump! You can't be tired — you ain't done nothin' yet!"

Later he yells, "I think the umpire could see better if he'd stand in front of the plate!"

In the middle of the Luray game, the public address announcer gives scores from other contests, and at the exact moment of silence between the announcement of the scores and the resumption of conversation in the stands, Fred yells, "What's the score of *this* game?" Again, the New Market stands erupt in laughter.

Nothing surpasses beating Luray, and in the end, the Rebels do so by a final score of 14-8. Both Burnside and Roth pitch an inning, and each gives up a couple of runs, but neither was hit real hard, and no one really cares.

The Rebels amass 27 base runners with 17 hits, 6 walks, and 4 hit batters.

At the postgame meeting, Lucas is pleased, but low-key as always. When he asks if anyone has anything to add, Sanchez Gartman pipes up, "The coaches are smilin'!" This is a good thing, especially after Lucas' man-to-team talk.

In the dugout, I say to Mo that now the Rebels must put together a string of wins and not fall back into the pattern of winning one and then losing the next. Sanchez, seated nearby responds before Mo can.

"Ain't gonna happen again," says Gartman, "we had a little heart-to-heart."

"So I heard," I reply. "Did it do any good?"

"I hope so," he answered.

Hoping is much easier than hitting.

A summer shower washed out the next night's contest against Front Royal, dampening any momentum from the victory over Luray. It was muted entirely the following evening when the Rebels manage only 6 hits while dropping a 4-1 decision to Haymarket. Heading into the July 4th weekend, and at the halfway point of the season, New Market's record stands at a mediocre 10-12.

Chapter 15
Fourth of July Weekend

"Seth's going deep right here," pronounces Ryan Stauffer, the quiet left-hander, who is perched on the picnic table next to me in the Rebel bullpen. It is the bottom of the 6th inning, and the Rebels are losing to Fauquier 5-2. I look at Stauffer, who is deadly serious; this is no mere hope.

"You think?" says Jay Lively.

I am privy to this conversation because I am, indeed, sitting in the Rebel bullpen. Nate Furry was actually the first player to invite me out to the pen, saying that I would gather "some great material" out there. James Weiner followed with an independent invitation, and I checked with Joe Hammond to make sure that I'd be welcome. I have been overwhelmingly accepted by the players, but I don't want to overstep my bounds. Bruce happily gave his approval, as did Lucas.

"Actually," added Lucas, "that's a chapter I'd like to read, because I'd like to know what goes on out there."

As word gets around to the other relievers, they are excited to have me, and I am grateful for their enthusiasm. I don a uniform that approximates the Rebels', including stirrups, of course. Stirrups were worn from before Mo's time to after my time, and they are part of what a baseball uniform should look like. Pants worn down to the shoe tops are a baseball abomination, and I have done what I can to encourage the classic look among the Rebels.

During batting practice, I take my place alongside the relievers, and shag fly balls. They seem to appreciate my attempt to make their routine my routine for the night. They are impressed by my glove, a Nokona infielder's mitt, and we talk gloves and who has and hasn't pitched recently. Lively leads a discussion on what "activities" should be undertaken that night. A fly ball comes sailing in our direction, and I am eager to show that I truly belong on the field, at least for an hour. I drift back to my left; and keep drifting, finally running under the ball, with a half over-the-shoulder catch.

"You made that look easy!" marvels Jake Guengerich, who is not yet 20. I accept the compliment, but don't have the heart to tell him that when I was his age, I would have been standing there waiting for it to come down.

After batting practice, I venture down to Lucas' office to get his take on the Haymarket game; yet the latest loss that came after a big win. Dan Rollins has already told me that the Rebels were "flat as hell," and Corey Paluga noted that there were some "atrocious" at-bats, but Lucas chooses his words carefully.

"It wasn't our worst played game, but it wasn't our best, either."

Within minutes, he is discussing his decision to send Zach Helgeson home on a single to right, with two outs and Kenny Mickens, who was 20 for his last 30, in the on-deck circle. Helgeson was thrown out and "that took the air out of us a little bit." Lucas continued to explain why it was a poor decision and talks about his intense desire to improve as a third-base coach. I am struck by the fact that he does not mention the lack of clutch hitting or the three errors committed by his team, and I tell him so. He seems half disturbed and half perplexed by my comment.

"It's about accountability and self-assessment," he says. "I expect it of those guys," he adds motioning toward the locker room, "and I expect it from myself."

* * *

Kivett is the first batter in the bottom of the 6th. During batting practice, he has hit practically every ball to right field, and he lifts a long fly ball in that direction. As Fauquier's right fielder drifts back to the warning track, we rise as one in the bullpen. The right fielder can finally drift no further, as he is against the wall, and the ball sails out of Rebel Park. Stauffer has called the homer, and Jay and I congratulate him. The Wave rolls back and forth across the bullpen as Kivett circles the bases. There is a real sense now that we are not only back in the game, but that we will somehow find a way to win it. *We*. In the stands or in the press box, I work hard at being an observer of batting stances and body language and the mood of the crowd. Not this night; this night I have been invited to the bullpen for the experience of sitting out there and the experience is definitely *we*.

"Boy, it would be sweet if we could come back and win this game!" I say to Stauffer.

"In front of our parents? You better believe it," he replies.

Indeed, this Fourth of July weekend is also the Rebels' annual Parent Weekend, when players' parents are extended a special invitation to take in the weekend games, New Market's 4th of July celebration, including the parade in which the Rebels will ride, and the picnic that brings together the actual families with the host families.

Immediately before the game, the players and both sets of families have gathered in the parking lot, waiting to be introduced to the crowd, and I am privy to bits and pieces of conversation.

"Hey, I like your socks," Steve Helgeson tells Zach, who is sporting his stirrups.

I talk briefly to Richie Gonzalez and to his dad Richard, who flew in from Puerto Rico the week before in order to watch his son play. Richie is now sporting stirrups, too, and I tell him that we'll never lose a game once the entire team dons them.

Two Rebel alumni are also here this weekend, including Larry Fielder from the 1967 squad and Nolan Nieman, last year's manager, and they are the first to be introduced.

Dave Beaver is on the P.A. system, for the Algers are a host family, and they are introduced next. C. B. runs onto the field, waving his hat to the crowd.

In no time, the first-base line is filled with host families, players, parents, little brothers and sisters, girlfriends, and fiancées.

"You don't see this in the big cities," says Mo, who has sidled up to me along the outside of the fence beyond the dugout where I am standing. "It's a piece of Americana," he adds, before being introduced himself and walking out onto the field.

The game does not begin well. Eric Alessio is roughed up for two runs in the first. The bullpen does what it can; that is, from a superstitious standpoint. Weiner calls for everyone to "bait your hooks!" and everyone goes through the motion of baiting a fishing hook.

"Now, cast!" he calls.

"Reel it in!" The "it" refers to a strike or an out, but instead, Gator left fielder Ryan Gauck doubles, knocking in the second run.

Between innings, half the relievers spell out "Y-M-C-A" when Bruce plays a classic that was already 10 years old when Ryan Stauffer was born.

Alessio settles down and holds the Gators scoreless in the next three innings. The conversation in the bullpen settles down as well. With Jake Pierce getting the start, George Carroll is in the bullpen, and he and fellow New Yorker Mike Roth become the center of attention.

George tells me that Weiner has been ragging him about his accent. "He'll say to me, 'Say what you had to drink with breakfast,' and I'm like, what, *cauwfee?*"

Indeed, Carroll and Roth stand out in a bullpen that also features a Virginian, a Tennessean, two Georgians, and two Alabamians. The conversation quickly turns to a subject that boys universally share, and a debate begins about the sexiness of a girl in cowboy boots. Somehow, this leads to the subject of "Guidos," a term for overly dressed, overly styled, overly self-impressed men.

Roth interrupts this conversation: "Don't call anyone a 'Guido'; that offends Italians. Just call him a 'douche bag.'"

Between innings, Brian Burgess allows no one else to warm up left fielder Kenny Mickens, who is ever thinking about hitting. Before Burgess throws the ball, Kenny assumes his batting stance and then swings as the throw comes to him, swipe-catching the ball with his glove. I look behind Burgess to see Roth chatting up two girls seated in the open back of a van parked beyond the bullpen.

"A little trick of the trade," says Carroll, who shows me a ball on which he has written his name and phone number. He leaves the pen and gives the ball to one of the girls.

Trey Alger and a couple of buddies are constantly hanging over the back fence of the bullpen, chattering to the relievers or running in one direction or another.

Alessio runs into trouble again in the 5th, and Matt Burnside leaves us and takes the mound. He allows an RBI single, before retiring the next three batters, and the Rebels trail 5-0. Their only hit is a first-inning double by Kivett. A lackluster loss to Fauquier on the heels of the same kind of defeat at Haymarket could send the entire season into a slide from which the Rebels might not recover. This team, however, seems to play at its best when things are at their worst.

They rally in the bottom of the 5th inning. One-out singles by Kevin Rufus and Zak Messer put runners on first and second. An error by the first baseman on a ball hit by Gonzalez scores Rufus, and Messer scores on Kenny Mickens' sacrifice fly. When the Gator first baseman botches the play, Jay Lively throws a shoe over the low fence and out onto the field, and calls of "*Das boot!*" ring out from the bullpen. To "boot" a ball, of course, is to make an error. This "boot," which is really an old tennis shoe, has been attached to a long piece of twine, and when play is ready to resume, Lively hauls it back into the bullpen.

Alsessio makes his way down to the bullpen, complaining of "sliders down the middle" that have not been called strikes. Rollins — who by now has assumed the role of pitching coach, thus allowing Lucas to concentrate solely on managing — has been chirping to the ump all night about his tiny strike zone. Burnside holds Fauquier scoreless in the 6th and gives way to Jake Guengerich in the 7th, the Rebels trailing 5-3 now, thanks to Kivett's home run.

The bullpen conversation has turned to which famous person each reliever looks like. Someone suggests that Steve Thiele looks like the "second son who was killed in *The Patriot.*"

"Turn this way . . . dude, you do!"

Meanwhile, lefty James Weiner has been instructed to get loose, that he's going in soon, and Burnside, who has returned to the bullpen after his night's work, asks him if he has a changeup. Weiner confirms that he does.

"Good. Then throw changeups. They swung through every one I threw," instructs Burnside.

While Weiner makes his way in, Spencer Clifft turns to SteveO and says, "What's the capital of Thailand?"

"Don't do it," warns the big right hander, and Spencer grins, but makes no move in Owens' direction.[1]

During the 7th-inning stretch, Bruce asks for a moment of silence in which to remember the veterans who have made possible the celebration of the nation's founding. Tacy Hawkins then sings "God Bless America." There is a sense in the stands and in the bullpen that *this* is the inning in which the Rebels need a rally.

---

[1] If you don't know this joke, you can consult an atlas and look up the capital of Thailand and then use your imagination. If you still don't get it, just move on.

With one out, Zak Messer hits a long home run to left center near the scoreboard. Jordan Pegram's hand injury has proven so severe that he is finished for the season, and Zak has become the regular shortstop. Slowly but surely, he has found his hitting stroke and now dramatically demonstrates that fact with his long home run. His home run is no more significant than his turn at second base on a Gator double-play ball in the top of the 6th. Receiving a good feed from Richie, he fired the ball to first with no thought whatsoever. It is the first play that I have seen him make in the field in over a week in which he didn't think about his throw. Zak is becoming "empty-headed," as ballplayers need to be.

We are doing the Wave once more, as Zak rounds the bases.

Following the homer, Richie singles and Mickens is hit by a pitch, and after McKinnon Langston flies out, Kivett walks to load the bases, bringing Sanchez Gartman to the plate. Sanchez has had a tough night so far, but I have faith in him: He has donned stirrups for the first time. He wandered into the coaches' office asking how to wear them. I showed him a simple way to roll the tops into his pants, and he thanked me.

"You had to educate me on stirrups, sir," he said to me. "I didn't know nothing about 'em."

"Any time," I tell him and now, in the bullpen, I say as much to myself as anyone, "C'mon, Sanchez. It's the power of the stirrups."

Sanchez usually pulls the ball, but this time, he hits a high fly to left center. From our perspective in the bullpen beyond the left-field fence, it looks like nothing more than a long out, but the center fielder keeps running, and at the last second, we see that he will not catch it. We jump up on the picnic tables, yelling. Sanchez has cleared the bases, giving the Rebels ... giving *us* a two-run lead.

In the bottom of the 8th, Weiner relieves Guengerich with one out. After fanning the first batter he faces, Weiner hangs a changeup, and center fielder Dan Baggett homers. After hitting the next batter, Weiner is relieved in favor of closer Brian Burgess, who gets Rich Pacione looking, to retire the side.

The Rebels tack on an unearned run in the 8th, and Burgess fans two more looking, in the top of the 9th, to save the victory.

"Everybody should be ecstatic about this win," Lucas tells his players after the game. "We got big hits when we needed them, and that's what it's going to take. It's about winning together as a team."

* * *

Saturday, July 4th dawned sunny and cool, by Valley standards, with low humidity. Games are not usually scheduled on this day because so many league towns hold festivals and celebrations, and New Market is no exception. Bruce Alger was at Rebel Park at 8:00 a.m. to assemble the float on which the Rebel players would ride, but he was able to take time out to participate in the "Old-Timers Workout" at Rebel Park, a hastily prepared event put together by Charlie Dodge and me. During our webcasts, we had invited parents to participate, but only Charlie, Melissa, Noah, Jay Hafner, Bruce, and I showed up.

I was accompanied by longtime friend Al Smith, who had taken hitting lessons with me from Mo and who had accompanied me during the Opening Weekend. Al helped Bruce with a computer problem back in June and was promptly listed as "Technical Advisor" on the Rebels webpage. Al and I have been playing ball together for almost twice as long as some of the players have been alive. Coach Corey Paluga was gracious enough to throw batting practice to us, and we reveled in days gone by. Best of all, no one got hurt, at least seriously hurt.

Al and I decided that the best way to keep from getting stiff was to keep moving, so we ventured down to the Community Park, and the "Americana" about which Mo spoke the night before reappeared before our eyes. We found Joe Hammond in the dunking booth, his mom, Beth standing well forward of the line, ball in hand, throwing at the target, which would send Joe into the tank.

"C'mon, mom! You gotta stand further back than that!" he yelled, just before his mother's toss sent him into the water.

Jake Guengerich, who picked up the win over Fauquier, was manning the moon bounce, which is sponsored by the Rebels. A boy of perhaps 10 was entertaining Jake with stories about his "girlfriend."

We saw Brian Burgess strolling hand in hand with his fiancée, Morgan, and it was hard to say who was wearing the bigger smile.

We saw the Owenses and Zach Helgeson and his mom, Lynn. We saw Sharon Smith, who was selling bottles of water for $1.00 on behalf of the Chamber of Commerce. There were pony rides, with ponies so small I am sure that Steve Owens could stand astride one and never come close to sitting on it. Several small children were hanging onto their saddles, however, as the little ponies paced their way around a little corral. Local institutions such as the Rescue Squad were selling pork barbecue, funnel

Jordan Pegram and family.

cakes, hot dogs, and the like.

Al and I got a sandwich and sat in the park. A band was playing "Johnny B. Goode." Al, whose commute takes him along part of the Baltimore Beltway and up I-95 to Aberdeen Proving Grounds remarked, "I feel like I'm in a different country. The people inside the beltways have no idea this world even exists."

"The funny thing is," I answered "those people inside the beltways would be mortified to realize that these people could care less what goes on inside the beltways."

Al laughed. "That's for sure."

It was 3:00 p.m. and time to return to Rebel Park to prepare for the parade. Al and I had figured on simply watching, but Bruce insisted that we be *in* the parade.

"You have to see what the players see in order to appreciate what takes place," he said.

The "float" consisted of a large flatbed trailer on which Bruce placed two benches, a feed trough full of ice and bottled water, and several bags of candy. It was decorated with appropriate bunting. The players would walk alongside the trailer handing out water and candy while the coaches, Bruce, Al, and I would ride in the back of the pickup that was pulling the trailer. Vic in the team bus would follow us, and we told Bruce that we would be happy to ride in it.

"No," he said with some exasperation, "you can't see it from there. You have to ride in the truck."

Mo arrived in pants made from multicolored fabric, the likes of which have not been seen since Joseph had his famous coat made during Old Testament times. I judged Mo's pants were not made at the same time as Joseph's coat, but it is possible that they came from the same bolt of material. Bruce put him in the truck cab so no one would see the pants.

The truck in which Mo was hidden, as well as the trailer, belongs to another member of the Rebel family, Wayne Kipps, whom Bruce describes as a "brother."

Slowly, Wayne pulled us onto the Old Cross Road leading into town, the original path of State Road 211, where we lined up and waited for the parade to begin. We were stopped across from a pasture full of cattle, and when a bull mounted one of the cows, he received an ovation from the players who, in turn, were constantly implored not to eat all the candy so that there would be some for the kids along the parade route.

Bruce had assigned Joe Hammond, Kevin Rufus, and George Carroll the task of bribing the judges at the reviewing stand with gift bags, explaining that the Rebels had won a ribbon 6 years in a row, and he wasn't taking any chances on losing this year.

At quarter after 4:00, we finally chugged our way up Old Cross Roads and turned south on Congress Street. Immediately, I knew why Bruce wanted me to see the parade from the inside out. Both sides of the street were 3 and 4 people deep as far as one could see. Some sat on their porches, and some sat in lawn chairs along the street. I saw faces alight and heard more than once someone cry out, "It's the Rebels!" Had the World Champion Phillies come riding down the street, they would not have received more sincere adulation. People waved, smiled, and yelled "Go Rebels!"

The boys quickly organized themselves so that a few remained on the trailer and pitched water and candy to their teammates, who were walking and handing them out. Meanwhile in the truck, we tried to spy older folks who might desire the water and direct the players in their direction. There were plenty of kids who, wide-eyed at these young strangers, smiled and stuck out their hands for candy. One tiny girl wanted some water and, of course, it was Steve Owens who delivered it. The smiles during the exchange, however, were of the same size.

There were familiar faces all along the route, including Front-Row Fred, the Hawkinses, Katie Getz, and Teahra Hough. Hough, a 2009 graduate of Strasburg High, began the year as the athletic trainer intern with Abbie, but could not continue in that capacity because she is not licensed by the Virginia Board of Medicine. Therefore, she moved into the press box, where she is largely responsible for the scoreboard, as well as assisting Bruce and Katie.

Melissa Dodge was taking photos as we went by, and I saw other fans, parents, girlfriends, and fiancées as well.

Eric Alessio hands out bottled water and candy during the 4th of July parade.

When we arrived at the judges' table, Joe, Kevin, and George presented their gift bags, and some players brought water bottles. Kevin took it upon himself to hug and kiss the one lady on the panel, and he was as graceful and smooth in doing so as he was in catching a fly ball hit into the gap.

When we passed the Southern Kitchen, the entire wait staff was outside under the awning, watching us go by and waving.

I saw what Bruce had wanted me to see: A town that gave its collective heart to a bunch of college kids for representing them. Even in this year of 2009, when cynicism for its own sake is as trendy as any new fashion, New Market does not look upon this bestowal of affection as old-fashioned or corny. The town seeks nothing in return for its affection; it is given to these boys for simply being willing to wear *New Market* on their chests.

Then, too, I saw the wonderment on the faces of the players for, as some remarked, they had never seen this many people in New Market before, and at least a couple speculated that many must have come in from neighboring towns. I saw wonderment, but little understanding. They are too young. One day, however — sooner for some and later for others — whether they make the major leagues or never play organized ball again, they will realize that for one summer, they were heroes to everyone from children, who themselves are a decade or more away from college, to some of the oldest folks who, perhaps, are enjoying their final summer.

* * *

After reaching the end of the parade route and turning down John Sevier Road, heading back to Rebel Park, two girls approach the float/trailer on which now ride all of the Rebels. They say "Hello" in a somewhat flirtatious manner that arrests all conversation. After a moment's silence, Spencer Clifft's voice rises above the drone of the truck engine, "Are you 18?"

Everyone cracks up, and someone yells that every girl in New Market is *under* 16, echoing Bruce's admonition from the team's first gathering. A trailer full of laughing ballplayers drives off the two girls, who indeed appear to be no more than 16 years old. Two blocks later, the trailer erupts in laughter again, this time at Jake Pierce, who standing and looking around asks, "Where are we?"

"Luray," someone yells.

Jake has had a rough day. He dutifully reported to the moon bounce at 7:00 that morning, and it was bad enough when no kids showed up, but when Richie Gonzalez, his relief did not appear, he was more than exasperated. Calling Richie to find out why he had not come to relieve him, Jake was informed that their shifts were for 7:00 and 8:00 p.m., respectively.

* * *

At 9:15 that evening, the fireworks begin. Al and I are sitting on folding chairs in a secluded spot in New Market. There are only two pickups parked here, but I hear a voice call out in the darkness, "Austin, is that you?"

I walk toward the speaker: "Vic? I thought I recognized your voice!"

"Man, this is the best spot in town to watch these fireworks. You can see great, and there's no traffic to beat," says Vic. "I'd hate for anyone to know about this place." "Don't worry, Vic," I reply, "I won't reveal it, because I'm planning on coming back here, too."

* * *

It has rained most of Sunday morning in New Market. It is unseasonably cool, and the clouds envelop Massanutten Mountain as we gather under the pavilions at 2:00 p.m. for the Parents Weekend picnic. Some of the folks recall the last time we gathered in the pavilion for a Rebel picnic and joke about the hailstorm. One main topic of conversation regards whether tonight's game against Staunton will be played. The scoreboard is continuously flashing the names and schools of each of the players, while host families lay their casseroles and bowls of baked beans and plates of brownies on the food tables.

After Dick Powell's blessing, everyone gets down to the serious business of eating fried chicken and side dishes, which have been piled high. As folks finish, Bruce rises to make several introductions. He tells the assembly that there are three groups without which Rebel baseball would be impossible: the players, their families, and the host families who take them in for the summer. He asks each combination of two groups to applaud the other.

He then explains to everyone that the Rebels attempted to bribe the parade judges, "for the simple reason that our float isn't very good," and tells of Kevin Rufus kissing the judge.

"Kevin, that lady hasn't been kissed like that in 30 years!" Bruce jokes. Mayor Larry Smith then pulls a gigantic red-white-and-blue ribbon from a box, and the streak of consecutive first-place awards, which now numbers seven, is intact.

Bruce calls on Lucas, who rises and introduces his coaching staff. Lucas is noticeably more comfortable and more polished than at previous gatherings. He notes that Corey Paluga's family could not be here, "but they do love him." Everyone laughs. He delivers the line with professional pitch and timing. After introducing all the coaches but Mo, Lucas has each player stand and introduce himself, any family he is with, and his host family.

As one player after another stands, I have the growing sense that we are being introduced to the various branches of a single family.

Lynne Alger introduces Mo for "a few words, and I do mean a few."

Mo rises and tells the crowd his "verbose" story. The parents have never heard this before, and they laugh heartily, as do the players who have perhaps only heard the story once. On a roll, Mo follows up by saying, "I've lost a little height lately," adding that the war did that to him, and more laughter ensues. He grows suddenly serious, however.

"But I'm no hero," he says, "I came back," and he sits down.

Bruce finally introduces Marvin Diamond and then asks, "Is that everybody?"

"That's everybody in town," answers Bob Lanham, and everyone laughs once more.

Lucas gets up from his seat to take a call on his cell phone and then makes the announcement that we all expected: "The game's been banged," he says.

Most disappointed are the Hammonds, who had arranged to stay through Sunday night in order to watch Joe's start against Staunton.

As the picnic breaks up and parents and players say their goodbyes, I look up from my notes to find Al folding chairs and loading them into a pickup truck and wiping down the extra tables that had been set up in the pavilion.

"What are you, the Director of Table Wiping now?" I joke. Al just laughs, but I recall what Bruce said to Becky Kipps, and it is obvious that Al "has it" regarding the Rebels.

On a lot of teams and in a lot of towns, it's all about *me*. On the Rebels and in New Market, it's all about *we*.

Chapter 16
The Struggles of Zach Helgeson

The rainout against Staunton did not blunt the momentum gained from Friday's night's dramatic victory. The Rebels got on a roll.

Against Harrisonburg on Monday, New Market scored five runs en route to a 5-3 victory behind the stellar pitching of Steve Owens. SteveO, who has seemed more contented than he has been all summer, threw one-hit ball over six innings. Joe Hammond relieved and gave up an unearned run in the 7th, and when Joe ran into trouble in the 8th, Mike Roth came on to retire the side.

"I cleaned up Joe's mess, and he gave me he gave me a hug for it," said Roth, adding, "that's what it's all about; picking each other up."

On Tuesday, the Rebels rallied for 5 runs in the top of the 8th to defeat Luray 8-3. The game featured a long home run to right by Sanchez Gartman and four solid innings of one-hit relief by the bullpen. It also featured five Rebel batters who were hit by the pitch. In the previous contest against Luray, four Rebels were plunked, including Zach Helgeson who had hit two home runs. Everyone in the Valley League knows that Wrangler manager Mike Bocock likes to intimidate opposing teams, and there doesn't seem to be much doubt that these hit batsmen are no accident.

What Bocock doesn't seem to realize is that no Lucas Jones team will ever be intimidated (was Gary Cooper intimidated in *The Fountainhead* or *High Noon*?), and it is especially difficult to intimidate Mike Roth, the native New Yorker, who at 6'6" and 230 pounds brings an intimidating presence of his own to the mound. In the previous contest, Roth hit the first batter he faced in the bottom of the 9th, and he does the same in this game, and this is Roth's way of "picking up" his hitters.

Roth has taken Jordan Pegram's spot in the Dodge household, and host mom Melissa has taken to calling him the "Hitman."

"I like that nickname," says Roth, who epitomizes the phrase, *big lug*. Roth won't admit intentionally drilling anyone, nor will he suggest that he was ordered to do so, but he makes it abundantly clear that he doesn't mind in the least doing "what needs to be done."

The victory over Luray moves New Market to 13-12, the first time that the Rebels have been over .500 since the first game of the 2008 season.

On Wednesday against Haymarket, Garrett Baker hooked up with Western Carolina teammate Mike Benedict in a pitchers' duel at Rebel Park. Baker is the tough-luck pitcher on the squad, his teammates having scored only 3 runs in his 30 innings of work. Kenny Mickens and Zak Messer lead off the bottom of the first with hits, and both come around to score, but those are the only runs New Market manages in Baker's 7 innings, and he departs trailing 3-2.

Shortstop Troy Zawadski — who is from Boston, Massachusetts, but attends Cleveland State Community College in Cleveland, Tennessee, and has taken Jordan Pegram's place on the roster — is hit by a pitch in the 8th and scores the tying run on a Kenny Mickens double. Both teams miss opportunities to score in the 10th. In the bottom of the 12th, Kevin Rufus is hit by a pitch for the 14th time this season and after stealing second, he advances to third on an error by reliever Matt Sushack, who tried to glove a dribbler up the first-base line by Richie Gonzalez, but missed.

This brings Mickens to the plate, this time with the winning run on third. Mickens hits a two hopper up the middle that shortstop Zeth Stone appears to have lined up when suddenly, the ball spins 60 degrees to Stone's right. Stone, who had been playing left field, makes a valiant effort to stop suddenly and lunge back to his barehand side, but he cannot quite reach the strangest looking hit that anyone has seen for some time. Mickens' spinning single, which he said he hit off "the middle" of the bat, scores the winning run, and the Rebels move to two games above .500.

After the game, a happy group of players gathers in the pavilion for a postgame meal of lasagna and salad. All except one.

"Hmm. Helgeson's still down there," says Zak Messer, who is sitting at a picnic table with Mo, Bruce, Jake Pierce, and me. It is half an hour after the game has ended. I glance in the direction of Messer's gaze and see Zach Helgeson, who had struck out three times and grounded into a double play, sitting on the bench. He is still in uniform, and he is staring out toward the empty diamond.

Baseball can do that to you. One night you hit two long home runs, and by the next week, you are convinced that you will never get another hit. Baseball is full of these streaks, but knowing that fact doesn't make it any easier to take. We can feel Helgeson's anguish, even at this distance.

We talk about the game a bit more, when Messer excuses himself, saying that he has to go. I figure that he wants to work out, but after a few more minutes, I realize that I haven't seen him pull out of the parking lot. I look toward the Rebel dugout, and there is Messer talking to Helgeson. After a few minutes, Zak and Zach leave the dugout and walk into the locker room.

If such signs of excellent team chemistry have been the most consistent aspect of the Rebels' season, so, too, have the injuries. Quiet Kenny Bryant, his shoulder still hurting, left for home immediately after the picnic on Parents' Weekend. Jake Pierce would be heading home soon as well. Removed from the Luray game in obvious discomfort, Abbie confirms that Pierce has a stress fracture in his spine. He has played through some serious pain, but he can no longer swing a bat, much less catch, and there is nothing for him to do but go home and rest. The easygoing Pierce will be missed.

George Carroll picked the wrong time to miss the bus to Winchester the next night. Lucas, adhering to team policy, would not play Carroll, and with Pierce shut down and about to head home, Jones was forced to use Sanchez Gartman behind the plate for only the second time this season. Gartman stroked a two-run homer in the first inning, tying him with Zach Helgeson for the team lead, but in the 8th, his passed ball opened the door for a five-run Royals rally, and by the end of the frame, New Market trailed 8-3. Winchester's five runs were, perhaps, conjured up by a marimba band composed of Royals players in the dugout who started playing a steady, foot-stomping beat on three empty ball buckets and two sets of crossed bats.

"That's Valley League Baseball, right there," laughed Bruce, who admired the spirit of the Winchester players, even if Rebel fans were grumbling about it; perhaps because the rally music was having the desired effect.

New Market had a counter to the efforts of Winchester's musicians, however. As the Rebels came off the field after the final out in the 8th, Mo

Weber greeted each player, imploring them, encouraging them, convincing them that they had five runs in them, too. And they did. Seth Kivett drove in the first run, and Matt Townsend's booming double drove in the second. Kivett scored on a wild pitch, and with two outs, Kevin Rufus walked, marking the fifth time he had reached base in the game. That brought up Troy Zawadzki's spot in the lineup, but Lucas sent in Zach Helgeson to pinch hit. After the rough night against Haymarket, Jones had sat his struggling first baseman, just to give him a chance to collect his thoughts. In any other profession, this would be known as a "mental health day." Helgeson fell behind 1-2, although he looked better at the plate than he did the previous night, and on the next pitch, he did something that he hasn't done before: He cut down on his swing and hit a little tapper toward the shortstop.

There's an old saying in baseball, that if you just put the ball in play, good things may happen, and tonight, the saying proves correct. Winchester's third baseman ranges far to his left, cutting the ball off from the shortstop, but he cannot get his body turned, and he makes an awkward throw to first that skips past the first baseman and two more runs score. The inning ends when Richie Gonzalez forces Helgeson at second, but not before the boys make a prophet of Mo and score five runs to tie the game at 8.

The game has been lumbering along at a slow pace, although Bridgeforth Field in Winchester is a pleasant enough place to watch a game. Located in Jim Barnett Park, the field holds a fairly large number of people, by Valley League standards, and indeed, over 900 are here this night when a local business has sponsored the game and everyone enters for free. It's 386' to dead center beyond which, and across the road, lies the recently constructed Daniel Morgan Middle School.

The worst part about a game in Winchester is having to listen to their insipid theme song, which is comprised of seven words repeated endlessly: "Are you loyal? To the Winchester Royals; are you loyal?" As if to make up for that assault on the senses, Winchester can boast that it sells the best hot dogs in the league. I have relish and onions on mine and count them as my green and my vegetable for my evening meal.

George Carroll is brought in to catch the bottom of the 9th, in spite of the fact that he missed the bus. Gartman is not used to catching, and his left hand is so sore that he can now barely swing the bat. Carroll's fellow New Yorker, Mike Roth, enters the game to pitch the bottom of the 10th, but after committing a throwing error on a ball hit by the leadoff batter, he surrenders a long double to Jordan Steranka, which brings in the winning run. In spite of the spirited 9th-inning rally, the Rebels fall 9-8. The game lasts four hours and two minutes.

The Winchester game has an effect on the next night's contest at home against Harrisonburg. Gartman's thumb is still sore, and he sits out against right-hander Drew Granier, who entered the game with a 3-0 record. Gartman's bat would be missed.

Joe Hammond starts this night and promptly walks the leadoff batter. It appears he will escape the inning with no damage done when, with two out and men on second and third, Turks' DH Mike Schwartz taps one out to Richie Gonzalez at second. Gonzalez mishandles the ball, allowing the runner from third to score, and then in a vain attempt to atone for the first error, commits a second on the same play when his glove-hand toss to Helgeson at first gets past Zach and the runner from second scores.

Those would be the only two runs that Harrisonburg would score all night. But they would be enough. Matt Townsend hit a home run to dead center field in the second, the ball sailing out over the 6 in the 365 sign, but that was the only run the Rebels would muster. Hammond and Granier matched zeros for the next 6 innings in what is the best pitchers' duel of the season so far, but Joe comes away with the loss on those two unearned runs.

Zach Helgeson tells me before the game that the roller he hit in Winchester that brought home the tying runs "may be what I need to get me going. Baseball's a funny game like that." Instead, however, Zach strikes out four times, the final two times looking, and his frustration begins to boil over. After the third strikeout, he barks at the umpire, who ignores Zach's words and glare. After the fourth strikeout, he controls himself until he gets to the dugout and then slams his helmet to the ground. To add insult to injury, the helmet hits a rake, which comes flying forward and hits Zach in the mouth, breaking a tooth.

Zach Helgeson

140

He has been stoic and analytical during this slump, but he has reached the breaking point. As all players in slumps are wont to do, Zach has tried to hit every pitch 400 feet and then 500 feet and then 600 feet as the slump continues. He is pulling off the ball badly. He is trying too hard. In baseball, you have to try easy. I feel for Zach, and I find myself trying to somehow *will* his head to stay on the pitch. This is why baseball players and fans are so superstitious: It seems that you can lose your game so fast that it must be some tear in the fabric of the Cosmos causing the problem because you *know* that your swing is the same. Hence, the problem must be that you are wearing the wrong undershirt or you put your socks on in the wrong order or you sat in the wrong seat in the dugout.

With back-to-back tough losses, the Rebels momentum is suddenly blunted. They have slid back to .500, going into the last game before the VBL All-Star game. The Saturday night contest is against division rival Woodstock, and it has become important. No one wants to slip under .500 right before the break.

In the bottom of the second inning, Zach Helgeson comes to the plate with two outs. He has been dropped to 7th in the order, and Corey Paluga has talked to him and worked with him earlier in the day. Paluga has taken over the club for the weekend because Lucas Jones has a wedding to attend. Zach bounces a sharp single through the hole on the left side, and I find myself literally heaving a sigh of relief. My wife Martha who is with me and who also knows about Zach's struggles grabs my arm. It is a meaningless single in terms of the game, as Helgeson is stranded at first, but it means something to Zach. And to us.

He tries not to smile when he comes into the dugout to retrieve his glove, but he cannot help himself. Corey greets him with a smile as well, and when he comes in for the bottom of the 3rd, Mo is there to shake his hand. Twice.

Zach will go on to strike out once, again pulling his head off the ball, and he hits a weak tapper back to the mound, but draws a walk in his final at-bat. "Last night, he wouldn't even have walked," says Mo after the game.

The Rebels do not need any help from Helgeson on this night, in any case. Starter Steve Thiele shuts out Woodstock over the first 7 innings, Kenny Mickens collects 4 hits, and Kevin Rufus contributes an RBI triple; but the big blow comes in the New Market 7th when Sanchez Gartman, his thumb obviously improved, launches a grand slam, again to right field.

Four relievers mop up for Thiele, and the Rebels defeat Woodstock by a final score of 8-3.

It is an important victory, restoring some of the momentum lost against Winchester and Harrisonburg, and overall, it has been a good week. The Rebels have gone 4-2 during this first full week of July, and the pitching efforts of Steve Owens, Joe Hammond, and Steve Thiele as well as the bullpen, coupled with several late-inning rallies by the offense, have given Rebel fans real hope for the playoffs.

I will take something else from this week, however, for after Sanchez Gartman hit his grand slam, the first teammate out of the dugout to congratulate him was Zach Helgeson.

Chapter 17
Is the Batboy Here?

Eric Alessio, Brian Burgess, Zach Helgeson, Kenny Mickens, and Richie Gonzalez represented New Market for the South Team at the Valley League All-Star game held in Woodstock on Sunday, July 13. The four Central Division teams were divided between the North and South Divisions along geographic lines. Hence, New Market and Harrisonburg joined the South Division, while Luray and Woodstock joined the North.

A home-run derby was held before the game in which both Helgeson and Sanchez Gartman participated. Neither hit a home run, nor did just about anyone else. Staunton's Todd Brazeal hit one to finish runner up to Front Royal's Steve McQuail, who hit all of two. With the deep dimensions down the lines and in the power alleys at Central High, and with a stiff breeze blowing in, it was extremely difficult to hit anything over the fence.

The game followed the pattern of the home-run derby, the South squad winning 1-0. Alessio started the game and was the only pitcher on either side to hurl two innings. Richie Gonzalez reached on an error in the 6th and scored the game's only run on a double by Harrisonburg's Bobby Brown, who was named the game's Most Valuable Player for the South squad. Brian Burgess retired all three batters he faced in the 9th to record the save.

Sixteen scouts attended the game and sat directly behind home plate. As a pitcher went into his windup, a garden of radar guns blossomed and then disappeared again as scouts set them down to record the speed of each pitch.

Brian Burgess admitted to being nervous upon entering the game. "I've never seen that many guns before!" he said.

The Rebel faithful, including the Kipps family, Melissa Dodge, and Melissa and Front-Row Fred, were in attendance. So was Generals Sign Guy Mike, and Haymarket Joe was there as the official photographer.

All the Rebel coaches were in attendance, and several players showed up in support of their All-Star teammates. After the game, we gathered at McDonald's and as they waited for their respective orders, Lucas talked hitting with Zach Helgeson. It was obvious that the conversation was more about encouragement than about technique. Zach struck out looking in his only plate appearance.

That Wednesday, the same group of Rebel All-Stars, with the exception of Alessio, represented New Market at the Mid-Atlantic Classic All-Star game in Waldorf, Maryland. After eight months of planning, the game had finally arrived, and the result left a very sour taste in the mouths of many Valley League fans. The VBL lost to the Cal Ripken Senior Collegiate Baseball League 2-1, but it was the highly questionable management of the team by Staunton's Lance Mauck and Luray's Mike Bocock that had fans upset.

Starting five Braves and two Wranglers, Mauck and Bocock seemed determined to make the game a showcase for their own players. This became evident in the 6th inning when, with the bases loaded and two out, Mauck let Luray's Drew Martinez, a left-handed hitter bat against southpaw Nick Cicio. Martinez, who came into the game with a .322 average, a .389 on-base percentage, and a .390 slugging percentage, grounded into a fielder's choice to end the inning. Sitting on the bench were three right-handed hitters, including Richie Gonzalez (.375/.430/.462), Kenny Mickens (.393/.518/.558), and the league's leading home run hitter, Steve McQuail (.300/.341/.633).

Any one of these three hitters would have been a better statistical matchup than Martinez, and when none were sent in to pinch-hit for the Luray outfielder, the coaches from other VBL teams who were in the stands, as well as the fans, became quite restless and began hurling pointed comments and barbs into the dugout.

Mauck was quoted in that morning's edition of Harrisonburg's *Daily News Record* as saying that because he was playing to win, "everybody's not going to get in, and that's the bitter shame of it all, but it is what it is."[1]

That is nonsense, of course, because, "it is" what Mauck *made it* to be. Neither Rockbridge's representative, nor either of the Fauquier players ever got into the game. Kenny Mickens logged half an inning in right field, and Richie Gonzalez struck out swinging in the 9th. Zach Helgeson never made an appearance, while Brian Burgess with his 0.00 ERA was left sitting in the bullpen, leaving Trey Alger, who served as the VBL batboy, the most active Rebel of the night.

For most of the VBL players, this all-star game will be the pinnacle of their baseball careers, yet the desire to win a meaningless game was allowed to supersede the opportunity to give everyone there an at-bat or a third of an inning pitched. Even in the major league All-Star Game, with home-field advantage in the World Series at stake, the respective managers find a way to play all of their players. Not so in the Valley League, and, in defense of Mauck and Bocock, they received no directive to do otherwise.

The trip to Waldorf from New Market takes approximately three hours, but that does not deter a cadre of hardcore Rebel fans, including the Smiths of New Market, the Smiths of Baltimore, the Dodges, Mo, Lucas, and several others from attending.

* * *

In between the two all-star games, the Rebels visited Staunton to take on Mauck's Braves in a makeup of the game rained out during Parent Weekend.

The boys are louder and more raucous on the bus than on any trip so far, their laughter cutting through the droning engine, the sound of which, along with a hot breeze, comes pouring in the open windows.

"It's hot as @#$%!" yells someone before we ever leave the parking lot.

"Hey, man, relax with that," McKinnon Langston hollers back, as he half nods in the direction of the young bat boy who is riding the bus this day.

---

[1]Helton, Marcus. "VBL Gets Rare Tube Time," *Daily News Record*, July 15, 2009.

Will Cooper, from McLean, Virginia, and a college batterymate of Jay Lively at George Washington University, joins the Rebels' as their latest, newest catcher. Cooper had arrived only a couple of hours before the bus departed, and he introduces himself to his new teammates, who welcome him aboard both the Rebels and the bus. Steve Owens is not present, however, as he is attending a tryout in front of scouts from the Angels and the Twins at Aberdeen High School — Cal Ripken's alma mater — in Maryland.

John Moxie Memorial Stadium in Staunton is an old park that sits in a tree-lined neighborhood. The lights here are terrible; the two poles in left and right center, respectively, contain only four bulbs each. The field itself slopes dramatically toward the right-field corner. While it is 340' down the lines, it is only 360' to center, but the small dimensions of the outfield are nothing compared to the dugouts, which are so tiny that they make Mo Weber look like a giant. The night's starter, 6'6" Mike Graham from Virginia Commonwealth and Fairfax Station, Virginia, cannot stand up in them. Constructed of stone, they contain only two metal benches and, therefore, most of the players sit on benches that have been placed alongside the dugouts. A large and enthusiastic crowd is gathering this evening.

"They were wound up today, weren't they?" says Vic about the players whooping it up on the bus as we watch batting practice.

"That means that they'll either play real well tonight or real poorly," I tell Vic.

For 5½ innings it was mostly the former, but for the final three innings, it was the latter, and the Rebels — who committed four errors, walked six, and hit 3 batters — lost in embarrassing fashion 16-7.

New Market falls behind early 3-0, then goes ahead in the 3rd on Sanchez Gartman's 6th home run of the season, a three-run shot that looks like each of his previous five long balls: a laser beam over the right-field fence. Staunton immediately ties the game in their half of the 3rd. The Rebels take a 5-4 lead with a two-out, bases-loaded walk in the 5th, but cannot push another run across. Again, Staunton ties the game in their half of the 5th.

The Rebels load the bases once more in the 6th, and once more receive a bases-loaded walk, but George Carroll's shot to right is hauled in and another opportunity to put more runs on the board is lost. Staunton then scores three runs in their half of the 6th.

In the top of the 7th, the Rebels load the bases again with two out and score a run on Kevin Rufus' single, but Seth Kivett strikes out on a 3-2 pitch to end the threat. Staunton then sends 10 men to the plate, scoring seven of them. The inning is punctuated by John Dishon's grand slam. Dishon flips the bat high in the air, as if to put a twirling exclamation point on the long blast, a gesture that is not appreciated by the Rebels. Spencer Clifft, who had given up Dishon's homer, sails his next pitch over Donovan Huffer's head. No one on the Rebel bench believes that Clifft's pitch was intentional; not so in the Staunton dugout, but other than some hollering and posturing, there is no other reaction.

The rest of the game is played without incident, Staunton adding one more run in the 8th to complete the scoring.

It is a game that does not sit well with the many Rebel fans who had journeyed an hour south. It certainly does not sit well with Lucas, and I hurry to right field for his postgame meeting with the players.

"Is the batboy here?" asks Lucas, as the last of the players gather. That question could only mean that he was about to use some words that the batboy shouldn't hear and, Lucas, just as Langston had done on the bus before the game, intended to see that he didn't. Lucas caught everyone off guard, however, by first congratulating his four all-stars and then saying that he was at a loss for words. He found them soon enough, although he did not direct them at his players:

"There is no point in bitching you out tonight. Just ask yourself if you're committed to this. Ask yourself over the next two days that you're off. Our number-one goal is to make the playoffs, and this is the type of game that can be used for a positive. This game was good for us because it shows us the commitment that will be required. For one thing, you need to come out with some fire and get a little @#$% about you."

Then, the words that the batboy shouldn't hear began to rain down, but again not at his players. Staunton had done some showboating in the late innings, flipping bats after big hits and stealing third with none out, and Lucas directed his ire at a Braves team that clearly held his own team in contempt. When he finished talking about the Braves, he came back to the Rebels and the profanity-laced tirade (well, it was a tirade by Lucas Jones' standards) became a sincere pep talk.

"The next two weeks will go by like that," he began, "and I wouldn't trade you. If we lose the next 14 games in a row, I wouldn't trade you. I believe in you, I care about you, and I trust you. Go about your business with a little chip on your shoulder. Commit yourselves to what we're doing over the next two days, and tonight will be the turning point of our season."

It is most appropriate to say that the Rebels came back with a vengeance three nights later against Luray.

Saying that his all-star experience in Waldorf was "disappointing, but I tried to stay positive," Kenny Mickens had to admit feeling satisfaction when he launched a three- run homer in New Market's 12-7 defeat of the Wranglers in the first game after the Mid-Atlantic Classic. Rebel fans certainly took it as an act of vengeance for the slighting of their all-star left fielder by Lance Mauck and Mike Bocock.

"Looks like an all-star to me, Bocock!" shouted a Rebel fan after Mickens' home run.

Kenny Mickens

Mickens admitted to having a sense that perhaps his homer would show Mike Bocock that, indeed, he could play, but in the typical fashion of a leadoff hitter, he said, "I'd have rather gone 4 for 4."

Richie Gonzalez stated that "It was an honor" to be selected, but he was disappointed that he didn't play more.

Brian Burgess was particularly upset that he had been told that he would pitch the 9th, but "never saw a batter." He added that what really bothered him and a host of other all-stars was that the game had become the Staunton–Luray show.

Zach Helgeson was much more direct, citing the "personal agenda" of Mauck and Bocock in playing their players, but in typical Helgeson fashion, he quickly added, "I understand not playing me, because I haven't done @#$% lately, but I'm more mad for the league and for my team." Both Helgeson and Mickens noted that tensions were rising in the dugout as the game grew late and no substitutions were being made.

The all-star break almost had much more far-reaching consequences for New Market than the slighting of its representatives, however. On the day before the game in Waldorf, Matt Townsend organized a tubing trip down the Shenandoah River that included McKinnon Langston, Sanchez Gartman, Richie Gonzalez, Troy Zawadzki, and fellow James Madison University teammate and newest member of the Rebels, pitcher Kyle Hoffman from Reading, Pennsylvania.

The group put in the river at Island Ford near Harrisonburg around 5:00 p.m., which was late enough, considering that the proposed trip was to take three hours. This "three-hour tour" turned into its own version of *Gilligan's Island*, as 4½ hours later, the boys still had not made their take-out point near Elkton where Kyle's car was parked. Townsend, Langston, Gartman, Zawadzki, and Gonzalez all clambered through hip-high mud along the banks, then made their way through multiflora rose patches and other assorted impediments before emerging from the woods at the Merck Pharmaceutical plant in Elkton. Gartman and Zawadzki scaled a fence topped with barbed wire to get help. They were promptly ushered into Merck's security office as were the others who were still waiting outside of the fence.

The boys' appearance no doubt convinced Merck security that this was not a raid by a pharmaceutical espionage team. Langston's white bathing suit was now brown with mud, Townsend in general was covered with mud, and all the boys were scratched and barefoot.

"Worst experience of my life," said Gartman.

"If we didn't have to babysit you, we'd have made it before sunset," replied Townsend. Gartman, as it turns out, can't swim.

"*Somebody* told me that it was only going to take three hours," said Gartman, glaring at Townsend.

"They *told* me three to four hours, but *unh-uh*," replied Matt, attempting to defend himself.

"I honestly thought I was going to die!" related Gartman, and I don't think he was kidding. "I made so many promises."

"You mean you'll have to go to church for six years' worth of Sundays now?" I ask.

"Yeah, something like that," he replied.

As bad as their plight was, the real problem was that Hoffman kept on floating down the river.

"I thought we were almost there," he explained.

An hour and a half after his teammates climbed out of the river, Hoffman finally spotted what he thought was a house light, only to find it was a safety light along some railroad tracks. "So then I walked up the tracks about a mile" said the 6'3" right hander, showing me the cuts on his pitching hand and the abrasions under his arms that six hours in an inner tube will cause.

Meanwhile, the boys at the Merck plant had informed security that one of their buddies was still on the river, and the search-and-rescue squad was called. Hoffman, who was also barefoot and still clinging to his inner tube, essentially walked right into the arms of the local fire police who had been called, and now that everyone was accounted for, the boys, Merck security, and Elkton's finest could relax. Shortly before midnight, all six Rebels were back to Matt Townsend's car near Island Ford, their 3-hour tubing trip incomplete after seven hours.

"I couldn't believe this was happening to me!" Hoffman said with a laugh. It was only half a laugh, though, as it will take some time — at least until the cuts and abrasions heal — before he can laugh fully at what will no doubt be one of the great misadventures of his life.

"Worst experience of my life," repeated Gartman. "I felt like survivor out there, and I don't mean the TV show."

With no players drowned and all players accounted for, what happened over the all-star break and during the game in Waldorf was of no consequence to Lucas Jones. As he told his squad after the debacle at Staunton, the number-one goal is to make the playoffs, and that means winning as many of the remaining 14 games as possible. The Rebels begin the home stretch of the season in grand style with the 12-7 victory over Luray.

Mickens leads off with a walk to begin the game, and Kevin Rufus follows with a home run. Luray ties the score in the bottom of the 1st, but Mickens' homer gives the Rebels a 5-2 lead, and they never look back. Zak Messer adds a two-run homer in the 3rd, New Market tacks on five more runs, and new catcher Will Cooper goes 3-for-4 with two RBIs. The game is not as close as the score indicates — the mop-up men out of the Rebel bullpen allow five runs over the last two innings. Brian Burgess records the final two outs, and though it isn't a save situation, he states that he was particularly satisfied that he could shut the door on Mike Bocock's squad.

Rain falls across the Shenandoah Valley on Friday, leaving Rebel Park too muddy for the game against Winchester that evening. This latest shower again lowers temperatures throughout the region as the Valley continues to enjoy a rare, cool summer. The Rebels, however, stay hot on Saturday afternoon at Harrisonburg. Behind the seven-inning, eight-strikeout performance of Garrett Baker, who finally picks up his first win, the Rebels defeat the Turks 4-1. Coupled with Luray's loss to Covington, the Rebels are now only half a game out of first place in the Central Division.

New Market's next contest is with the Fauquier Gators at Athey Memorial Ballpark in Warrenton. In another bit of All-Star revenge, the Gators defeated Lance Mauck's Staunton Braves 5-4 in 10 innings the night before. This put Fauquier half a game in front of the Rebels in the wild-card standings with 12 games to play.

Athey Memorial Ballpark is on the campus of Fauquier High School. The diamond is well-maintained and sports very fair dimensions, but it is totally lacking in atmosphere, at least on this night. The crowd numbers perhaps only three dozen people at the start of the game.

The Rebels go up 2-0 in the 1st inning on a long single by Zach Helgeson and a sacrifice fly off the bat of Zak Messer.

In the stands, Lynne Alger informs Rebel fans that a new game is being played in her house. "Yeah, it's called 'Find George's Jersey,'" she says, referring to "son" George Carroll, "and it usually starts about five minutes before the bus leaves. Only George usually doesn't find it."

Kay Helsley is in the stands, of course. She has not missed a game this year, and she encourages her host son Kevin Rufus to take a "nice level swing, now," a phrase that, along with "Find a gap, now!" she uses often.

"Listen to your mother!" hollers C. B. Alger, who brings the same wit to the webcast booth, where he occasionally assists with color commentary. Some have started referring to C. B. as the Rebels' future general manager. I think it's more likely that he'll be the future mayor of New Market. Or President.

The Rebels score one more run in the 5th and three more on no hits in the 8th to defeat Fauquier 6-0. Eric Alessio wins his 4th game of the season, striking out 6 batters over 6 innings, while Seth Kivett strokes three of the Rebels six hits. Luray defeats Covington 11-1, so New Market remains half a game behind the Wranglers with the season now three-quarters complete.

Lucas told his team at the beginning of the season that they should divide the schedule into quarters and seek to improve during each one. After starting 4-7, the Rebels improved to 6-5 in the second quarter, and then 8-3 in the third. Nine of the final 11 games are against divisional opponents, an exception being the Monday contest against Front Royal, which is a makeup game from July 1. The Cardinals sport the best record in the Valley League at 21-13, and the game proves to be an exciting affair that includes both the thrilling and the strange, and in the end, it is never finished.

Delayed almost half an hour by wet grounds from afternoon rains, New Market jumps out to a 1-0 lead only to have Front Royal go in front 3-1 on a Steve McQuail triple in the 5th. In the 6th, the Rebels take a 4-3 lead when Richie Gonzalez is hit with the bases loaded, and Kenny Mickens follows with a two-run double.

The Cardinals tie the game in the 7th on a sacrifice fly to Kevin Rufus, who makes another spectacular catch against the center-field wall. Tripping over the uneven ridges in Rebel Park's warning track, he falls backward, hitting his head against the wall, but reaches out while on his back and catches the ball.

In New Market's 8th, Gonzalez strokes a two-out single and appears to steal second, taking third on an apparent throwing error, but the home plate umpire rules that Mickens has interfered with the throw, and Gonzalez is declared out.

Front Royal then executes a two-out suicide squeeze in the top of the 9th, plating the go-ahead run off the healing Kyle Hoffman as rain begins to fall. New Market loads the bases with one out in the bottom of the 9th, when the skies really open up and play is halted, not to be resumed on this evening.

And so, after an exciting night of baseball, the game remains a suspended game to be played Sunday, the 26th at noon before the Rebels venture to Harrisonburg for a 5:00 game and the Cardinals journey back to Haymarket.

Batting practice before the next night's contest against Harrisonburg is a lighthearted affair. The pitchers are taking BP as a reward for allowing no earned runs in Joe Hammond's effort against the Turks on the 10th. There are many catcalls, groans, and cheers whenever a ball approaches the wall.

"Did he get it? No!" someone shouts when a ball short-hops the fence.

Jake Guengerich shows off a pretty quick swing, however, and puts one off the very top of the short fence in front of the Rebel bullpen. It misses by the width of the baseball from going out and is the closest any pitcher comes to hitting a home run.

The better a pitcher hits in batting practice of course, the more he thinks he should get some at-bats in a game, and Jake is becoming convinced that his offense might become valuable to the Rebels. Since he played middle infield early in his high school career, it well may be. Backup infielder Troy Zawadzki returned to Tennessee. Lucas is now left with no backup middle infielders and no chance to recruit anymore as the deadline for adding to the roster passed the day before Zawadzki decided to return home.

It will not matter on this night, for around 6:00, rain begins to fall. Again. Lucas has already had his players tarp the field, and it is removed at 7:45 when the rain stops. The players had not finished rolling the tarp back onto the roller, however, when the rain begins again and the game against Harrisonburg is postponed soon thereafter. With all scheduled rain dates filled, this game will have to be played on July 31st, one day after the regular season is to have concluded.

There was nothing to do but eat. Mo and I ventured to Jalisco's on Congress Street and were soon joined by Bruce. We talked baseball and ate salsa and chips and burritos until past closing time. Soon after parting company, my phone rang. It was Bruce.

"Just wanted to let you know that we're in first place," he says happily. "Luray lost tonight 6-5 to Woodstock."

Both teams are at 18-15, but New Market's better divisional record gives them the lead. This gives even greater significance to the Wednesday night game, which happens to be against Luray. That is, of course, if the unusually rainy weather holds off long enough to play. As Wednesday afternoon drifts by, dark clouds cover the Valley sky.

Chapter 18
These Boys Won't Want to Go Home This Summer!

S anchez Gartman does not take playing baseball for granted.

"Last summer, I came home with a 2.5 GPA, and my daddy had two applications waiting for me 'cause that wasn't good enough. I worked 12 hours a day painting light poles in a plant. He even took my Charger and made me drive an old truck we had sitting in the yard. So at the end of this year, I came home with a 3.5, and he let me come to New Market to play ball."

And play ball he has. "Chaz," as his teammates call him, leads the Rebels with seven home runs and a .610 slugging percentage through the first 34 games. His 25 RBIs is tied with Zach Helgeson for the team lead, while his .310 average ranks third on the club. Even his outs are hard-hit balls.

"Ungodly power," is the way Corey Paluga describes Gartman's ability to drive a baseball, and Mo Weber sees Sanchez as the one player on the team at this point with professional hitting abilities.

Yet, this is the first time in his life that he has used a wooden bat.

"After my first double at Woodstock, I said to myself, 'Oh, snap!' maybe I can do this [hit with a wooden bat], but I was scared of the inside pitch," relates Gartman, picking up a bat and adding, "With metal, if you hit it here [indicating the handle of the bat] you can still get hits, but with wood, you'll just sting your hands or break the bat.

"I called my coach at home, Kelly Ahrens, and he helped me. Mo helped me with the 'L' and as long as I use my lower half, like Mo tells me, I can get to that inside pitch."

The "L" to which Gartman refers is formed when the batter turns on the back foot, thereby clearing his hips. His back foot and calf will automatically form an "L." It is only by clearing the hips that a batter can reach the inside pitch and pull it; all seven of Gartman's home runs have been to right field.

Gartman has made a quick adjustment to using wooden bats, even though he had to try seven different models until he found one that he liked. His USC–Sumter teammate, Kevin Rufus, tried four wooden bats before settling on a model.

Rufus is another player who finally "just got comfortable." The left-handed hitter's comfort has obviously increased at this point because his swing has quickened, and he is now driving the ball to right field.

For the second straight day, rain began to fall immediately upon the conclusion of batting practice before the Wednesday game against Luray. Ryan Stauffer, the lefty reliever has been a very popular guy these last few days, as he is a meteorology major.

"We gonna play tonight?" is a question that has often been directed toward Stauffer for the last three nights.

Another question that has been making the rounds for some time among a certain group of older ladies in the upper right corner of the Rebel bleachers is Who is going to win the "Sweet Cheeks" Award? This award has nothing to do with a player's skills. If you sit near that last row in the corner, you are certain to hear "Bend over a little more!" and see camera flashes pop when any potential winners come to bat.

This year's finalists are Seth Kivett and Kenny Mickens, both of whom take the news of their finalist status with good humor.

"May the best man win," says Seth, while shaking Kenny's hand. "Maybe I should bend over and tie my shoe next time I come up," he adds.

The game against Luray is played despite the pregame shower, getting under way only two minutes behind the usual start time of 7:37. The Wranglers waste little time in jumping all over starter Mike "Moonlight" Graham, as Stauffer refers to him, for seven runs in the second, an inning highlighted by left fielder Pablo Bermudez's grand slam. The Rebels get one run back in their half of the second on doubles by Zak Messer and Richie Gonzalez and then send 11 men to the plate in the third, scoring six times on seven hits to tie the score. Zach Helgeson, who struck out in the first, booms a double to left center to plate one of the runs, and Gonzalez smacks a two-run double to right.

Graham is lifted after two innings in favor of Stauffer, who slams the door on the Wranglers, pitching three innings of 2-hit relief.

Steven Thiele relieves Stauffer and issues a leadoff walk to Bermudez, who steals second and scores on Dan Bowman's two-out single in the 6th. The home half of the 7th, however, presages the weird weather that is to follow.

Kenny Mickens leads off with a double that appears to be a long out to right center, the Luray center fielder tracking the ball all the way. At the last instant, however, right fielder Bowman steps in front of him, and the ball hits off Bowman's glove and falls for a double. It is then that Kevin Rufus steps to the plate, and with the count 2-2, pulls a ground ball to second, advancing Mickens to third. It is textbook baseball. Rufus reaches for an outside pitch and intentionally grounds to the right side, ensuring that Mickens can move up 90 feet, and he is warmly greeted by his teammates as he enters the dugout.

Seth Kivett, perhaps celebrating the fact that he has, indeed, defeated Mickens for the Sweet Cheeks Award, laces a single through the hole on the right side with Luray's infield drawn in for his third hit of the game. Kivett, who has been nursing a sore hamstring, has turned in a gritty performance, taking third on a short single to right in the 5th inning, despite the leg problem. He reaches third with no effort now in the 7th when Sanchez Gartman walks and Zach Helgeson is hit yet again by a Luray hurler. With a 2-0 count on Messer, the third pitch is a wild one, but bounces off the padding at the base of the backstop and right back to catcher Alex Haitsuka. Kivett breaks for home immediately, but Haitsuka's throw to the pitcher is a good one. And Kivett is ruled out. Seth jumps up in disbelief.

"He never tagged me," said Seth afterward. "He reached back to tag me a second time; I never felt the first one. I knew it was going to be bang-bang when I saw the ball bounce right back to the catcher, but with the sore hamstring, I couldn't stop, so I just kept going."

Had Kivett stayed at third, the Rebels would have had the bases loaded with a 3-0 count to Messer. For his part, Messer swings at the next pitch, grounding out to third. In the span of only two pitches, the Rebel rally evaporates.

That is the only thing that evaporated on this night, however. With the excitement in the bottom of the 7th, no one paid any attention to the fog that was slowly obscuring the trees beyond the center-field fence. By the time the Rebels took the field for the top of the 8th, advertising on the left field wall was unreadable. The right-field wall was quickly obscured, then the outfielders became barely visible, and the scoreboard was soon just a white hazy blur. In less than five minutes, fog had rendered the rest of the game unplayable, so in the end, nothing was determined this night between the two teams with the best records in the Central Division.

Eric Alessio (#19), Zach Helgeson, and the fog that descended on Rebel Park during the game against Luray on July 22.

"Man, strange stuff happens every time you're here," exclaims Jay Lively, who is the first player I see after play is halted. I attempt to defend myself, but I no sooner get done explaining to Jay that I've seen quite a few normal games when John Combs greets me with, "Every time you show up, weird stuff happens!" Of course, the Rebels have been through a hailstorm to end all hailstorms, a blackout, and now a fogout; they have had nine games postponed or suspended as a result of rain, a total that equals over 20% of the schedule. And they still have eight more games and now two suspended games yet to be played. No wonder Lucas Jones looks bewildered.

"I'm worn out!" he says, shaking his head during the postgame meal. "And it's not the games; it's watching the weather and raking the field and trying to decide whether it's worth putting on the tarp or not and having Stauffer tell everyone that we probably won't play tonight!"

"Don't worry," I tell him, "I figure tomorrow night, the sinkhole that is probably under Rebel Park will open up, swallow Rufus whole, and you'll be without a ballpark. You'll have discovered New Market Caverns and have a new tourist attraction, but you won't have a ballpark."

Lucas gives me a look that indicates he believes this might really be a possibility. We are joking, but the strain of being a first-time manager is clearly getting to him. He knows that the Rebels could have and probably should have been leading when the game was suspended. He knows that Troy Zawadzki's departure has left him short one player. He is worried about his pitching. He is worried about the weather. He is worried that the Rebels, should they win the championship, are facing the possibility of 21 games in the next 21 days, a grueling schedule, even by major league standards.

Lucas Jones does not have to worry about one thing, however, and that is his team. And it is *his* team. He picked them for their attitudes as much as for their abilities, and they are showing no signs of any strain. To a man, they seem ready to play anywhere there's a field dry enough or with visibility good enough.

Little things indicate this. Before the game, some players arrive as early as 4:15, and I find myself in a group that includes Helgeson, Messer, Gartman, James Weiner, Dan Rollins, and Will Cooper. A stranger would never pick out Cooper as the "new guy," for everyone is talking baseball in the parking lot and Cooper acts, and is treated, as if he has been with the Rebels since May 31st. No one complains about the rain or being tired, nor are they ready for school to start. This is especially true of Zach Helgeson, despite struggling so mightily over the last three weeks. With strikeouts still piling up and hits still hard to come by, it is Helgeson who points out to me, with a disbelieving shake of the head that, the Harrisonburg Turks, upon hearing the news that the previous night's game had been postponed, *cheered* the announcement.

"When I heard them cheering, I thought that meant we were playing," said Zach.

Mo repeatedly says that you can't measure a player's heart. True enough; but next to Zach Helgeson's name, you can simply write "more than enough."

The same is true of Zak Messer, whose confidence at the plate has grown almost visibly since Father's Day. Always intense, Messer's intensity is now crossing over into ferocity, and it sometimes gets him in trouble. In the 4th inning of the game against Luray, he hits a leadoff double and takes off for third when the ball gets loose in the infield. He is safe—barely—but it was a fundamentally poor decision and I halfway expect to see Mo coming out of the dugout to strangle Zak. That is, if Lucas doesn't beat him to it. Zak hasn't yet mastered the idea that aggressiveness must be tempered with patience; that the best thing one can do in certain situations is nothing. With a struggling pitcher on the mound, the best thing to do on a 3-0 count is to leave the bat on your shoulder. Nevertheless, to be this close to such unbridled intensity is a restorative, a rejuvenator, a potion that turns back time and returns to me the feelings of my own youth, even if the speed and strength and reflexes don't return with those feelings.

I know that no one should take even the slightest chance of making the first out at third base, but there is a certain beauty in the thoughtless drive that propels a young man to third, that sends him headfirst into the dirt, defying convention headlong, willing to risk a tongue lashing or even a benching for that extra 90 feet that says, "You *can't* get me out!" The pained look that flashed across Lucas' face when Zak barely beat the tag was obvious to anyone paying attention, but Zak never saw it. He was too busy pounding the dirt once with his fist and uttering an almost primitive sound of triumph.

Always an encourager, Lucas must feel incredibly encouraged the next day when a lengthy feature article on Richie Gonzalez appears in the *Northern Virginia Daily*. Gonzalez is quoted as saying, "I think [Lucas] did a great job of getting people that he thinks will match each other [and whose] personalities get along pretty well. He did a great job recruiting for this team. Our team chemistry, from day one, it looked awesome. It's one of the best teams I've played on."[1]

The fact that the Rebels are more than ready to play is never more apparent than in Thursday night's game against Winchester. This game is also delayed when the Royals arrive late because of an accident on I-81 and the fact that the field must again receive special attention after yet another shower. The Royals, riding an 11-game winning streak, are within one game of first-place Front Royal in the North Division, but the Rebels dispatch them with quiet precision. Behind Steve Owens' strong six innings in which he allows only two runs, New Market defeats Winchester 4-2. After losing the opener at Harrisonburg, Owens has now reeled off six straight victories to lead the Valley League, and Brian Burgess records his league-leading 8th save. Seth Kivett adds another RBI single.

---

[1] Stafford, Jeremy. "For the love of the game: New Market's Richard Gonzalez brings passion for baseball to Valley League," *Northern Virginia Daily*, July 23, 2009.

Saying that he was "overswinging," Kivett confers with his coaches and his dad and comes to the conclusion that he should simply concentrate on "watching the ball hit the bat." Seth tells me that he was taught in college to hit everything the other way, but the right-handed swinger is starting to pull the ball with authority now "for the first time since high school."

"It feels good!" he tells me with his seemingly ever-present grin. "Sweet Cheeks," as some of his teammates are starting to call him, will have much more to smile about by the time Friday's contest with Harrisonburg concludes.

Of course, it wouldn't be a day in the Valley in the summer of 2009 if there weren't some rain or at least the threat of rain, and it pours in New Market until about 1:00 in the afternoon on Friday. Working feverishly to rake out the infield once again, the Rebel coaching staff is aided mightily by Harrisonburg coach Bob Wease, who not only helps prepare the infield, but brings along 10 bags of Turface for Lucas to use at Rebel Park. Turface is an absorbent blend of soils used, among other applications, to help make wet fields playable. New Market has already used two pallets of Turface, including the final 16 bags the night before. This is twice the amount budgeted, and Lynne Alger has decreed that Lucas can spend no more on the magic dirt.

Wease even sweeps out both dugouts for good measure, while Lucas and the coaches put the finishing touches on the infield.

Lucas, in his leather gloves and broad floppy hat, looks like a farmer pondering how much seed to order as he stares across the infield and, indeed, Corey Paluga has created exotic swirls of little furrows with the three-wheeler and the spike-tooth drag. "Weatherman" Ryan Stauffer is the first player to arrive, appropriately enough, and immediately grabs a landscape rake.

Bob Wease's gracious gesture goes unrewarded in the game, however, when Garrett Baker carries a no-hitter into the 5th and allows only two hits through seven innings of work. Jake Guengerich and Mike Roth complete the shutout, and the Rebels move a game in front of Luray when the Wranglers lose to Woodstock 5-3.

Seth Kivett, the top of his calf now actually black and blue from his torn hamstring, walks in the 3rd and endures three different 3-2, two-out pitches on which he must run. While clearly uncomfortable, he never shows how much pain he is in. In the bottom of the 5th and with the Rebels clinging to a 1-0 lead, Kivett launches a mammoth home run — to left field — which clears the Rebel bullpen and bounces close to the first row of cars parked in the grass beyond. In his excitement, he half runs around the bases, his smile broader than ever, and he admits he didn't even attempt to lose the smile.

It is by a consensus of opinion the longest home run anyone remembers being hit at Rebel Park. "And the highest," adds Bruce Alger.

As if hitting this titanic blast weren't enough, he makes a Brooks Robinson-like play in the top of the 8th when he charges a dribbler, barehands it, and rifles a throw to first for the out. With Gartman and Rufus suddenly in mini-slumps — they are a combined 5 for 22 in their last 3 games and are striking out frequently — Kivett is picking up the slack. That's what successful teams do.

They also have fun. Peering out into the Rebel bullpen from the webcast deck, where Charlie Dodge and I are broadcasting the game, we can see several Rebel relievers wearing bright-green shark hats on top of their baseball caps. Team photographer, host mom, ardent fan, and Charlie's wife, Melissa scrounged these items from her basement and handed them off to Jay Lively. Melissa had bought them for a previous team, but "they just weren't feeling it." This group of Rebels "feels it" and then some.

"Where did you get these?" asked Lively, almost breathlessly of Melissa after the game. "We need 15 more; one for everybody. If we can't get these, we might get some Rastafarian hair ... whatever we can get for everybody in the bullpen."

Later on, I relate this story to Mo who laughs and looks longingly — not into space really, more into time — and says, "These boys won't want to go home this summer." Then he adds, "That's very unusual."

Of course, at the rate games are being cancelled, they may never get home in any event. Just as the players are gathering to board the bus the next night for Luray at about 4:45, a line of dark clouds that had appeared on the horizon at around 4:00 are now positioned over New Market. The weatherman had predicted only a 20% chance of showers on this day, but by 4:45 it is raining; by 5:00 it is pouring on the other side of the mountain in Luray as well. Vic Moyers never gets the bus out of the parking lot before the game is cancelled.

Vic would soon have more important matters that would consume his attention in any case. Just as Lucas was getting the call that the game in Luray was postponed, Vic received a call informing him that two thirds of the roof on the Shenandoah Flea Market had blown off when a small tornado descended just north of New Market and was now scattered across the parking lot and over 500 yards of the pasture on the other side of Route 11. This is the place where Vic displays his refinished furniture that, unbelievably, was untouched, save for a little rainwater that he was able to wipe off after entering the building. Several people were inside at the time, but remarkably no one was hurt.

Three days later, the National Weather Service determined that a "microburst" of 70-mph winds blew into an open garage door in the back of the building and lifted the roof off. That might explain how the roof came off, but not how some of it ended up 500 yards across Route 11. Whatever it was, a picnic table that had sat in front of the flea market and that took four men to lift disappeared altogether. At this point in the summer, no one would be surprised to see a plague of locusts descend on New Market.

Ryan Stauffer, the meteorology major, explains to me that if that much wind entered a small opening, it would create a funnel effect and magnify the force. Parts of the roof weren't *carried* that far; they essentially ended up that far when the roof, literally, blew apart.

Stauffer does some research which reveals that the summer weather pattern has indeed been unusual. He finds that this has been first time since 1979 that the maximum daily temperature for the area has not reached at least 90 degrees in either May or June. Furthermore, he discovers that the total rainfall for April-May-June — 19.74 inches to be precise — is the second highest total *ever*, the record being 21.69 inches during the same period of 1889.

With no ballgame to watch, Bruce, Mo, and I venture to the Southern Kitchen to eat and to talk about baseball.

"Lucas is worried about getting all these games in and getting the field in shape," Bruce tells us, "and I told him not to worry; there's a pallet of Turface at the hardware store waiting for us."

"So the treasurer consented to buy another pallet?" I ask.

Bruce laughs. "The treasurer knows nothing about it."

"My lips are sealed!" I say.

The question of the moment, however, is not what the treasurer's reaction would be to the president's unauthorized purchase of Turface, but whether Rebel Park will be in playable condition by noon tomorrow when the remainder of the suspended game against Front Royal is to be played.

That question is answered at about 11:30 that night when rain again begins to fall and seemingly keeps on falling for half the night. By 9:00 on Sunday morning, it is official: The suspended game is postponed. There is no sense in using up all that new Turface and working for 3 hours on the field for what might amount to one pitch.

* * *

At the end of every inning, baseball broadcasters will often give fans a summary by saying, for example, "There were no runs, on one hit, no errors, and a man left. At the end of three innings, there is no score." To follow suit, "For the week of July 19th, there were three Rebel wins, no losses, two suspended games, a postponement of a suspended game, two rainouts, and no open dates left."

* * *

The rainouts are giving more time for Zach Helgeson to work on his swing.

"I'm closer to being good than it looks," he tells me one day in the picnic pavilion. "Guys are making perfect pitches, like last night, for example" — and Zach proceeds to explain the sequence and the pitch selection and how he pulled off a ball ever so slightly and he fouled it back instead of hitting it hard somewhere. "I haven't seen a mistake in so long..."

Zach is quick and strong and highly intelligent, and he refuses to believe anything except that with his next game and his next at-bat, he will break out of his slump. He points out to me that with very little playing time at the University of Maryland, he has essentially gone from high school to playing in a college all-star league.

"I got thrown into the fire here," he says, and there is not the slightest hint that he is making any excuses when he says this. He is merely pointing out why it is taking him longer to adjust.

I pursue this conversation with him and ask what adjustments he needs to make. Zach explains to me that his hands aren't becoming still at the same moment that his front foot comes down.

"Why not just keep your foot still and set your hands to start with?" I ask.

Zach looks confused, ever so briefly. No question that I've asked of him before, regardless of topic, has ever given him pause. "I don't think I could hit that way," he says with half a laugh, and perhaps knowing that I'm about to ask "Why not?" he launches into an explanation of something he heard former major league second baseman and manager Davey Johnson say about the swing versus timing.

I listen, and what he says makes sense, but the advice that Mo has given him, more than once, comes back to me: "See the ball, hit the ball."

The next day, I find Zach along with Zak Messer swinging at Corey Paluga's soft tosses in the batting cage.

Helgeson does not start at Harrisonburg against the Turks on Sunday afternoon, however. I don't bother to ask him how he feels about this because I *know* that he will say that the success of the team comes first and that Lucas must do something to get more production from first base. And Zach will be right, and he will express himself with a grace that extends way beyond his years and yet, I wish that at some point soon, he would take a bat and smash something and curse fate and shed bitter tears and cry out to the baseball gods, "Why me?" Zach would never do this, of course, but it would make *me* feel better.

Instead, George Carroll will make his debut at first base against the Turks. A backup corner infielder in college, George has been taking ground balls in practice, and a bad elbow has prevented him from catching. The Rebels are once again down to one catcher, and the load has been wearing down Will Cooper, just as it did Jake Pierce.

New Market jumps out to a 6-0 lead in the first inning against Harrisonburg when with two out and none on, Seth Kivett singles. This is promptly followed by four walks, two infield hits, a hit batter, and an error. The Turks give every indication that they are done with the season. By the end of 5 innings, the Rebels are cruising 10-2 behind Eric Alessio. Alessio, however, has been fighting a serious cold, as have several other members of the pitching staff, and he is removed from the game.

Kyle Hoffman comes on to face five batters, retiring none, but he is hurt by two Rebel errors, including Carroll's second of the game. As good as George has looked in practice, he looks just that bad in this game; uncomfortable, even nervous. Jay Lively is then brought on and strikes out the side with an assortment of excellent off-speed pitches.

Lively promptly runs into trouble in the bottom of the 7th, recording only one out before giving way to Spencer Clifft, who records no outs. Jake Guengerich comes on and allows an RBI single to the first batter, which makes the score 10-8. The bases are loaded and the next batter, catcher Parker Brunelle, hits a sharp grounder right at George Carroll. For a split second, it seems that he is about to flinch, but recovers himself, fields the ball cleanly, and steps on the bag. His teammates are yelling "Home!" and bad elbow and all, he throws a strike to Will Cooper, who puts the tag on the runner who doesn't even bother to slide. The throw doesn't have much on it, but it is chest-high and is easily handled by Cooper.

The Turks tack on another run in the 8th, when with two out and a man on, a ball rolls right under Kivett's glove at third, and the error is followed by a single.

With the score now 10-9, Kenny Mickens leads off the Rebel 9th with a single to right, but is forced at second on Kevin Rufus' attempted sacrifice. Mickens slides late and headfirst, almost belly-flopping into the bag, and Turk shortstop Victor Croglio takes exception, for some reason.

"That's @#$%&*!@#$" he yells at Kenny, who replies, "I'm very tough to piss off, but you're starting to."

"Kenny's nice even when he's mad!" laughs Seth Kivett afterward.

More words are exchanged, however, and both dugouts empty, but nothing dramatic occurs. Both sets of fans, however, are riled up and rooting hard, but Brian Burgess, who was brought on to record the final out in the 8th, closes the door, albeit not without encouraging the Turks' fans even more when he allows a two-out single to Brunelle. The game is 3 hours and 13 minutes of sloppy baseball, but in the end, it is a New Market victory, and they are a season high six games over .500 at 21-15.

There is often a fine line between being loose and losing focus. Today, the Rebels seem to have crossed that line, especially once they went up 10-2. Pitchers were crowding each other for fly balls during batting practice before the game, giving the appearance of a wide receiver and three defenders going up for a Hail Mary pass at the goal line. One player was running around with his helmet on backward. And then there was the matter of a certain excursion to a Harrisonburg bar the night before, which resulted in several hangovers.

This is a polite, intelligent, friendly group of young men, but the politest, most intelligent, friendliest young man on earth is still under the influence of the world's most dangerous substance: testosterone. Even as it propels you with grace and speed across the outfield to make a spectacular running catch, it is also propels you into bars to do dumb stuff.

The Rebels would soon lose more than their focus.

Chapter 19
Disaster

On the second pitch of Monday night's game at Woodstock, Kenny Mickens was hit in the back of the head. He lay sprawled in the batter's box for a few minutes, then got up, joked with Abbie, and made his way to first. The Rebels failed to score, and Kenny took his position in left field. He soon started feeling "loopy," however, and came out of the game after flying out in the third.

Kenny developed a headache, but was showing no signs of a concussion. Nevertheless, when Bruce Alger arrived at the game just moments after Kenny had been removed, he insisted that Abbie take Mickens to Shenandoah Memorial Hospital, about 2 minutes away. Doctors performed a CAT scan, which showed a small area of bleeding. Kenny was immediately taken to Winchester Medical Center where a neurologist was on call and where Kenny would spend the next two nights under observation in intensive care. No procedure was required, and Mickens was released with no real restrictions save one: no more baseball for the rest of the summer. Just like that, the Rebels lost their leading hitter for the remainder of the season.

In that fateful third, Kevin Rufus struck out, but reached first on a wild pitch. He stole second, then third, and came home on a balk. This would be the only run that the Mid-Atlantic Classic All-Star Ian Marshall would give up in seven outstanding innings. The River Bandits scored the go-ahead run on a bases-loaded walk in the 8th, and the Rebels' winning streak came to an end. Luray, which had been trailing in its game against

Harrisonburg 6-0, got a grand slam from D. J. Hicks in the bottom of the 8th and pulled out an 8-6 victory. This meant that the Rebels had lost their grip on first place and now trailed the Wranglers by a half game. Therefore, Tuesday would be a very big night: The fog game was to be completed before the regularly scheduled game at Rebel Park with Luray.

* * *

"When are you sitting in the dugout?" Lucas Jones had asked me the week before. I was hoping to receive an invitation to do so and, within a few days, Bruce had secured permission, the only caveat being that I had to be in uniform. *Had* to be? My immediate thought was that Bruce will be lucky to ever get it back. Heck, I might never take it off.

Before Tuesday's games, I ventured into the coaches' office to draw my uniform.

"Two? Four? Five?" asks John Combs, referring to the numbers on the uniforms that were left hanging in the office.

"Four," I answer immediately. It was the number that I wore all through high school. It's my number, and I always notice any ballplayer who wears "4." I am even issued a white BP jersey with a red "4" on the back, which I wear while shagging fly balls and talking about the crazy weather with Ryan Stauffer. The Rebels are nonplussed by last night's loss. This evening, some members of the bullpen arrive with the foam shark hats, while others have obtained foam monkey hats. Stauffer tells me that they "definitely lost focus" during the 10-9 victory over Harrisonburg, but the fact that they were in a 1-1 game in the 8th against Woodstock shows that it was quickly regained. For his part, however, the recent slumps of Kevin Rufus and Sanchez Gartman have Mo worried.

Upbeat in spite of the loss of Mickens, the fans are eager for the evening's contests. Front-Row Fred has arrived with two cowbells, a big one and a little one. He is greeted by Zach Helgeson, and when Fred asks me which one he should use, I tell him to get two more and play "Take Me Out to the Ballgame." He laughs.

I have grabbed an iced tea from the concession stand, but I look out to see Gartman back in the cage. I run out to shag for him, and he hits almost every offering from Corey Paluga to the opposite field.

"I've been trying to pull everything over the fence," he tells me by way of explaining why he is focused on hitting everything to left. Hitting the other way requires that a batter wait longer before swinging, and Gartman figures that this will help him stay on the ball, instead of jumping at the pitch or starting his swing too early in his effort to pull the ball.

After BP, I go to my van and pull on the regulation home uniform, and the first person to see me is Mo.

"How does it feel to have the uniform on again?" he asks with a big smile. Mo understands the thrill.

"It feels great, Mo," I answer with a grin.

I venture into the dugout where several players have already gathered. No one does a double-take at my appearance. A couple of guys even tell me that I'm "looking sharp." I am both humbled and thrilled by the acceptance. I find a spot and sit down.

A dugout is full of grit and spit and sunflower seed shells, all covered in a fine dust. It is often a profane place, although there is a minimum amount of that in the Rebel dugout. The dugout offers one of the worst views of home plate of any seat in the ballpark, and no view of the home crowd. The wooden bench, which runs most of its length, is durable and venerable and shows the marks of 1,000 sets of cleats. With prevailing westerly winds, the Rebel dugout, which opens to the east, is hot and stuffy; the mere act of picking up a loose baseball and rubbing it mindlessly is enough to make one break a sweat.

In other words, it is a wonderful and glorious place.

The Luray players arrive just before the resumption of the suspended game at 6:00 p.m. They come over the mountain via car caravan, in direct violation of the league's transportation policy.

The game is resumed in the top of the 8th with the score tied at 8. A one-out error by Zak Messer puts a runner at first base. A. J. Wirnsberger, the Luray Wrangler second baseman, then singles him to third, and he scores on a single by Jacob Wright. Wirnsberger is cut down at the plate by a strong throw from Matt Townsend in right. Wright tries to hurdle catcher Will Cooper, but Cooper stays with him and tags him out.

What hurts the most is the fact that Wright appears to have looked at strike three, but the umpire, Jim Clayton, rules it a ball.

"Wow! Wow! Wow!" snaps Lucas from the corner of the dugout nearest home plate, "That's terrible!"

Clayton walks toward Jones.

"You want to go now, Lucas?" he asks menacingly.

Lucas says no more. This time.

Matt Townsend, the Rebels' leadoff batter in the bottom of the 8th hits a weak flare to shortstop, and upon returning to the dugout, is immediately assailed for a scouting report from his teammates: "What's he got?"

"Is he coming down and in?" Helgeson asks. When Townie confirms that he is, Zach emits a sarcastic, "Great."

In the top of the 9th, with Alex Foltz the batter and one out in the inning, Clayton begins to raise his right arm, getting it as high as his hip, and we hear the "st-" in "strike" when he stops himself from calling Foltz out on strikes. In the middle of calling a strike, he has called a ball. No one in the dugout has ever seen an umpire freeze in the middle of a call.

"You can't do that!" screams Lucas, who bolts from the dugout. Clayton tosses him immediately for arguing balls and strikes. The argument does not last nearly as long as the howling from the New Market fans. It is a call that Lucas Jones will later say "changed the complexion of our season," for what will occur later in the inning.

Foltz doubles and eventually scores when Messer commits another error, and the second and final run in the inning scores on a squeeze play. The final out is also recorded on the same play when, with the attention of the two umpires focused on home and first, respectively, Wrangler left-fielder Pedro Bermudez intentionally cuts third base in an attempt to score a second run as the throw is headed to first. In the major leagues, with four umpires and television cameras everywhere, this play would be clever if a team could get away with it. In a college summer league game with only two umpires, it is a bush-league play. And there is no doubt in the Rebel dugout that it is a designed play.

Bermudez is caught between third and home, and Cooper lunges at him to make the tag, which he does while falling to the ground. He picks himself up and walks into the dugout heading straight to Abbie.

"I think I broke my elbow," he says as calmly, as one might say, "I think it's about 3 o'clock."

Cooper has landed not hard, but awkwardly on his elbow while making the tag, and when he holds it up, it is clear that something is definitely wrong. There is a bulge where no bulge ought to be.

The Rebels lose the game and their catcher, and the complexion of the season has indeed changed.

Carol Lanham volunteers to run Will to Shenandoah Memorial in Woodstock. I spy Coop as he is heading to his car for his wallet shortly before leaving Rebel Park.

"Man, you are one stoic dude to just walk in and say, 'My elbow is broken.'" I tell him.

He half shrugs. "I heard something pop. . . . I was a little nauseous a few minutes ago, but I think that's just the Advil that Abbie gave me."

On the way to the hospital, Will tells Carol that he wishes this had happened during the school baseball season.

"Why?" she asks, somewhat surprised.

"'Cause this is the most fun I've had playing ball," he says matter-of-factly.

Not only have the Rebels lost their catcher, they are about to lose their trainer, only she will depart because of injured feelings.

George Carroll and Abbie have not gotten along, ever since George's elbow started hurting. He can't understand why he cannot have an MRI immediately — it would be done right away in New York — but as Bruce tells him, "Here, you wait for the wagon to pull up some time during the week and then you get one," referring to the mobile lab that services the New Market area. It appears that this is the city mouse who doesn't understand the country mouse, and vice-versa. For his part, George is frustrated at being hurt, and the natural scapegoat for that frustration is the trainer. Before Cooper leaves the dugout, George says to him, "Maybe Abbie is wrong," in an attempt to encourage Will, but Abbie, overhearing the remark, takes it as an insult to her skills.

There are words, at least by Abbie, who storms off to Bruce in the press box. She quits the team, leaving Bruce scrambling to find a replacement, as a certified trainer must be provided by the home team, according to league policy. Abbie calls a friend on the New Market Rescue Squad, who arrives just before the start of the regularly scheduled game.

I spy Bruce walking across the parking lot. He wears the expression of a guy whose host son is in the hospital, whose trainer has just quit, and whose team is now 1½ games out of first.

* * *

No one is dejected, despite losing the suspended game. Brian Burgess gives me a high-five without saying a word, as he strolls past me wearing his shark hat over his Rebel cap. A container of cookies, which Sharon Smith baked and sent to the dugout before the beginning of the suspended game have been consumed voraciously. Seth Kivett is trying to convince Dan Rollins that he can catch, bad hamstring and all. Indeed, Lucas will be forced to go with a makeshift lineup now that will feature first baseman Helgeson in left, left fielder Gartman behind the plate, and catcher George Carroll with his bad elbow at first.

At the end of the first game, I give Joe Hammond, the second-game starter, some unsolicited advice. After all, I have to do *something*—I'm wearing "R-E-B-E-L-S" on my chest this night.

"You go be the father, Joe," I tell Hammond, urging him to assume the demeanor of a dad who stays calm in a family crisis. "Just go out there, be calm, do your thing, we'll win the game and everything will be just as it was before the night started."

Joe nods politely, but he is in that zone where all starting pitchers go before a game, and he says nothing. Nevertheless, I feel that I have now contributed something. The very first batter of the game flies to Zach in left field, who makes the catch. It draws a loud ovation from the dugout, including applause from the coaches.

"Mo, you always say you can't hide 'em!" laughs John Combs after the catch, referring to the baseball axiom that whenever a player is out of position, the ball will always find him. Combs, as the outfield coach, keeps the spray charts; that is, charts indicating where the batter has hit the ball in the past. He directs his outfielders accordingly: "Pull side, now!" he booms from the corner of the dugout or "Off field!" or "Give me two steps left!" and the outfielders move one way or another.

Hammond, however, gives up hits to the next four hitters following the fly out, and the Rebels trail 3-0.

"C'mon, let's show 'em who we are!" says Mo, exhorting the Rebels as they come off the field in the 1st, just as he did at Winchester in the 9th. The Rebels are retired three up and three down in the 1st, however, and Hammond surrenders another run in the top of the 2nd. In the bottom half of the inning, Helgeson singles to right with two out and is stranded at first, but I am thrilled — as is he — to see him make solid contact and hit the ball to the opposite field, just as Sanchez Gartman was working on during batting practice.

"Nice single the other way!" I tell him as I hand him his glove when he comes into the dugout.

"I have no idea how I did that!" he exclaims, and now I am even more pleased that he finally has no explanation for something that has happened at the plate. Perhaps he just saw the ball and hit it.

In the top of the 3rd, Zak Messer almost commits another error, George Carroll leaping to make the catch and then deftly touching the bag with his toe.

Zak calls to him, and when George looks up, Zak taps himself as if to say "That was on me."

"Don't worry about it, man," George verbalizes back.

With two outs, Kevin Rufus again crashes into the center-field fence, but this time he is unable to haul in the baseball, and another run scores. Rufus is not hurt, but the Rebels are now down 5-0.

In the bottom of the 3rd, I retreat to the far end of the dugout. Perhaps this is the spot from where I can affect the fabric of the Universe and induce Karma or the ghost of Abner Doubleday or a random microburst or something to grant the Rebels some runs. It appears to work. With two outs, Rufus walks and Richie Gonzalez reaches on an error. Seth Kivett promptly doubles home both runners.

"Thataway, Sweet Cheeks!" someone yells from the dugout.

I spy Helgeson and explain what I am doing at the far end of the dugout.

"Well, wherever you were sitting when I was hitting, go back there!" he says. He's not joking, and I return to the back of the bench, next to his glove, when his turn comes up, but he grounds out to third. Still, it was decent contact and not another strikeout.

"We gotta keep our swag up," says Gartman, who patrols the dugout in the bottom of the 4th with his hat on sideways. "Swag" is short for swagger, and he is doing his part to influence the baseball gods, too. Sanchez' hat has no magic in it, however and the Rebels fail to score.

After one teammate strikes out and slams his helmet to the dugout floor, Kivett turns to me and says, "Everybody knows *that*'ll get you more hits."

In the top of the 5th, Carroll makes a sensational, over-the-shoulder catch to end the inning. It is his third great play of the night. Zach Helgeson runs in from left field, straight to George to congratulate him.

In the bottom of the 5th, Kyle Hoffman shows Sanchez how he wants him to signal the pitch so that he can best see it from the mound. Later, Sanchez sees me in the dugout, "We don't look good tonight," he says and proceeds to tell me what has been wrong with our pitchers. "We kind of lost our swag," he adds.

In the bottom of the 6th, a girl, standing beyond the Wrangler dugout along the first-base line almost loses her head. Literally. Thanks to Sanchez, who rather than driving the ball the other way, pulls a vicious line drive that slams into the top rail of the wooden fence and ricochets into right field. The girl had her back turned to the diamond and was talking to a friend. Had it been 3 inches higher, it would have struck her in the head. Had it been two inches lower, it would have screamed through the slat and into her torso. There was a collective sucking in of breath in the dugout, followed a split second later by a chorus of "WOW!" even as the ball was bounding across right field.

I am in the near corner of the dugout now, trying to entice a run or two out of the Cosmic swirl, standing where all the coaches gather. Dan Rollins, who calls most of the pitches, has constructed a comfortable seat by sticking an unused base into a milk crate, which in turn has been placed on top of a cinder block.

Spencer Clifft comes on to pitch the top of the 7th, giving up an unearned run and is incredulous when Rollins informs him in the bottom of the inning that he is done for the night.

"Are you kidding me?" he asks rhetorically — and angrily — and throws his glove down before storming off. He does not head to the locker room or his car, however; he heads back to the bullpen. The entire episode strikes me as symbolic of the evening: Everyone is frustrated, but no one has quit on the season.

The Luray left fielder makes a sliding catch in the 8th, which prompts Kevin Rufus to begin a conversation on outfield play.

"You should never make a sliding catch; always make a diving catch," he says, explaining that diving will bring the outfielder two to four feet closer to the ball because instead of leaning away from it, the fielder is heading toward it. In other words, the glove gets to the ball faster. It is a hard thing to learn because it is an unnatural movement to throw your face *toward* the ball. "I used to practice diving during batting practice, and my teammates were like, 'What are you doing?' I told them that I was learning to be an outfielder," says Rufus.

It is now the bottom of the 9th, and the Rebels are trailing 9-3. They have stunk for 10 full innings now, counting the completion of the suspended game. I slide toward the far end of the dugout again and grab hold of the handle on the field liner. Ryan Stauffer gives me a look as if to say "Can't you find one place to be in?" and I explain that I'm trying to find the spot that will generate some runs. And, indeed, Zach Helgeson leading off, surprises everyone in the park by dropping a bunt down the third-base line for a single. Matt Townsend promptly follows that with a long home run.

"Put in the book that we planned out a bunt hit and a home run!" exclaims Zach when he reaches me in the dugout, a smiling Townsend right behind him. There is life in the Rebels yet. When the Wranglers change pitchers, I walk to the center of the dugout.

"Shouldn't you be over in your spot?" asks Stauffer.

It's just a pitching change, I assure him, and I move back when the action is ready to resume.

The Rebels load the bases and with one out, Seth Kivett hits a sacrifice fly to center making the score 9-6. With two on and two out, Sanchez Gartman represents the tying run, but Gartman grounds out to first, and the Rebels are now 2½ games behind Luray.

The team gathers in short left field for the post-game talk. What can a head coach say to a team in this situation? It's not as if they're not trying. Words can't make hits fall or pitches graze the outside corner, but they can keep a team fighting, especially in the face of adversity.

Lucas tells his team the story of Jeff Taylor, the man who was killed by a line drive while throwing batting practice to his son. It is the same story that he told at the Grandstand Managers Club banquet, and he alludes to his earlier speech.

"We will play the rest of this season for Jeff Taylor. I told those people at the banquet that we would play hard every day. There are a slew of things that have gone wrong this summer. Now is not the time to start complaining about how many innings you're getting or who's playing where. All I'm asking is that you just play hard. I'm not talking about winning the division title or making the playoffs or anything. Sure we're undermanned; no one thinks that we have a shot now. Please promise me that for the next four days, you'll play your asses off. I beg you. If you do, I promise you that you'll feel good about yourselves, no matter what happens."

And with that, Lucas and his coaches left the players to mull his message.

Shortly thereafter, Zach Helgeson sees me. "What do I always tell you?" he asks pointedly. "It's never about individuals. It's always about the team."

From left to right: Mo Weber, Steve Thiele, Bruce Alger (standing in back), Eric Alessio, Joe Hammond, Ryan Stauffer, Steve Owens, Kyle Hoffman, Mike Roth, and Dan Rollins.

The post-game meal is a giant sub, and the pitchers insist that Melissa Dodge take their picture seated behind it, under the pavilion. Often, some of the pitchers will run immediately after the game while their teammates eat. Someone—usually another pitcher—always makes sure, however, that enough food has been saved for them before anyone is allowed to go back for seconds. Before tonight's meal is completely gone, Will Cooper returns in time to eat a section of the sub, his right arm in a sling, his X-rays in hand. Everyone wants to see them, and they clearly show a piece of bone that has broken off. Soon everyone has left.

* * *

Sometime after midnight, I slowly pull off my uniform.

* * *

By the time I arrive at Rebel Park the next day at around 11:00 a.m. it is raining lightly. There is one car in the parking lot, and I wonder for a moment who has come to work out in the rain. Then it quickly dawns on me that it is Will Cooper's car.

I finish a short run and get a call from Bruce. He has had an excellent talk with Lucas about Abbie and other matters. Abbie has reconsidered, and is willing to return. She and Lucas talk, and the situation is resolved.

With his van in the shop, Bruce calls me and asks if I would drive him to Winchester so that we can pick up Kenny.

"He called and said, 'Pops, come and get me,'" says Bruce with a chuckle.

We retrieve Kenny from the hospital and on the way home receive a call that the game against Harrisonburg has been canceled. While at lunch, we receive a call saying that Bob Wease has declared the game back on. Of course, Lucas has already sent out a text to his players telling them that the game has been postponed, but now he must try to reassemble the troops. We get Kenny to Rebel Park shortly before the bus is scheduled to depart for Harrisonburg, and his teammates are happy to see him. Two teammates are missing, however, as Lucas has been unable to reach Richie Gonzalez and Mike Graham, the scheduled starter, to tell them that the game will now be played. The afternoon is wearing on, and we must leave. Halfway there, contact is made with Richie and Mike, and the two make their way on their own to Mauck Field.

As the bus is about to turn into the parking lot, an ambulance comes speeding by with its siren wailing.

"Must have heard we were coming," I remark to John Combs.

Graham is given the start, but has not had sufficient time to warm up and is yanked after an inning, trailing 1-0. Ryan Stauffer, who pitched two scoreless innings the night before, allows an unearned run in the second, then retires the side in the third. With two out in the top of the 4th, Turks catcher Parker Brunelle lofts a lazy fly ball to left field. Kevin Rufus immediately yells "In! In!" to Helgeson in left, but Zach breaks late, and the ball drops in front of him. Three more hits lead to two runs, and the Rebels now trail 4-0.

With a chance to get back in the game, New Market loads the bases with none out in the 5th, but fails to score. It is perhaps the moment in which the game is lost. It is definitely the moment when the fans without any conscious effort or design go from rooting to hoping. I catch Sharon Smith's glance in the next section of stands. We exchange knowing looks, and what we know isn't good.

The Turks, who appeared to be finished only three nights before, add single runs in the 5th and the 7th and tack on six runs in the 8th. Hope has now turned to despair. I again look over at Sharon Smith, who is sitting with her face in her hands, staring bleakly at the action on the diamond.

The Rebels add a meaningless run in the 9th on an error and a sacrifice fly from Kivett and lose their fourth straight by a final score of 12-3. They have managed only six hits in the game.

There are no new injuries tonight, but Seth Kivett has aggravated his hamstring on a swing in the 7th when fouling off an 0-1 pitch. Kivett singles and limps down to first base, where Abbie comes out to check him. Kevin Rufus comes over from second and puts his arm around Kivett's shoulder. Lucas probably would have removed Seth from the game had there been anyone else to put in; although Kivett, no doubt, would have protested all the way to the dugout.

Lucas has given his final, best speech the night before and so, after this game, he simply informs his team that they will have a pitchers' batting practice before the next game. He and his staff leave, but Joe Hammond is saying something at the center of the group. He tells his teammates that it is "gut-check time" and that they have a chance to do something that very few guys do: "win a championship in one of the premier summer leagues in the country."

As his teammates are pondering these words, Kenny Mickens steps up and says simply, "F@#$ it. We need to win one more game to make the playoffs. Let's go have fun the next three days."

As the players make their way to the Turks' concession stand for their post-game hot dogs and hamburgers, I spy Bruce Alger, who is looking shell-shocked.

"This is the first time all season I've realized how tired I am," he says.

* * *

Desperate for a catcher, Bruce Alger appeals to Dave Biery, league president, for special dispensation to sign one. There is precedent on Bruce's side, and Biery grants permission. Were it not for the fact that this is the most specialized position on the diamond, no such consideration would have been granted. An attempt is made to sign Steve Cochrane out of Spartanburg, the catcher who was on the original roster, but could not play because of summer school obligations. He has finished summer school, but declines the invitation. Several others are considered, but, eventually, a call is put in to Nate Furry to come back and help out. He accepts.

It is good to see Nate back in a Rebels uniform, and I ask him why he has returned.

"I heard you needed a helping hand," he tells me.

"I got a theory on why you left," I inform him. I tell him about what I thought I saw in his face in the June game against Woodstock; that he made a throw that he knew that he shouldn't have and in that instant, he had simply had it.

"That's about it," he says, giving me a look to suggest that he was impressed with my "diagnosis." Now that we are face to face again, I say nothing about playing for the thrill of the grass or that he will one day look back fondly and proudly on his career. It strikes me as too intimate a thought to express to him here on the warning track in front of the dugout and, besides, he *is* back and playing and, therefore, requires no perspective on his summer. Perspective is something that comes to those whose summers are past.

Instead, I tell him that now he must hit the home run that puts the Rebels in the playoffs; that it will make for a great story.

He laughs as he walks away to join a group of teammates and while some still privately question the fact that he walked out on them once, they accept him back into the fold. As he talks and jokes and plays catch with them, it is as though he has never left.

That night in Rebel Park, with Furry behind the plate, Steve Owens took his 6-1 record to the mound, but recorded only two outs while giving up two two-run homers. His fastball never tops 80 mph, and he is removed from the game, his shoulder hurting. A scout from the Los Angeles Angels was supposed to be at the ballpark this night, but he does not show. It is just as well. Mike Graham, who pitched only one inning the afternoon before in Harrisonburg, is brought on and records the final out of the inning. He will pitch seven more, allowing no runs over that span in an effort Jones labels the "best outing from a starter all summer" — in spite of the fact that it came in relief. He and Furry, teammates at VCU, are completely in sync, and Jones will credit his new, old catcher with calling "a good game."

Nevertheless, the Rebels, who are not hitting and trail 4-0 before they even come up to bat, manage only eight hits and two runs and lose by a final score of 5-2. Time and again New Market put runners on base, but cannot get a big hit when it is needed. Ultimately, they strand 13 runners. In the 6th, Furry draws a bases-loaded walk with one out, but they fail to do any further damage. Again in the 7th inning and with a run in, the Rebels load the bases with one out, but fail to score.

Woodstock has now vaulted into second place in the division. Four days before, the Rebels led the Central Division. Now, they must win at least one more game just to capture one of the two wild-card spots. To do that, they must get a hit when it counts. And they must do that without their leading hitter, with only one catcher, with an injured third baseman, and with three of their most important hitters in slumps.

Chapter 20
Redemption

Yet another rainstorm hits the Valley late in the morning on Friday. Some players question whether the game will even be played, but the sun comes out in the afternoon and at 4:00 p.m., the coaches and players begin working on the infield at Rebel Park. Four wheelbarrows of mud are scraped from the home-plate area, and the dirt is replaced by Turface. The infield is raked and dragged and raked some more and, in the end, 25 bags of Turface are used to make the field playable.

Lucas Jones is looking more than a little dazed. His team is on a five-game losing streak, it has rained yet again, and now he has lost two more players. George Carroll has been totally shut down: The MRI that he finally has taken reveals a torn UCL. This leaves the Rebels with no reserve position players.

"I've lost 13 pounds this summer," Lucas tells me, as his players continue to work on the field.

Lucas Jones

"Did you rake it off or worry it off?" I ask.

"A little of both," he answers.

As the team continues to work on the field during the time normally taken by batting practice, I spy Charlie Dodge, whom I will be helping with the webcast this evening.

"I have a good feeling about tonight's game, Charlie," I say to him, "I really do."

"Me, too," says Charlie, as we walk to the broadcast deck.

We have reason to be optimistic, with Garret Baker and his 2.47 ERA starting this contest against Harrisonburg. That and the fact that we are baseball fans. Give us 24 hours, and even after the toughest loss, we have the ability to imagine a 12-game winning streak. Or at least imagine winning that one game that will put us in the playoffs.

Our optimism is considerably muted, however, in the very first inning when Baker gives up a two-run homer to the third batter of the game, Tom Nichols. He gives up a total of three runs in the first on a whopping six hits and, once again, the Rebels are in a hole before they even get a chance to swing the bat. Walks to Rufus and Kivett, who pull off a double steal, and RBIs by Gartman and Gonzalez get the Rebels right back into the game, however.

Baker settles down and allows zero runs and only three hits over the next six innings. His Harrisonburg counterpart, Clint Dempster, matches Baker 0 for 0. In the 2nd and again in the 6th, the Rebels put two men on with two men out on a walk and an error, but fail to come up with a big hit.

In the 7th, Rufus and Kivett lead off the inning with singles and again pull off a double steal. With Sanchez Gartman at the plate, a wild pitch sends Kevin Rufus flying in from third. For the second time in a week, however, the ball bounces off the backstop padding almost straight to the catcher, who throws to Dempster covering for the out. Saying the tag was late, Lucas Jones argues the play, but to no avail.

Charlie and I and every New Market fan in attendance are thinking the same thing: How much longer can the baseball gods keep us from getting a break?

The wild pitch was ball four to Gartman, and it put Kivett on third. For the second time in the game, Richie Gonzalez comes through with an RBI single, this one a bouncer up the middle. Gartman rounds second and heads for third. "And Gartman is going to be thrown out at third — except, he's ruled safe!" I exclaim to listeners on the Internet. The throw from Ryan Eden beat Gartman by a considerable margin, and splendid photos by Melissa Dodge

Sanchez Gartman is safe at third ... despite being tagged out.

showed Sanchez to be out by a good two feet, but safe was the ruling. Perhaps *this* was the break we needed.

It wasn't. Gartman was left stranded at third when Helgeson and Townsend struck out and the inning ended. Even worse, Harrisonburg immediately went ahead in the 8th on a two-out error by shortstop Zak Messer. In the bottom of the 8th, Messer draws a two-out walk, Rufus is hit by a pitch, and they pull the Rebels' fourth double steal of the night, bringing Seth Kivett to the plate. The ever-gregarious George Carroll, out of uniform because of his elbow, appears in the front row next to Fred. Rising and waving his arms, George proceeds to lead the Rebel faithful in a chant of "Sweet Cheeks!" but to no avail. Kivett, the team's hottest hitter over the last 10 days, pops out to second.

This is agony. Twelve runners left stranded through eight innings. One thrown out at the plate on a controversial call ... Everyone sporting a Rebel hat or shirt is of one thought: Can fate be this cruel?

Charlie and I tell our audience that we must *will* in a run from the broadcast booth. Turks manager Bob Wease has brought in Drew Granier, his best pitcher, to close out the 9th. It was Granier who held the Rebels to only one run in 8 innings back on July 10th, but it was Matt Townsend who accounted for the Rebels' run in that game with a homer, and Matt will bat third in the inning.

Sanchez Gartman leads off the bottom of the 9th, however, and he walks. After stealing second, he takes third on a ground ball to his right at short. It is a violation of one of baseball's cardinal rules, but the ball slows down considerably when it hits the 1,000 pounds of Turface that has been spread about in the infield dirt, and Gartman is able to advance. Matt Townsend now strides to the plate with the tying run on third and only one out.

Everyone in both sets of bleachers, in both dugouts, and on the broadcast platform is anxious. Rebel fans know that the season could be hanging in the balance. What happens next seems to unfold in slow motion. Granier throws a pitch low and away that skips past Parker Brunelle. Remembering how Rufus was thrown out in the 7th, however, I look to see where the ball is bouncing, rather than down at Gartman. It is not careening back to Brunelle off the padding. It is bounding off to his right, and only now do I look for Sanchez ... who is frozen at third. He hasn't moved on the wildest wild pitch of the year. Suddenly thawed out, he darts for home, and I can't believe that Fate is so sadistic that Gartman will be cut down in the next second trying to score. Brunelle, however, has turned to the inside, to his left, rather than outside to his right. And so on one step in the wrong direction, the game turns. Brunelle grabs the ball and heaves it desperately to Granier covering, but the throw is high and the ball ticks off the end of Granier's glove. Sanchez Gartman is safe. The Rebel bleachers roar and George Carroll launches himself off the front row like a rocket.

Later, Gartman will tell me that he didn't see the ball on the ground, and he thought that Brunelle was trying to deke him. Of course, his dugout wasn't trying to deke him when they immediately began screaming "GO!" but in this case, Sanchez is, indeed, safe and not sorry.

Still, maybe Fate is merely teasing us. Townsend strikes out and Helgeson grounds to third for the final out in the inning. The game is only tied, and in extra innings, anything can happen.

On the broadcast platform, we note the moon off to our right that is shining above Massanutten — a waxing gibbous moon, as Noah Dodge points out to the Internet audience. The events on the field would make one think that we are under a full moon, however.

Brian Burgess, who was brought on for the final out of the 8th, is still pitching in the 10th. With one out, he hits Jack Posey and walks Mike Schwartz, and again, the crowd holds its collective breath. Burgess retires the next two batters, however, and the side is retired.

McKinnon Langston, New Market's DH leads off the 10th and drops a perfect bunt down the third-base line for a hit. Nathan Furry then sacrifices Langston to second, but when Zak Messer pops to short and Kevin Rufus lifts a popup behind first base, it appears that Matt Burnside, who has come on to run for Langston, will be stranded. Rufus' ball is nothing more than a routine popup, but neither Schwartz at first, nor Raymond Quinones the second baseman is set under it. Right fielder Matt Wease, seeing some confusion, comes racing in. Quinones looks at Schwartz, who is still backpedaling. To the amazement of everyone, perhaps especially Quinones and Schwartz, the ball drops untouched. With two out, Burnside is running all the way and scores easily.

As Matt crosses the plate, a 10,000-pound burden that has been shouldered by players and fans alike seems to lift from Rebel Park and float up and over Massanutten Mountain. The Rebels have clinched a berth in the playoffs.

* * *

After another delicious meal served up by the Kipps family — it is Mexican night — the players leave Rebel Park singly and in groups of two or three. Only the coaches, the Dodge family, Bruce, and I remain, and I slowly become aware of additional action taking place in the outfield. Noah Dodge is throwing a tennis ball to Jake Guengerich, Matt Burnside, and Mike Roth, who are taking turns to see who can propel the fuzzy green ball into or over the Rebel bullpen. C. B. Alger is patrolling the warning track hauling in some flyballs and watching others sail over the fence. Soon, Dan Rollins joins the group. Everyone is smiling and laughing, and I am witnessing a celebration.

This is not a celebration of the pennant-clinching victory, however; it is a celebration of boyhood. It is a celebration by boys just entering their teens and boys who have just left them, playing a game that they have made up on the spot, under the lights on a midsummer's night in a little ballpark in a little town in Virginia.

* * *

August 1st arrived and with it summer; at least, it finally felt like summer. The distant mountains were swathed in haze, though not so thick as to obscure them. White, cumulus clouds played a lazy game of tag as they drifted north over Massanutten Mountain, and the droning of traffic out on I-81 could barely be heard above the locusts' crescendo chirping from tree to tree and back again.

At 1:00 on this Saturday afternoon, the suspended game against Front Royal would finally be played. The players drifted in as slowly as the clouds, although Zak Messer was there — of course — when I arrived at Rebel Park, which was 10:45 a.m. Soon, Guengerich, Roth, Gartman, and the man of the hour Zach Helgeson appeared. Helgeson was coming to bat with the bases loaded in the bottom of the 9th and one out when the game was suspended.

Many of the players arrived with breakfast from McDonald's in hand, and not a few appeared to have done some playoff partying the night before. All the girls in New Market might be under 16, according to Bruce, but apparently every girl in Harrisonburg is over 21.

"There's the one-hit wonder!" cried Spencer Clifft, referring to last night's winning hit, upon seeing Kevin Rufus.

No one is in a hurry to do anything this morning; there is no BP or infield/outfield, so I wander into the coaches' office, and we talk about what changes need to be made in the playoff system, and the Rebels' shortage of players.

"We're one pitch away from having no chance," says Jones almost wistfully, referring to the fact that if anyone gets hurt from a pitched ball and cannot play, à la Kenny Mickens, then New Market will have to resort to putting pitchers in the field.

As the conversation breaks up, Lucas looks at John Combs and says, "Get somebody ready because if we tie, one of those hung-over bastards is going to have to pitch!"

The Rebels do not tie, however. Zach Helgeson strikes out and Zak Messer pops out and the Cardinals capture a 5-4 victory and the number-one seed in the VBL playoffs. The suspended game, the resumption of which had to be postponed, is concluded in two minutes, or about 58 fewer than it takes Front Royal to travel to New Market.

After the game, Lucas introduces me to his parents, Roger and Jackie Jones, as the guy who is writing a book about the team. We talk about the number of things that have gone wrong, from the unusual weather to the various injuries.

"Ah, the book would be boring if you guys had gone 30-14 and swept the playoffs," I joke.

Corey Paluga slams his bag down in mock anger. "No, it wouldn't!" he protests. "That would be the best damned book I ever read! I'd keep it on my nightstand."

"With a wreath around it," interjects Mo.

* * *

The final game of the season, which is the rainout from July 25th, is finally played that night in Luray. If the Rebels win, they can move from the 6th seed to the 5th seed, but Lucas had given permission to Matt Townsend and McKinnon Langston to attend a wedding, back when there were plenty of players and plenty of wins. With a lineup that features Matt Burnside at designated hitter and Steve Owens in right field, the Rebels lose 7-4. Again, there is no offense, and Owens collects one of New Market's five hits.

New Market has lost seven of its final eight games and all of their bench players. The Rebels finish with a record of 22-22 and take a strange path to get there: In between their 1-5 start and 1-7 finish, New Market goes 20-10.

In any case, New Market finishes as the 6th seed in the eight-team playoffs, and that means they will face arch-rival Luray in the first round, set to begin the next day. It comes as no surprise to anyone, however, that it pours all through the morning of August 2nd, and the first game has to be postponed. August 3rd is sunny and warm, however, and the playoffs finally begin at Bulldog Field in Luray.

Chapter 21
This Could Be the Last Game

"**W**hy are they pinch hitting for Furry?"

The question ran through the bleachers full of Rebel fans at Bulldog Field. Why, with the score now 5-4, thanks to a Matt Townsend home run leading off the 11th inning in the first game of the playoffs, would you remove your only catcher? Especially when all you had to pinch hit was a pitcher?

We knew the answer even before we had finished asking the question. Nate Furry had been beaned in the top of the 9th. It appeared to be a curveball that struck him in the helmet where the visor joins the earflap. Initially stunned, he took first base and then caught the next two innings, saving the game for the Rebels in the process. In the bottom of the 10th, Luray loaded the bases with one out when Kevin Bond hit a ground ball to Seth Kivett at third. Kivett's throw home was wide to the first base side, but Furry, keeping a toe on home plate, stretched out full and caught the ball, landing with a thud in the process. The Rebels got another ground ball to escape the jam, and now here they were with the lead when Townsend sent a ball crashing off the Wrangler trailer beyond the left-field fence. A lead and no catcher.

Everyone was remembering Kenny Mickens, who had been beaned the week before and also stayed in the game for two more innings before having to come out with a concussion, and I am remembering what Lucas had said to me in his office just two days before: "We're one pitch away from having no chance."

"Well, there's the ambulance!" said someone, and we looked behind the Rebel dugout to see the Luray Rescue Squad loading Nate into the back on a stretcher. He was starting to show some serious symptoms of a concussion in the dugout, so the ambulance was called. He waved to everyone in typical Nate Furry fashion, but even at a distance, we could see that it was doubtful that he knew exactly who he was waving to. Buddy Weiner, James' dad, volunteered to drive to Page Memorial and look after Nate there.

Now in their most crucial inning of the season, the Rebels once again were forced to use their left fielder, Sanchez Gartman, behind the dish and insert reliever Matt Burnside into left field.

Brian Burgess was on the mound, but this was not the sure thing that it had been all season for the Rebels. Burgess entered in the 9th to a thunderous ovation and cries of "Lightning!" from the Rebel fans, with a 4-2 lead to protect. With little bite on his "Frisbee," as his teammates called his wicked curveball, Burgess had given up two runs, the final one coming on a two-out pinch hit by Tyler Truxel. It was Burgess' first blown save and first earned run of the season, and he was now in his third inning of work.

Burgess had come on to relieve Jake Guengerich, who had pitched a scoreless 8th in relief of starter Eric Alessio. The Rebels' ace enjoyed a three-up, three-down first inning, but struggled through the next six, although he allowed only two runs. It could have been more, but the Rebels were playing stellar defense, turning a nifty 5-4-3 double play in the 2nd and a 5-5-3 double play in the 4th. In between, Alessio helped his own cause by picking off Drew Martinez for the final out of the 3rd. In the 5th, Eric hit two Wranglers back to back, but Kivett again turned a 5-5-3 double play, and in the 6th, the Rebels turned their fourth twin killing, this one Richie Gonzalez to Zak Messer to Zach Helgeson.

In the top of the 7th, Helgeson bounced a single through the hole on the left side to plate Gonzalez who had walked, giving the Rebels a 2-1 lead. Matt Townsend, who had also walked, took third on the throw and scored when McKinnon Langston stroked his third hit of the game through the middle. Kevin Rufus had accounted for their first run an inning earlier with a line-shot home run to center field. Helgeson was thrown out at the plate for the final out of the 7th, with the Rebels leading 3-1.

Alessio yielded a leadoff single to A. J. Wirnsberger, who scored on a wild pitch to close the gap to 3-2 in the bottom of the 7th. The Rebels got that run back in their half of the 8th on a Zak Messer RBI single.

And now, with a 5-4 lead, Brian Burgess would be facing the top of the Wrangler lineup in this bottom of the 11th. After striking out Alex Foltz, Burgess walked Truxel to bring the winning run to the plate in the person of Pablo Bermudez, Luray's speedy left fielder. With no curveball and an increasingly shrinking strike zone — Burgess is uncharacteristically and visibly upset with several calls — Brian throws perhaps his best fastball of the year past Bermudez on a 3-2 count for the second out. The Rebel faithful, who had exchanged cheers and jeers with the Luray crowd all night, begin to applaud. Some stand. By no means is the game over, how-

ever, as the dangerous D. J. Hicks steps into the batter's box. Hicks, who leads the Wranglers in RBIs with 39, has been worked carefully by the Rebel staff, having been walked four times in the game already.

Brian Burgess was not about to let the game get away from him a second time, however. Hicks hits a comebacker, which Burgess snares. He runs halfway to first before tossing it to Helgeson, and just like that, the Rebels, now down to eight position players, take the opening game of the playoffs 5-4.

Brian Burgess

Most teams, seeing their closer blow a save and witnessing their only catcher being carted off in an ambulance, might have understandably shrunk from the monumental pressure of winning a tight game in someone else's ballpark. The Rebel players, however, are the least surprised bunch on either side of the mountain. Despite stumbling across the finish line, the Rebels had given no indication before the game that they would do anything but win.

Burgess and his housemate Alessio had played golf that day at the Shenvalee, and Eric conceded that after Brian's round of 80, Eric had lost the summer-long golf match. Sanchez Gartman had spent part of the afternoon working on his swing in the batting cage with skipper Lucas Jones and was joined later by Nate Furry. Of course, the bus erupted with laughter before Vic took the boys over the mountain when it was discovered that Lucas, after asking his players three different times if they were sure that they had packed their blue jerseys, had forgotten his own.

And it didn't hurt team morale to have Kenny Mickens and Will Cooper riding the bus to Luray. Cooper had returned after one day of "sitting around and watching TV." With his arm immobilized from hand to shoulder and hanging in a sling, he explained that his elbow had been 90% cracked to start, and that he might have split the remaining 10% simply by opening a door. Most of the bone had died, and the surgeon was forced to scrape it in order to stimulate fresh growth. A bone-marrow infusion and a few pins completed Will's surgery, and he had returned to finish the season, even if he couldn't play.

Upon arrival, Vic and I stood outside the dugout to watch batting practice. Joe Hammond was getting in his laps and as he passed us, he stretched out his arms in dramatic fashion and began singing along to Celine Dion's "My Heart Will Go On."

"I think these boys are ready to play!" said Vic laughing and proving to be rather prophetic. Vic had to watch the top of the 11th inning standing beside the bleachers, however, rather than in his seat next to me. Having gone to the concession stand when Townsend hit the home run, he attempted to return to his spot, but as we began to tell him that he was not allowed back in, lest he ruin the good luck that had been created by his departure, he simply waved us off and stood by the side of the bleachers. He returned for the bottom of the 11th by mutual consent, but I feared we might have to call an ambulance for Vic when, after Burgess' one-out walk, he muttered, "I can't take this @#$%!"

He survived, however, as did Burgess and the Rebels, whose faithful crossed back over the mountain happy and contented. And indeed, there were many cars headed across Massanutten this night. All the regulars and then some had packed the New Market side of the stands, including Kevin Dietrich, the 3-year Rebel who "graduated" in 2008. Kevin had hitched a ride with his dad, who was on his way to New York, and was dropped off in New Market so that he could see his summer-league alma mater play its arch rival.

One Rebel fan spent his time not in the stands, but in the bullpen. Desperate to find a bullpen catcher — the shortage of position players left no one around to even warm up the relievers — Dan Rollins issued a uniform to one of New Market's webcasters, Kevin Barb, who had graduated in June from Stonewall Jackson High, where he had played baseball. The only problem was that Kevin played outfield and admitted to having great difficulty catching Burgess, whose ball, at least while warming up, was moving quite a bit. Obviously proud of wearing Rebel gray, Barb displayed a slightly swollen thumb and a very large smile after the victory.

One person who was not there was Lynne Alger, who was simply too nervous to attend. She had spent her time getting updates on the cell phone and preparing the post-game meal.

For his part, Mo Weber, who drove separately to the ballpark from his home in Luray, was so excited that he, too, drove back over the mountain just to share in the moment.

"I'm as pumped up as the boys!" he exclaimed, and indeed, they were pumped. There was quite a bit of whooping and hollering on the bus, as we departed Bulldog Field and headed up Massanutten Mountain. With the light of the full moon bathing Page Valley in hazy, translucent white, the atmosphere seemed filled with magic. With Furry out, Burgess flat, and no players left, we had won a game that we probably had no business winning. Magic indeed.

We crested the summit of the mountain and began to descend when the beckoning lights of Rebel Park came into view. Lynne and the rest of the Alger family awaited us there with a dinner of fried chicken, baked beans, macaroni and cheese, and other delectables.

"This is a good Southern meal," noted Spencer Clifft with great satisfaction.

Seated at a table with Guengerich and Clifft, I talked baseball with the two relievers while we ate, but before we finished, the Weiners, with Nate Furry in tow, arrived. Nate, still wearing his dust-caked gray pants, fixed himself a plate. He did not require a CAT scan, but one look at our "new" catcher suggested that the Rebels might be losing him again. And they did.

Carol Furry, Nate's mom and a registered nurse, insisted that Nate come home to Salem for a CAT scan. Her maternal sensibilities seemed well founded, considering that Nate still had a headache and felt "out of it."

The Rebels took the loss of their only catcher in stride. With all that had happened, had that giant sinkhole actually opened in center field and swallowed Kevin Rufus, they would have just collectively shrugged, stuck another pitcher out there, and told him to watch his step.

* * *

Game 2 was played the next evening at Rebel Park on August the 4th. It is my 30th wedding anniversary, and when Martha asked me in April what I wanted to do on this special occasion, I replied "Hopefully, we'll be in New Market for a playoff game." That was the honest answer but apparently not the correct one. With an understanding and a love and a friendship that comes from 30 years of being together, she abandons thoughts of a cruise or the Florida Keys and arrives in New Market, ready to root for the Rebels.

Before the game, I am shagging fly balls during batting practice, and I notice Ryan Stauffer doing the same in bare feet. He has referred to Mike Graham as "Moonlight," and now I address him as "Shoeless" Ryan. I half expect to hear voices from the fields beyond the center-field fence telling me to "Go the distance." Stauffer is not channeling Shoeless Joe Jackson, however. The poison ivy that he contracted weeks ago has never disappeared and, in fact, has now worsened considerably. His foot is blistered to the point that it appears burned, so he is shagging barefoot. While it is annoying and even painful to Ryan, his condition does not even make the top 10 injuries that the Rebels have suffered this year.

The fans, Martha included, are excited, but apprehensive. No one wants to go back to Luray, and there is a sense that this is a must-win game. Steven Thiele takes the mound for New Market and records two quick outs before a Zak Messer error and a shallow single to center field off the bat of D. J. Hicks produce a run in the first. Zak has had his trouble in the field all year, and it stems from the fact that he tends to field the ball "under his jock," as Mo says. That is, he fields the ball too close to his body and too upright, rather than fielding the ball approximately 18 inches in front of his body, with his knees bent and his butt low. He never seems to form "the alligator" on anything hit directly at him; that is, putting his bare hand above his glove hand, ready to clamp down on the ball and gobble it up, as an alligator might gobble up a meal.

The Wranglers score single runs in each of the first three innings, including another unearned run. The Rebels score an unearned run of their own in the second when, with none out, Gartman and Gonzalez single and Gartman scores on a throwing error by Luray pitcher Drew Rucinski, who throws wildly to first on a Messer sacrifice. Gonzalez takes third on the play and Messer second, and when Matt Townsend walks, New Market appears to be in business. Just as befell them throughout the final week of the regular season, however, the Rebels fail to score when Helgeson and pitcher-turned-left-fielder Matt Burnside strike out and Kevin Rufus grounds out.

The Wranglers score two more in the 5th to go up 5-1, but New Market makes it 5-4 when Seth Kivett launches a three-run bomb over the centerfield fence and into the trees beyond.

Thiele shuts down the Wranglers in the 6th, and Spencer Clifft throws two more innings of shutout baseball. With one out in the bottom of the 8th, Steve Owens is sent up to pinch hit for Burnside and promptly delivers an infield single. Burgess runs for the big man, and while Brian has assured me before the game that he could pitch "five innings," there is no way that Lucas and Dan Rollins will pitch him tonight, after he pitched three innings the night before. Burgess reaches second on a two-out single to right by Langston, who is hotter than he has been all year, which brings Seth Kivett to the plate. Down 0-2, Kivett works the count to 2-2, fouling off several pitches, before smashing a ball to left field. It is slicing away from Pablo Bermudez and for an instant, it appears that the Rebels will take the lead, but the fleet-footed outfielder makes a running catch in front of the Rebel bullpen. The play saves the game for the Wranglers.

In the bottom of the 9th, Zak Messer singles with two outs, keeping the hopes of the Rebel faithful alive, especially with Matt Townsend coming to bat. The same thought flashes through everyone's mind, including Matt's: Could he do it two nights in a row? Was there really magic in the moonlight? Quite unromantically, Townsend walks, and while it pushes the tie run to second and puts the winning run on first, it brings Zach Helgeson to the plate. Zach, who had singled the previous night to knock in a run in the 7th and pinned the right fielder against the wall in the 9th, has struggled again this evening, and his last at-bat is no different. He strikes out for the fourth time, and the Rebels lose the game, 5-4.

The fans are glum as they file out of Rebel Park, for the consensus has been that the Rebels needed to win this second game; that it just isn't likely that they can go back to Luray and win another game in their park against their fully manned squad, while the Rebels are trying to land safely in the semifinals on a wing and a prayer and whatever magic there is in the moonlight.

"We don't want to have to go back across the mountain," has been the refrain.

Lucas Jones approaches me during the post-game meal and tries about six different ways to begin a sentence that will explain this typical Rebel loss and finally blurts out, "I'm speechless! My stomach is in knots...I truly don't know what to say."

After the meal, I talk to Clifft and Sanchez Gartman, who are busy pulling blue tarps across the home-plate circle and the mound, respectively.

"Man, how many runners did Zach leave on base tonight?" asks Clifft in his soft, Southern accent. He says this without acrimony or accusation. After a bit of thinking, we come up with the answer: "A lot."

"I feel bad for the guy," I say.

"Me, too," they respond in unison, and in that moment, I began to feel better about the Rebels' chances. They are still a *team*. There is no finger-pointing, no complaining about a teammate's failure.

Gartman immediately begins to discuss his own failures: that he is still jumping at the ball with his characteristic double toe tap.

"That's all right," he says, the tarps now covering the mound and home plate, "Seth's hitting the ball well, and I'll get myself straightened out. We'll be all right."

The three of us head back to the pavilion where only the coaches now remain, and Sanchez immediately asks Corey Paluga to work with him on his throwing. Luray, knowing that Gartman is playing out of position behind the plate, took advantage of the situation and stole three bases in four attempts. Gartman has taken this rather personally, and he is determined to prevent it in Game 3.

"They were treating me like a scrub," he says evenly, but with obvious irritation. He could have asked to work on his hitting — always more fun — or he could have figured, as have the fans, that sweeping the Wranglers in Luray isn't likely and, therefore, there is no point in working on anything. The only thing Gartman was figuring on, however, was what needed to be done to win that third game.

And indeed, at 4:15 the next afternoon, one hour before the bus is to leave for Luray, Sanchez Gartman is behind home plate, working on his throwing mechanics and firing baseballs to Paluga, who is covering second.

By 4:45, it is obvious that the entire team is clueless. That is to say, they have absolutely no clue that they aren't supposed to win.

Ten of them had visited Jay Lively at Bryce Mountain Resort and had spent the day riding the zip line.

Brian Burgess arrives and announces "I'm putting you guys on my back tonight!"

Joe Hammond arrives and asks Bruce Alger how much a new uniform costs, and Bruce asks him "Why?"

"Well, hypothetically, let's just say that I left it on top of my truck and then took off for Woodstock."

"Well, then hypothetically, you'd be a dumbass," replies Bruce.

"Well, it's a good thing I didn't!" grins Joe, pulling his uniform from his bag and relating how the "hypothetical" had almost happened.

We boarded the bus at a leisurely pace and waited for Vic to put it in gear and take us over the mountain.

"Do we have everybody?" hollers Matt Townsend.

"Yeah, all 21 of you," answers Lucas. That can't be right. Twenty-one? Is that all we have left? I look to the back of the bus and, indeed, it looks empty, compared to that Opening Day trip to Harrisonburg one day shy of exactly two months before.

Before we are out of New Market, the laughter and hollering have started. Townsend and Gartman call to me from the back of the bus to find out if they are in the book yet. I assure them that they are. As we reach the summit, Townsend yells, "Hey, Skip! How do I look?" And when we all turn around, there sits Townie, an impish grin on his face and a Luray Wrangler hat on his head. Everyone laughs.

We arrive at Bulldog Field, laughing all the way. Upon parking the bus, Vic wishes good luck to every player or small group of players as they hop off the bus.

"That's the most carrying on I've heard the whole year!" he says. "Those boys are pumped."

And they were just getting warmed up.

"Coach!" Townie calls to Lucas, "Can I hit in this shirt tonight?" Townsend is wearing a red shirt, rather than the gray New Market T-shirt that is standard for batting practice before away games.

"No," is Lucas' short reply.

"Good!" answers Matt, gleefully. "I was just seeing if you were still about the team!"

I ask Matt about his at-bat in the last inning of last night's game; if the thought of another game-winning home run had crossed his mind.

"That was all I was thinking!" he replies. "Same pitcher, too. That pitch I fouled back ..." he leaves the sentence unfinished, shakes his head and smiles, obviously wishing that he could go back in time and take one more swing at it.

Mo Weber is into the spirit of the day as well. Gartman has forgotten his gray BP shirt, and he "does not want to get into trouble." The 5'5", 130-pound Mo Weber promptly pulls off his shirt and gives it to the 6'0", 210-pound Gartman. Corey Paluga, witnessing all this, is left to stare at the shirtless Mo, who flexes at him, and then without a word, enters the dugout to don his game jersey.

Batting practice soon turns into a spectacle of a different kind. Messer, Langston, and Kivett begin launching bombs out of Bulldog Field. So many home runs are being hit off or over the Wrangler trailer that it appears to be under attack. In fact, Lucas grabs his glove and positions himself in the parking lot. Gartman hits them out; Richie Gonzalez hits a couple out to left; even pitcher Matt Burnside asks if I had seen the ball he had hit over the fence.

"What the hell has gotten into our guys today?" asks Dan Rollins of no one in particular, as Lucas chases one ball after another.

As it turns out, the star of the show had not even taken center stage yet. With a remarkably compact swing, Steve Owens turns on pitch after pitch, sending balls flying over the trailer, and clearing the fence in center field. With the shortage of position players, Steve will be pressed into service in left field tonight. Thinking he was only getting two turns in the cage, he grabs his glove and heads for the outfield.

"You tired or something?" asks Seth Kivett, "You've got another turn coming."

"No, no! Sign me up," says Steve, quickly putting his batting helmet back on and launching two more home runs when his turn comes around again.

I had talked to SteveO earlier as he was hitting fly balls before BP began. He had not been drafted as he expected. No one signed him as a free agent. No scout had turned up to watch him pitch as he had been told would happen. He had been removed from his last start with arm trouble, yet here he was these last two weeks, seemingly more contented and happier than he had been all summer. I ask him if I am reading him correctly.

"Yeah, you are."

"Well, then, what's going on?"

"It's a great group of guys," he answers immediately. He pauses then and smiles and says, "Hey, I'm hitting ... it's beautiful! It's beautiful."

Steve gives me a look as if to say, "You know what I mean," and I think that I do. His dreams of professional baseball in disarray, Steve Owens is contented, for he is happy with what he has: good teammates and a chance, perhaps a final chance, to play the game of baseball. Rather than cursing the end, if it is indeed the end, he has seized this time, determined to enjoy every moment of it and thereby blessing it. And indeed, what is perhaps the shining moment of his entire career is yet to come.

Following Steve into the hitting cage, Matt Townsend, the host of today's pre-game show — and it *is* a show — steps in and fouls off Corey Paluga's first offering, then misses the second entirely.

"Now I'm swinging for real!" he calls out, and everyone is laughing at him and with him. Even Corey is doubled over behind the L-screen, laughing.

Soon, Townie launches one over the fence.

"Smell that!" he cries.

I approach Townie between turns and ask him what in the world has gotten into him today.

Without hesitation he replies, "This could be the last game; you gotta enjoy it."

* * *

The question, of course, for everyone in the stands is Can the Rebels sustain the kind of firepower that they have displayed in batting practice once the game begins? By the time the first pitch is thrown, almost everyone from New Market *is* in the stands. Vic is to my right, with Dan Hawkins to his right. The Kipps are two rows in front of me while Front-Row Fred is further down and to our right. Kay, Carol Lanham, Katie, Tearha, and the Smiths are also in the stands. Tacy and Melissa are seated on the back row, and Bruce and Trey Alger are immediately behind us. Jay Hafner is seated to my left. Will Cooper is missing, however, as are the Dodges. They are running late, but they call me right after the 1st inning begins, and I give them a cell phone play-by-play until they reach Bulldog Field during the 2nd.

Fortunately, there is a great deal to tell them about. Kevin Rufus draws a leadoff walk and takes third on McKinnon Langston's double. Richie Gonzalez knocks in Rufus with a ground ball to second, and Langston scores when a grounder off the bat of Seth Kivett rolls under third baseman Cory Johnson's glove for an error.

The Rebels are throwing tough-luck lefty Garrett Baker, in what is now the newest most important game of the season. He issues a leadoff walk to Alex Foltz and a single to Pablo Bermudez, but escapes trouble when A. J. Wirnsberger flies out to center and D. J. Hicks grounds into a 3-6-1 double play, with Baker making a sensational stretch for the ball at first.

The score remains 2-0 heading into the bottom of the 3rd when with one out, Drew Martinez singles, bringing Alex Foltz to the plate for his second look at Baker. Foltz lifts a deep fly ball to left field. The Luray fans have a great look at the play, seated as they are along the first-base line and they rise, cheering, certain that Foltz has tied the game. Owens runs back to the chain link fence and reaches, but this is surely a home run. We reassure ourselves that the game is only tied, but Steve takes a step — maybe two — toward the infield and pulls the ball from his glove, casually tossing it in to the infield. Almost simultaneously, the Luray fans sit down as we stand up and cheer. We never saw the ball disappear into Owen's outstretched glove, but the ball and Steve's huge smile tell us in an instant that our two-run lead had never disappeared, even if the ball had.

"If he'd been 6'8½", he wouldn't have caught it!" exclaims Bruce, who had left his seat behind us and happens to be standing down the left-field line when Owens reaches across his body and back over the fence to make the catch.

It is a phenomenal grab, better than the catch that Pablo Bermudez made in Game 2. The fact that a pitcher, pressed into service as an outfielder, has made this catch makes it all the more ... magical.

The 4th inning proves to be Kevin Rufus' turn to play magician. In the stands, we've been saying that we need to score again before Luray scores a run in order to really take control of the game. Rufus singles in Matt Townsend who had walked, giving us the run we have been craving, but it is in the bottom of the 4th that Kevin pulls a rabbit out of the hat.

Baker hits Wirnsberger, leading off the inning, then loads the bases on a single and a walk. He strikes out Dan Bowman, then runs the count full to Cory Johnson. Johnson fouls off four pitches before finally striking out, and it appears that Baker will wriggle out of more trouble. The next batter, catcher Alex Haitsuka, however, launches a ball to center, and we alternate between watching the ball and watching Rufus and calculating all the while if they will intersect. They do, but only for an instant. Running full out, Rufus crashes into the center-field fence just as he gets a glove on the ball. Both Kevin and the ball fall to the ground. Owens, hustling over from left field, picks up the ball and gets it back in. Haitsuka has cleared the bases with a triple, tying the score, but Rufus' leap has kept the ball in the park. Unfortunately, Rufus is now crumpled on the ground. Lucas Jones can stick guys in left and right, but Kevin Rufus cannot be replaced in center. After several minutes, he rises from the middle of a concerned circle that includes most of his teammates on the field, Lucas Jones, and members of the Luray Rescue Squad. He stays in the game, and Baker retires Martinez on a ground ball to Zach Helgeson for the final out of the inning. It is 3-3, but it could have been worse — in many ways.

It gets better in a hurry. Gartman leads off the top of the 5th with an infield single, and Seth Kivett promptly hits another home run to dead center field to give the Rebels a 5-3 lead. Gartman takes his time jogging around the bases from first, but Seth, excited and half-running all the way, almost catches his teammate at third base. They cross the plate not 5 feet apart.

The Wranglers get one run back in bottom half of the inning on back-to back doubles by Wirnsberger and Hicks, but the damage is minimized by yet another New Market double play that has preceded the doubles.

Again, the Rebels respond immediately to Luray's scoring. Langston and Gonzalez open the 6th with singles, and Gartman delivers a mammoth three-run homer into the trees in right center field on the first pitch he sees. He has stayed back on the ball, and just as he had told me after Game 2, he is doing his part to ensure that the Rebels "will be all right."

After Kivett strikes out, Zak Messer sends a solo shot over the Wrangler trailer in left just as we had seen from so many hitters before the contest began. Batting practice has indeed carried over into the game. With 12 outs to go, the Rebels lead 9-4.

We are going crazy in the stands. Front-Row Fred yells out to Steve Owens, who is in the on-deck circle, "Hit like I do!" to which a chorus of "NO!" fills the bleachers, followed by a wave of laughter.

Still, the Wranglers are a good-hitting team, and we are in Luray. It's not over yet.

Jake Guengerich comes on to start the top of the 7th and runs into immediate trouble by surrendering a leadoff double to Foltz. He strikes out Bermudez and Wirnsberger, but the latter reaches on a wild pitch third strike. That's a bad omen, and everyone in the stands knows it, especially when it brings the dangerous Hicks to the plate. Hicks singles to center, driving in Foltz and sending Wirnsberger to third, bringing to the plate shortstop Jacob Wilson. Guengerich has not been his usual self, bouncing many pitches to Gartman, and we are squirming in the stands. A substantial lead seems to be melting before our eyes and, indeed, Wilson sends a blast toward center field.

"Uh oh," I mutter.

It's a three-run homer. Only it isn't. Before Wilson even crosses home plate, and for no reason that we can discern, the Luray bullpen is jumping up and down in anger, as though every member had received a hot foot. Then we see that the two base umpires—there are three umpires for these playoff games—are conferring just beyond second base, and now they are waving their arms. They are saying "ground-rule double"! We saw the ball bounce, and apparently the umpires are saying the ball bounced out of the park.

While the Wrangler bullpen is livid, Mike Bocock gets halfway to the umpires, puts up a mild protest, and returns to the third-base coaches' box. This surprises everyone, for Bocock had missed Game 1 while serving the last of a three-game suspension for bumping an umpire.

"He must be on pro-bation!" cries Vic when Luray's manager fails to erupt.

"I thought you were going to say that he was on Pro-zac," I answer and, indeed, Bocock is strangley undemonstrative.

Only one run scores on the play as the umpires return Wilson and Hicks to second and third, respectively. Guengerich strikes out Bowman, walks Johnson to load the bases, and then retires Haitsuka on a popup to Messer at short. Everyone in the stands exhales. We're still ahead 9-6.

James Weiner relieves Guengerich to start the 8th, and the Wranglers start another rally on an error and a single, but Weiner, who strikes out Bermudez, then induces another double play and escapes with no damage.

By now it has been raining steadily for an inning. Jackets and umbrellas have spouted everywhere. Front-Row Fred has his jacket pulled up over his head.

"Fred looks like a nun," I say to Vic.

"That's the ugliest nun you'll ever see," yells Vic.

We all laugh and await the bottom of the 9th. I look around and I have the strongest sensation that I am at a family reunion. We are not related by blood or marriage. We are not even related by New Market Rebels baseball, although that is surely what brought us together, but it is not what unites us now. We are not only there for the players who sport "New Market" across their jerseys, we are there for each other. We are a community, centered not around a single town, but around a single purpose: to be a part of and to contribute to something greater than ourselves. It might only be a little baseball team in Virginia, but it is ours, and from it has sprung a sense of belonging and a host of friendships.

Misery loves company, of course, and should we lose this game, there is no one else with whom we would rather commiserate. Conversely, joy is magnified in a multitude, and should we win, this is nearly the perfect multitude. So, here we sit, in the rain, together, rooting for this extension of our family out there on the field. We have agonized with them over every error and every strikeout, and we have celebrated with them after every home run hit and every double play that has been turned. And now we rise to cheer wildly for Brian Burgess, who has come on for the save.

"Lightning!" yells Vic.

Burgess is sharper than on Monday night, but he still doesn't look quite right, surrendering a one-out walk and a two-out single, putting runners on first and second and bringing the tie run to the plate in the person of Alex Haitsuka. The baseball gods wouldn't suddenly turn on us now, would they? Not with only one out to go. Not after lending us a little magic.

Haitsuka lifts a towering foul ball toward the stands along the first-base line, and it appears that it will be out of play. It is hit so high, however, way up above the short lights, that it has time to spin back toward the field. I take my eye off the ball and look down at Zach Helgeson. He is indeed tracking it.

A popup in foul territory to the off field often spins back toward the diamond, making it a more difficult catch than one hit straight up. The degree of difficulty is increased by virtue of the fact that this ball is hit above the lights and, therefore, a fielder — Zach Helgeson — will lose sight of it temporarily.

Staring up into the rain, Helgeson is staying with that popup, drifting, drifting as it spins back toward the first-base coaches' box.

New Market Rebel fans count down the outs in the bottom of the 9th of Game 3 at Luray.

There is a split second of silence as we wait for the ball to reach the nadir of its descent, which it does, finally in Helgeson's glove. We have won.

Shouts of victory, and high-fives and fist bumps permeate our stands. We are relieved. We are happy. We are exhausted. I run out onto the field for the team meeting, calling Martha on the cell phone as I go. Lucas gives me a simple thumbs-up, and I hold the phone aloft so that she can hear Lucas' words of congratulations to the team. I call Al.

"We did it!" I shout into the phone.

"I know! The score was just posted on the league website, and I was just about to call you."

With Martha and Al having shared the moment as best they could over a cell phone, my multitude is complete.

After the game, the Battle of the Mountain trophy is presented to Bruce Alger at home plate. Trey has asked to accompany his dad for the first time, and the father asks the son to take it to the team. Trey hands it to Brian Burgess, who hands it to Lucas, who hands it to Mo, who clutches it tightly while wearing the broadest of grins.

Vic and I stand at the bus, greeting players as they arrive.

"That was a home run," says Kevin Rufus before we could even ask him about the ground-rule double. "It landed five feet over the fence and hit a macadam path back there."

It was immediately obvious what had happened. Only grass extends beyond the outfield fence in most parks and, therefore, a home run usually nestles into it with a gentle thud. At Luray, however, the umpires saw the ball bounce, unaware that they were looking *through* the chain-link fence, and they immediately ruled it a ground-rule double.

Magic.

We already know that we will face Haymarket in the playoffs. In fact, the Senators have swept Staunton, and now with Luray dispatched, there is not only a feeling in New Market, but throughout the entire league that the all-star insult that took place in Waldorf has been avenged. Indeed, the Rebels' triumph means that the four lowest seeds in the Valley League playoffs have all won.

Would the magic last?

Chapter 22
I've Never Had As Much Fun Watching Baseball As I Have This Season

The inspired victory over Luray represented the last that the New Market Rebels had left. There is really no such thing as magic. When a series of improbable plays occurs — a catcher making a diving stab of a wide throw for a forceout that saves the game, even as he is beginning to feel the effects of a concussion; a pitcher playing left field who takes away a home run by reaching far over the wall; a home run that is ruled a ground-rule double — we are fooled into thinking that we have witnessed the impossible, and if it's impossible, but it happened anyway, it must be magic. In any case, Magic is no match for a lefthander who throws an outstanding changeup and curveball and strikes out nine hitters in six innings. That's what Haymarket's Grant Sasser did to the Rebels in Game 1, as New Market fell 6-0 to the Senators at Rebel Park. The next night in Haymarket, the Rebels lost 5-3, and their season came to an end.

No one could foresee that McKinnon Langston's single in the first inning would be the Rebels *only* hit of the first game; and though they went on to load the bases in the 1st on a couple of walks and Langston's hit, they could not score. They loaded the bases in the 3rd and again in the 8th on hit batters and walks, but as happened time and again over the last two weeks, with the exception of the Luray series, they could not get a big hit when they needed it.

As if to dispel the notion of magic, Will Cooper could not even attend this game. Asking his father to take him home before the finale at Luray, Will is running a fever and will spend the next day in the intensive care facility with an IV hooked into his one good arm. The mystery illness will pass with no long-term effects, but Cooper is now finished, even as a fan.

There was one bright spot for New Market, however, and it occurs not on the field, but in the press box. There, Jane Harper, Bruce's mom, and Tacy Hawkins commandeer the public address microphone from Bruce and lead the crowd in singing "Happy Birthday" to him during the 7th-inning stretch. Everyone sings; it is everyone's way of saying "thanks" to Bruce for all the time and effort that he has given to the Rebels.

Toward the end of the game, a motion is made in the bleachers to give the boys a standing ovation, but Kay Helsley vetoes that idea saying that it "would make them think we don't believe they can come back home for Game 3." So, Melissa Dodge leads everyone in singing "High Hopes," a song that Kay describes as most fitting, "even though we didn't know enough of the words to get much sung, except the chorus."

Joe Hammond starts the second game, and I am confident that he will pitch with his usual grit and determination. I had told Bruce the night before that he is the kind of guy who, if he loads the bases with none out, will not panic; he will simply work at getting the next batter out.

Haymarket, indeed, loads the bases in the 1st inning when the first three batters of the game reach on two walks sandwiched around a single. Hammond gets a double-play ball off the bat of Tom LaStella, however, and only one run scores. The Rebels tie it in the 4th on a single by Seth Kivett, a double by Richie Gonzalez, and a groundout from Matt Townsend.

The 5th inning is uneventful, unless you have been watching Rebel baseball all season. Evan Noelle hits a routine grounder right to Zak Messer at short. It is the play that Zak has had the most difficulty with throughout the year, but as the ball comes to him, he bends at the waist and at the knees. He puts his hands about 18 inches in front of his body, his glove hand on the ground and his top hand above, as though forming the mouth of an alligator. The ball disappears into Zak's glove from which he retrieves it and throws on to first for the out. Zak Messer had fielded what would be his last groundball of the season, perfectly.

The Senators take the lead with three runs in the 6th. More significantly, on a wild pitch that plates the lead run, Sanchez Gartman hurts his back. We see it from the stands as Sanchez grabs at his lower back, and he can barely squat down behind the plate. He finishes up the inning, but must be removed before the bottom of the 7th because of back spasms. In the bleachers, we look at one another, not surprised — not after this season — but stupefied nevertheless. You mean the baseball gods are messing with us *still*?

Seth Kivett (l.) and Kenny Mickens (r.).

Seth Kivett, who has not caught on a regular basis since high school, now goes behind the dish. Zach Helgeson moves to third for the first time in the season; pitcher-now-left-fielder Steve Owens becomes the pitcher-now-left-fielder-now-first-baseman. Matt Burnside takes over in left.

The first batter of the inning drops a bunt down the third-base line. The Senators are testing Helgeson, as well they should, but to Rebel fans, it feels as though they were kicking us when we are down. Helgeson, however, races in, scoops up the bunt, and fires to first for the out, which prompts wild cheering and even finger-pointing at the Haymarket bench. It is a play that makes us start thinking that perhaps this ragtag bunch that is left can pull out this game and maybe even the series. It makes us all believe in magic for the moment, or at least hope for some magic anyway.

The Rebels load the bases in the top of the 7th with one out, but score only once on Langston's sacrifice fly.

The Senators add an insurance run in the 8th off James Weiner, even though Steve Owens has made two fine plays on ground balls at first. Even so, the Rebels are down to their final three outs. Before the inning ends,

Charlie Dodge says, "I think that we should all stand and cheer when they come off the field, in case this is our last chance to show them how we feel." No one vetoes the idea this time. And so, as a dejected group of Rebels come in for the 9th, four of them coming in from positions they hadn't played the entire season, we stand and cheer.

Indeed, the Rebel bleachers are packed again. Kay Helsley, the Dodges, the Hawkinses, the Powells, the Kipps family, the Alger clan, the Smiths, Richard Torovsky, and Lucas' parents are all there. Zak Messer's entire family, including the two dogs, is in attendance. Melissa and Front-Row Fred are there, of course, but Fred had yelled himself hoarse at Luray and isn't much of a factor in the cheering. The others make up for it. When the Haymarket public address system plays the "Charge!" call on the bugle, it is met with a resounding "Go Rebels!" which drowns out the Senators fans. The bugle call is begun a second time, but is stopped after about three bars, because there is no way that the home crowd was going to compete with the noise raised by the raucous Rebel faithful. The noise and cheering was heard in every inning down through the 9th.

Zach Helgeson would lead off New Market's final inning. No one had struggled more than Zach over the season's second half. Consequently, no Rebel had more fans rooting for him than Zach did. We watched him night after night as the strikeouts mounted and the frustration grew. Yet, he never cursed an umpire, never threw his bat, at least where we in the stands could see it; he never took his slump into the field, and he never made excuses. A soccer player can have a lousy game and 95% of the crowd will never notice, but when a baseball player is all alone in the batter's box and he strikes out or pops up, everyone knows that he has failed. Zach endured the public failure with a certain grace that had engendered a growing admiration among the fans. He was not just an adopted son to us, he *was* us. Most of the New Market fans are middle-aged or older, which means most of us have endured failure or adversity. He was displaying grace and perseverance at 20 that most of us wish we had at 40.

Down in the count early in his first at-bat, he suddenly began fouling off pitches and finally worked a walk.

"Hey, he's seeing the ball better!" exclaims Dan Hawkins as Zach takes first. We all happily agree and, indeed, that many fouls indicate that Zach is keeping his head on the ball.

In the 4th inning, Helgeson laces a line drive down the third-base line that is snared by the third baseman. Everyone in the stands was encouraged on Zach's behalf. It finally appears that Zach is keeping his head on the ball, especially when he draws another walk in the 7th and scores the Rebels' second run.

Now in the 9th, he lifts a lazy pop fly to right field. It is perhaps his worst at-bat of the night, but it is contact. The second baseman goes racing out, and the right fielder comes racing in, and neither can catch the ball. And so, in his final at-bat of the season, Zach Helgeson gets a hit.

With Helgeson at second, having taken the extra bag when the right fielder bobbles his single, Steve Owens is called out on strikes on a pitch that appears to be inside. The Rebel dugout erupts with anger. I look over, and all but Gartman, who can hardly stand are up on the top railing hollering at the umpire and cheering on Kevin Rufus, the next hitter. There is no quit in them, even yet. Rufus' groundball moves Helgeson to third, and he scores when Langston, who continues to be New Market's hottest hitter, drives him in with a single to right. Richie Gonzalez now represents the tie run.

My phone rings. It is Al calling from Yuma, Arizona, where his work had taken him, and he wants an update.

"You want me to stay on the line and give you a play-by-play?" I ask.

"That would be great," replies Al. "I was there at the beginning, and I kind of want to be there at the end."

And so it was. Haymarket, taking no chances, brought on fireballing left hander Jake Leathersich, who struck out Gonzalez on a foul tip. As catcher Evan Noelle jumped up out of his crouch, the ball firmly in his glove, the realization swept through the dugout and the stands that there was no more baseball to be played this season.

Lucas Jones gathers his players in left field as he has done after every game.

"I appreciate you guys sticking it out until the end," he tells them. "We had the tie run at the plate in the 9th. We battled all year."

He talks to them about the relationships that they had formed, reminding them that what he had said two months ago had come true. "I told you that for the first two weeks you wouldn't say a word to each other, but after that, we wouldn't be able to shut you up. And that's been the case."

I looked around at what was left of this Rebel team as Lucas spoke. They were tired, relieved even that the end had come, yet it was a sad-looking group of baseball players.

"I couldn't have asked for a better group of guys to have as my first year as a head coach," continues Lucas, "and I'll do anything for you. It's been an unbelievable experience for me."

There were 20 of them left, Jay Lively having departed earlier in the day for home, where he could ignore family commitments no longer. Fifteen others had worn the Rebel uniform at one point or another in the season, but were not here now.

"It doesn't always work out the way we want it to work out. That's life. But I wouldn't trade you for any other team," concludes Lucas, who then asks if any of the other coaches have anything to say.

None did but Mo Weber. It was hard to hear Mo, standing as I was on the edge of the group, but one word stood out: "proud."

The players gathered in, raised their hands together, and shouted "Rebels!" one last time.

They made their way to the bleachers for a final post-game meal of pizza, but the bleachers were not empty. Charlie and Melissa Dodge were there thanking the players for their efforts, as were the Kipps family. Becky Kipps appeared to be on the verge of tears. Katie Getz and Teahra Hough were well past the verge. Trey Alger had had the good sense to bring sunglasses, which he was now wearing. There were hugs and handshakes all around, and one last booming shoutout from Haymarket Joe, only this time it was "LET'S GO, REBELS!" as a salute to a valiant effort from a battered team.

Having driven separately, I drove back to New Market to await the bus. Mo rode with me. Through the darkness on I-66 and then on I-81 we talked baseball. As we approached New Market, we could see the lights at Rebel Park. When we pulled into the parking lot at 12:30 a.m., the Algers were there, waiting in the pavilion. Lynne had been crying, and Bruce was staring out at the field. We got out of my van and were greeted by the smell of wood smoke — it was another cool evening and someone must have been using a wood stove — as if Summer had left and Fall had arrived since the game had ended.

I start to approach Bruce, but think better of it. There are no questions left to ask, and I already know what he is feeling.

"I can't believe it's over," he says.

"We didn't get to the top of the mountain tonight," says Mo.

"No, but we could see it from there," Bruce replies. "We were still battling in the top of the 9th ... I can't wait to get started on 2010, which reminds me," he says to Mo, "You're fired."

They both laugh.

The bus arrives shortly thereafter. Steve Owens is the last one off. There are more hugs and handshakes and "thank you's," and Eric Alessio, the team barber, shaves out John Combs' Mohawk with a pair of shears. All the coaches, save Dan Rollins who had a job interview, had gotten Mohawk haircuts to fulfill a promise made if the Rebels beat Luray. Apparently, there was no magic in the Mohawk, either.

Wyatt Estep, age 10, who served as a bat boy on occasion for the Rebels and became one of the teams' favorite fans, collected every player's address so that he could write to them.

"He already sent Kenny Mickens a card," says Vic. Kenny had to catch a flight back to Los Angeles after the Game 2 loss to Luray. Though he did not serve as the bat boy against Haymarket, Wyatt had asked to ride the bus back in order to spend a little more time with the players before they left, and both his parents and Vic had agreed.

Players continued to say goodbye to the Algers, to each other, and to me. More than a few told me that they couldn't wait to read the book.

"Me, too," I told them.

Zach Helgeson promised a full literary criticism, and I told him that I had no doubt that he would analyze my efforts thoroughly.

Steven Theile even told me that it was "fun having you out there shagging."

Everyone thanked Vic for getting them up and down the Valley safely.

"It's harder for me this year to see them leave," he said, the emotion of the moment obvious in his eyes.

Most of the players turned in their uniforms and headed for home that night or returned to their host homes one last time for a short rest and an early departure. Vic and I stayed until all the players had left, and he hugged me goodbye. We had had a great time this summer watching those boys who were just here a few moments before. As it was, Vic had to get up early himself, as he was displaying his furniture in the Shenandoah Flea Market parking lot for the Route 11 Yard Crawl, a giant yard sale that snaked its way along Route 11 the entire length of Shenandoah County. Vic drove off, as did the Algers. It was 1:30 in the morning, and the lights were off at Rebel Park.

* * *

The next morning, I stopped by the Southern Kitchen for some breakfast. I was not wearing any Rebels gear, but the hostess recognized me anyway.

"Are your games all over?" she asked.

"Yeah, we lost last night, but we had a good season," I told her.

"I heard!" she said cheerily.

After finishing my sausage gravy, I headed to the coaches' office at Rebel Park one last time, where Lucas and John were awaiting Rufus, Gartman, and Owens, who still had to turn in their uniforms.

"So, what was the highlight of the season for you guys?" I ask them.

"SteveO's catch," answers John immediately.

"Yesterday," responds Lucas. "We had the tie run at bat in the 9th. It was a typical game in terms of injuries, but we gave it a good effort. We lost the right way."

Soon Dan Rollins stumbles in, looking as if he hasn't slept in two months and then Kevin Rufus stops by to turn in his uniform. He lays his home #25 on a big pile of blue jerseys and his away #25 on a big pile of gray jerseys. A pile of gray pants and a pile of white pants rest on the carpeted floor, which show clumps of dirt from spikes now packed away. We say goodbye to Kevin, and he leaves for South Carolina.

Mo Weber enters the office dressed in a coat and tie. He is headed to the funeral of Ardis Beaver, Dave's wife, who had died 4 nights before, the night New Market lost to Luray. Dave had attended the semifinal opener against Haymarket; Rebel Park offered a comfortable place to be, and its inhabitants offered understanding company, so he and his grandchildren took in the game. When I had heard the news, I thought back to the banquet and to the plaque that Bruce had presented to the Beavers.

Mo, of course, had stopped in because he wanted a little more baseball before the final uniform was returned.

I ask Rollins about his highlight and he, too, answers, "Steve's catch! I just can't get over it." He then proceeds to tell us, however, that he will never forget Mo joking with him as they would line up for the National Anthem every night, trying to make him laugh.

John jumps in, saying that Steve's catch was the onfield highlight, but "seeing Mo holding the trophy after beating Luray" might be the biggest highlight of the season. "He damned near had tears in his eyes," Combs had told me earlier.

Sanchez Gartman walks in. We are all pleased that he is even able to walk. He talks to us about heading to Newberry College in his hometown, now that he has finished his two years at USC Sumter Junior College, and that he wants to be a catcher.

When he departs, I ask Mo for his highlight.

"Owen's play," he answers. "Here is a guy who is ready to quit in the middle of the year, but he came back with a passion...Furry coming back. . . . The steady play and improvement of Seth at third base...Guys like Chaz who wouldn't tell you how hurt he was ..."

We were still waiting for SteveO who, as it turned out, was delayed getting to Rebel Park because he had to fight his way through the Yard Crawl traffic. It took 40 minutes to travel down from Mount Jackson, when it should have taken 15. He threw his #27 on the pile.

As Steve does so, Mo heads for the door, but not before turning and saying, "You know I'm a sharp guy because I live on the edge of town."

The Rebels played 49 games, which means that Lucas, Dan, and John were hearing this line for at least the 50th time.

"It's the same jokes all the time," smiles Mo, who could not depart even now without telling us a story about managing in Schuylar, Nebraska, in 1950. Finally, he leaves with Steve Owens right behind him, and I am struck by the thought that Mo and Steve were the long and the short of it.

That was it.

I head out of the parking lot and drive north on Route 11. Making my way slowly up the road, bargain hunters and treasure sellers seemingly everywhere, I arrive at the Shenandoah Valley Flea Market.

"Austin!" cries Vic Moyers upon seeing me.

"Hey!" I yell as I approach him, "I had one more goodbye in me before I headed out of town."

We shake hands.

"Ole Joe Hammond went by this morning. He blew the horn and waved," relates Vic, but we soon dispense with the small talk and speak frankly of how happy we each are that we have become friends. Indeed, I spent more time with Vic this summer on the bus and watching games everywhere from Fauquier to Covington and all points in between than I had spent sitting in my own living room with Martha. We had shared peanuts and opinions; we had shared the parade and the fireworks on the 4th of July; we had shared the glory of defeating Luray and the sad realization that the boys had done all they could, but were no match for Haymarket.

We shake hands again and hug.

"I've never had as much fun watching baseball as I have this summer," he says.

"Me, too, Vic" I answer.

Me, too.

EPILOGUE

Haymarket became the Valley League champions for the first time in their history by defeating Covington in the finals 3 games to 1 in a matchup of the bottom two playoff seeds. As one might expect, the deciding Game 4 in Covington was postponed a day because of rain.

New Market's players returned to their respective homes and then their schools, where some began posting photos of their summer on their Facebook pages. Jay Lively's photo album was entitled "Best Summer Ever."

Many players thanked Bruce Alger for the opportunity to play ball in New Market before they left for home, and Bruce gave them, as he has given grateful ballplayers on all the teams before them, the same response that he gave to Dan Rollins, who sent Bruce a heartfelt e-mail expressing his gratitude for a great summer: "In regard to thanking us, you can best do that by giving someone else a chance to chase their dream, if and when you have the opportunity to do so in the future. That thought is the principal foundation of our program and is one of the reasons we continue to be successful year after year."

New Market's fans have returned to their "regular lives." The Dodges left for the beach after the final Haymarket game and reported that "sun and sand help with baseball withdrawal." Larry and Sharon Smith made a point of watching the Little League World Series to help ease them off Rebel baseball. Kay Helsley reported that she was not as sad to see this season end as she has been in the past because "First, we made it to the playoffs (and even the 2nd round), which we hadn't done for several years — so this was some closure that they had really fought the battle ... Second, their bodies were so bruised and injured that you felt selfish to say they should have gone further."

The Algers vacationed in Florida for 10 days, where they relaxed and slept regularly and ate right, and upon their return, their house didn't seem so empty, devoid as it is now of ballplayers. They breakfasted with Seth Kivett on their way down to Florida, and Jordan Pegram stopped in to say hello. They visited Dale Brannon and his family while there and went to Tropicana Field to see Tampa Bay play the Orioles as guests of the Brannon family. Former Rebel and oldest brother Evan Brannon now works as a scout for the Rays.

When former Rebel Chris Ray (2002) came on to pitch for Baltimore, Bruce "nearly jumped out of his seat" with excitement," according to Amanda Alger who had joined her family on their vacation from her home in Orlando. He recited to Amanda all of Ray's numbers while with New Market.

"How do you remember all that stuff?" she asked.

"I don't know; I just do," replied her dad.

Of course, when the Algers returned home, work began on the 2010 season.

"I am anxious to see what Dad will do with the Rebels in the future," noted oldest son Greg, who looks forward to the day when his schedule will permit him to join his father as part of the Rebel organization.

Kivett and his "house brother" Kenny Mickens will continue to play together in college. Seth from Bearcreek, North Carolina, and Kenny from Los Angeles, California, have become such fast friends that Kenny has decided to enroll at UNC–Pembroke. Catchers George Carroll and Will Cooper are recovering from their surgeries.

Dan Rollins will be applying his coaching skills at George Washington University, where he was hired as an assistant shortly after the season ended. Corey Paluga will be doing the same at Stevens Tech in New Jersey. John Combs returned to his graduate assistant duties at Rio Grande and spent the autumn coaching fall baseball and rooting for Ohio State football.

Lucas Jones took a much needed vacation to Las Vegas before returning to Randolph Macon. Jones' ultimate goal is to coach at the Division I level, and he will need to make himself available over the coming summer for interviews. Though asked to return to New Market for the 2010 season, Lucas declined the offer after much soul searching.

"I certainly owe the town of New Market, Bruce Alger, and the entire organization extreme gratitude for the opportunity to coach the 2009 Rebels team. I have built positive, lifelong relationships that extend past the diamond, and I have nothing but posititves as I reflect on my experiences in New Market," said Lucas.

For his part, Bruce Alger did not hesitate to offer the job to the man he wanted for the job, bypassing his board of directors for the first time in such a situation. And so, on September 21st, the last full day of summer, Corey Paluga accepted the position of head coach of the New Market Rebels for 2010. John Combs and Dan Rollins happily agreed to return as his assistant coaches.

The Legend of the Valley will continue. Mo Weber, perhaps energized by the exciting victory over Luray, will return for another summer of bus rides and batting tips. For Mo, the magic was apparently not in the moonlight, but in the Battle of the Mountain trophy, and having raised it on high, the desire for at least one more taste of triumph burns brightly.

* * *

The batter swings and the summer flies
As I look into my angel's eyes
A song plays on while the moon is high over me
Something comes over me.[1]

Something indeed, comes over me. A certain sadness perhaps. The same sadness that seems to hang over Rebel Park in its quietude and emptiness like the pockets of fog that sometimes gather in the dales of Massanutten Mountain. Already, the 2009 New Market Rebels will reassemble here only in the mind's eye. I have this sense that if I glance back at the field, really quickly, perhaps glance out of the corner of my eye, I will catch a glimpse of some past game. Perhaps if I am totally still and listen hard enough, I'll hear the crack of the bat and laughter. Perhaps, if I wait until the moon is full and walk out to the warning track, that old

---

[1] From "The Riddle," by John Ondrasik. The first line of this quotation is the best summary that I have ever read of how baseball fans feel about their passion.

wooden fence will tell me how Kevin Rufus crashed into it or how one of Gartman's home runs sailed over it. After all, *it just happened!* They were just there, playing yesterday, last month, last year. How could a thousand moments disappear into the past so quickly?

I console myself with ghosts that are yet to be; the 2010 Rebels and the Rebel teams that will follow and perhaps some summer, grandchildren in the stands munching on nachos and asking, "Was that a hit or an error, Grandpa?"

And so, I look and I listen as I sit in Rebel Park, and I realize that it is not really empty. It is just waiting. Waiting for the winter to pass and the college baseball season to end. Waiting for the warmth of the late spring sun, which will bring life to old friendships that have blossomed in the stands, just as the wildflowers blossom in sprays across the Shenandoah Valley. Waiting for the cry of "Play ball!" that will bring the Rebel family together once more.

Appendix A

Valley Baseball League Town Population Figures

Town	2007 Population*
Haymarket	1,219 (360,411)
Harrisonburg	44,039
Winchester	25,733
Staunton	23,834
Waynesboro	21,656
Front Royal	14,565
Fauquier	8,877
Lexington	7,026
Covington	6,168
Luray	4,858
Woodstock	4,265
New Market	1,845

*Based on U.S. Census Bureau 2007 estimates.

Technically, Haymarket is the smallest town in the Valley League with some 600 fewer residents than New Market, but it is located in Prince William County in Northern Virginia on the outer edges of metropolitan Washington, DC. Prince William's population, shown in parentheses above, is 5 times greater than Rockingham County, the next most populated county with a team in the VBL. Shenandoah County's population—at an estimated 40,403—is one ninth the size of Prince William's, and contains both New Market and Woodstock.

Appendix B – 2009 New Market Rebels: Batters

Player	Avg.	GP-GS	AB	R	H	2B	3B	HR	RBI	Slg. %	BB	HBP	SO	OB %	SB-Att.	PO	A	E	Fld. %
Mickens, Kenny	.365	35-32	126	25	46	15	1	1	22	.524	19	11	32	.484	1-4	43	1	1	.978
Gonzalez, Richard	.331	47-47	169	22	56	10	1	0	31	.402	27	5	18	.438	7-8	90	117	13	.941
Cooper, Will	.280	8-7	25	3	7	0	0	0	3	.280	3	3	4	.419	0-1	60	2	0	1.000
Messer, Zak	.278	43-41	169	25	47	12	2	4	21	.444	15	0	34	.332	8-11	76	100	19	.903
Kivett, Seth	.276	48-46	174	34	48	8	0	4	26	.391	39	1	43	.407	6-6	61	91	14	.916
Gartman, Sanchez	.263	45-41	152	30	40	7	1	8	32	.480	42	4	41	.432	4-4	87	7	4	.959
Carroll, George	.250	18-14	56	11	14	0	0	0	11	.375	8	2	19	.358	1-1	135	13		.943
Rufus, Kevin	.241	45-45	170	37	41	3	2	2	16	.318	26	18	52	.397	24-29	90	7	0	1.000
Pegram, Jordan	.241	13-13	54	9	13	2	2	1	8	.352	5	0	6	.305	2-2	15	39	9	.947
Pierce, Jacob	.234	14-14	47	7	11	0	0	0	4	.277	5	0	12	.308	0-0	98	9	3	.982
Owens, Steve	.222	6-4	18	0	4	0	0	0	0	.222	0	1	7	.263	0-0	10	4	2	.824
Langston, McKinnon	.221	31-29	113	7	25	0	0	0	9	.239	19	0	36	.328	1-2	3	4	3	.700
Helgeson, Zach	.193	48-45	166	23	32	8	0	5	28	.331	25	10	71	.332	2-3	353	16	3	.992
Townsend, Matt	.193	37-35	135	17	26	3	1	4	12	.319	15	4	48	.292	7-8	48	4	1	.981
Leskiw, Matt	.162	12-9	37	6	6	0	0	0	3	.189	6	1	13	.295	3-4	20	0	3	1.000
Bryant, Kenny	.148	13-5	27	1	4	0	0	0	0	.222	2	0	16	.207	2-2	23	0	0	1.000
Burnside, Matt	.125	6-2	8	1	1	0	0	0	0	.125	0	0	2	.125	0-0	0	2	0	.667
Furry, Nate	.094	10-9	32	3	3	0	0	0	4	.125	2	2	11	.189	0-0	73	10	1	.976
Zawadzki, Troy	.083	5-3	12	1	1	0	0	0	1	.083	0	1	5	.154	0-0	6	9	2	.882
Burgess, Brian	.000	1-0	0	0	0	0	0	0	0	.000	0	0	0	.000	0-0	6	7	2	.867
TOTAL	.251	49-49	1690	262	425	80	10	29	231	.362	258	63	470	.369	68-85	1308	514	88	.954

Appendix B – 2009 New Market Rebels: Pitchers

Player	ERA	W-L	App.-GS	CG	SV	IP	H	R	ER	BB	SO	2B	3B	HR	Opp/Avg
Burgess, Brian	0.32	3-0	19-0	0	10	28.1	18	3	1	8	34	3	1	0	.175
Thiele, Steven	2.30	2-1	8-4	0	0	31.1	24	11	8	13	27	2	0	0	.211
Baker, Garrett	2.53	3-3	10-10	0	0	64.0	65	26	18	16	55	12	2	2	.266
Alessio, Eric	2.96	5-0	10-9	0	0	51.2	52	20	17	19	32	12	0	0	.267
Weiner, James	3.38	1-1	22-0	0	0	18.2	21	7	7	15	13	3	0	1	.284
Guengerich, Jake	3.71	1-2	23-0	0	0	26.2	27	16	11	13	30	6	1	2	.281
Hoffman, Kyle	3.86	0-1	4-0	0	0	4.2	4	4	2	4	3	0	0	0	.222
Owens, Steve	4.33	4.33	8-7	0	0	35.1	30	22	17	16	38	5	0	5	.214
Graham, Mike	4.33	0-2	6-5	0	0	27.0	34	18	13	12	15	8	2	3	.291
Stauffer, Ryan	4.91	1-2	13-2	0	0	25.2	36	19	14	6	11	9	1	1	.330
Hammond, Joe	5.03	0-4	12-6	0	0	39.1	41	27	22	25	34	8	2	0	.270
Harman, Brett	5.62	0-2	3-3	0	0	16.0	19	15	10	6	14	1	0	2	.284
Clifft, Spencer	5.79	1-1	23-0	0	0	23.1	21	19	15	20	14	3	2	1	.231
Kline, Derek	6.00	1-1	2-2	0	0	9.0	10	10	6	4	10	2	0	1	.286
Burnside, Matt	7.71	0-1	8-1	0	0	11.2	16	14	10	9	10	4	0	0	.333
Lively, Jay	11.88	0-1	13-0	0	0	16.2	28	23	22	15	14	6	0	2	.373
Roth, Mike	12.00	0-1	9-0	0	0	6.0	11	8	8	5	6	3	1	1	.393
TOTAL	4.13	24-25	49-49	0	2(team)	436.0	458	262	200	206	360	88	12	23	.268

ABOUT THE AUTHOR

Austin Gisriel grew up in Baltimore County playing baseball and rooting for the Orioles. Early on, his chosen career path was to take over third base for the Birds when Brooks Robinson retired, and it was only a lack of talent that prevented him from accomplishing this goal. Gisriel turned to teaching and free-lance writing, penning articles on baseball for *The Sun* (Baltimore), *Baseball Digest*, and other publications. Married in 1979, he and his wife Martha reside in Williamsport, Maryland, but hope to retire to New Market, Virginia. They have two daughters, Rebecca and Sarah, either one of whom would have been named "Brooks" had she been a boy.